DATE DUE

	NOV 2 7 2006

DEMCO, INC. 38-2931

Digital Libraries

Digital Libraries and Electronic Publishing
series editor: William Y. Arms

Digital Libraries, William Y. Arms

Digital Libraries

William Y. Arms

The MIT Press
Cambridge, Massachusetts
London, England

© 2000 Massachusetts Institute of Technology

Set in Sabon by The MIT Press.
Printed and bound in the United States of America.

Library of Congress Cataloging-in-Publication Data

Arms, William Y.
Digital libraries / William Y. Arms.
p.   cm. — (Digital libraries and electronic publishing)
Includes bibliographical references and index.
ISBN 0-262-01880-8 (alk. paper)
1. Libraries—United States—Special collections—Electronic information resources. 2. Digital libraries—United States.
I. Title. II. Series.
Z692.C65A76   2000
025'.00285—dc21   99-14773
                                                                          CIP

Contents

Series Foreword

Since 1990, digital libraries and electronic publishing have moved from esoteric interests of a few visionaries to activities that are beginning to rival traditional libraries and traditional publishing. The catalysts have been technical (personal computers, the Internet, the World Wide Web), but contributions have come from every discipline that values the dissemination of high-quality information. Many of the challenges associated with building the new libraries are social, economic, or legal rather than technical.

Digital libraries are being implemented by people who work within conventional libraries, but also by people who do not consider themselves librarians or publishers. The World Wide Web has created new professions. Research in digital libraries has become a vibrant academic subdiscipline, with computer scientists working alongside economists, sociologists, lawyers, and librarians. An interdisciplinary body of expertise is emerging.

To write books about digital libraries may seem a contradiction. Most researchers in this field rely heavily on the Internet for current information, but these same people are very conscious of the strengths of conventional publications. Innovation and current research are widely reported in articles and papers published in journals and magazines and presented at conferences; much of this detailed material is openly available online. A book provides an opportunity to be more contemplative and to give perspective to a field. The aim of the MIT Press series on Digital Libraries and Electronic Publishing is to provide a context. The hope is to have created a series that is valuable to both specialists and nonspecialists. The specialists will see how other leaders in the field view the state of the art, recent research, and longer-term trends. The nonspecialists will be introduced to the initiatives that are leading to the new generation of libraries and publishing.

William Y. Arms

Preface

In 1995, some colleagues and I created *D-Lib Magazine*, an online monthly that has become the voice of digital library research and implementation. We started *D-Lib Magazine* because digital libraries are bringing together people from numerous disciplines who know little about one another. Our aim was to create a magazine that would inform people of the vast array of expertise that is feeding this field. Computer scientists are often unaware of the deep understanding of information that librarians have developed over the years. Librarians and publishers may not know that the Internet pioneers have been managing online information for decades. Both librarians and publishers are aware that their fields are subject to external economic and legal forces, but have only limited knowledge of the implications.

The first few years of *D-Lib Magazine* show how prescient this vision was. Among the topics covered are the latest metadata workshop, implementation projects at the Library of Congress, user interface principles applied to search and retrieval, a historic review of Z39.50, a digital library of Japanese folk tales, the JSTOR approach to legal issues, and methods for handling alternative character sets. Nobody is an expert in all these areas, yet to be a leader in digital libraries requires some appreciation of all of them.

This book is my attempt to survey the entire field of digital libraries. Computers and networks are of fundamental importance, but they are only the technology. The real story of digital libraries is the interplay of people, organizations, and technology. How are libraries and publishers using this new technology? How are individuals bypassing traditional organizations and building their own libraries? Where is all this leading? The answer to the last question is simple. Nobody knows. I have tried to avoid speculation and to concentrate on describing current activities, trends, and research. Thus, the "panels"—each addressing a significant aspect of digital libraries, technology, application, or research—are the heart of this book.

Inevitably, the book reflects my own experience and biases. In selecting the examples, I usually choose those that I know personally, with an emphasis on work by American universities, but I am conscious of the good work that is being carried out around the world. Some of my biases are undoubtedly unconscious, but others are quite deliberate. I am definitely biased toward digital libraries that provide open access to information. As a reader, I am thrilled that the Internet gives me access to huge amounts of information that is completely unrestricted; as an author, I publish my research online so that everybody has access to my work.

Acknowledgements

Because I know so many of the people whose work is described in this book, I have been shameless in asking them for help. Amy Friedlander, the founding editor of *D-Lib Magazine,* has been a constant guide. My wife Caroline introduced me to digital libraries when she was a graduate student at MIT in 1966. Now at the Library of Congress, she helped with many sections throughout the book. Individuals who have made comments on the manuscript or checked specific sections include Robert Allen, Kate Arms, Steve Cousins, Gregory Crane, Jim Davis, Peter Denning, Jack Dongarra, George Furnas, Henry Gladney, Steven Griffin, Kevin Guthrie, Larry Lannom, Ron Larsen, Michael Lesk, Ralph LeVan, Mary Levering, Wendy Lougee, Clifford Lynch, Harry S. Martin III, Eric Miller, Andreas Paepcke, Larry Page, Norman Paskin, Vicky Reich, Scott Stevens, Terrence Smith, Sam Sun, Hal Varian, Howard Wactlar, Donald Waters, Stuart Weibel, and Robert Wilensky.

Earlier versions of chapter 4 were provided to the Fundação Getulio Vargas and the Ticer Summer School. A sketch of chapter 8 was presented at the SGML/XML Conference in 1997. Panel 6.3 is from the U.S. Copyright Office. The figure in panel 7.3 is based on a figure by Henry Gladney. The list of elements in panel 10.3 is from the Dublin Core web site.

Digital Libraries

1

Libraries, Technology, and People

This is a fascinating period in the history of libraries and publishing. For the first time, it is possible to build large-scale services where collections of information are stored in digital formats and retrieved over networks. The materials are stored on computers. A network connects the computers to personal computers on the users' desks. In a completely digital library, nothing need ever reach paper.

This book provides an overview of this new field. Partly it is about technology, but equally it is about people and organizations. Digital libraries bring together facets of many disciplines, and experts with different backgrounds and different approaches. The book describes the contributions of these various disciplines and how they interact. It discusses the people who create information and the people who use it—their needs, motives, and economic incentives. It analyzes the profound changes that are occurring in publishing and libraries. It describes research into new technology, much of it based on the Internet and the World Wide Web. Among the topics are technical aspects of computers and networks, librarianship and publishing, economics, and law. The constant theme is change, with its social, organizational, and legal implications. One book cannot cover all these topics in depth, and much has been left out or described at an introductory level. Most of the examples come from the United States, with prominence given to universities and the academic community; however, the development of digital libraries is worldwide, with contributions coming from many sources. Specialists in big American universities are not the only developers of digital libraries, though they are major contributors. There is a wealth and diversity of innovation in almost every discipline, in countries around the world.

An informal definition of a digital library is a managed collection of information, with associated services, where the information is stored in digital formats and accessible over a network. A crucial part of this definition is that the information is managed. A stream of data sent to earth from a satellite is not a library. The same data, when organized systematically, becomes a digital library collection. Most people would not consider a database containing financial records of one company to be a digital library, but would accept a collection of such information from many companies as part of a library. Digital libraries contain diverse collections of information for use by many different users. Digital libraries range in size from tiny to huge. They can use any type of computing equipment and any suitable software. The unifying theme is that information is organized on computers and available over a network, with procedures to select the material in the collections, to organize it, to make it available to users, and to archive it. In some ways digital libraries are very different from traditional libraries, yet in other ways they are remarkably similar. People do not change because a new technology is invented. They still create information that has to be organized, stored, and distributed. They still need to find information that others have created, and to use it for study, reference, or entertainment. However, the form in which the information is expressed and the methods that are used to manage it are greatly influenced by technology, and this creates change. Every year, the quantity and variety of collections available in digital form grows, while the supporting technology continues to improve steadily. Cumulatively, these changes are stimulating fundamental alterations in how people create information and how they use it.

To understand these forces requires an understanding of the people who are developing the libraries. Technology has dictated the pace at which digital libraries have been able to develop, but the manner in which the technology is used depends on people. Two important communities are the source of much of this innovation. One group, the information professionals, includes librarians, publishers, and a wide range of information providers, such as indexing and abstracting services. The other community contains computer science researchers and their offspring, the Internet developers. Until recently these two communities had disappointingly little interaction; even now it is commonplace to find a computer scientist who knows nothing of the basic tools of librarianship, or a librarian whose concepts of information retrieval are years out of date. Since the introduction of the web, however, there has been much more collaboration and understanding. Partly this is a consequence of digital libraries becoming a recognized field for research, but an even more important factor is the greater involvement of users. Low-cost equipment and simple software have made electronic information directly available to everybody. Authors no longer need the services of a publisher to distribute their works. Readers can have direct access to information without going through an intermediary. Many exciting developments come from academic or professional groups who develop digital libraries for their own needs. Medicine has a long tradition of creative developments. The pioneering legal information systems were developed by lawyers for lawyers. The World Wide Web was initially developed by physicists for physicists.

Economics

Technology influences the economic and social aspects of information, and vice versa. The technology of digital libraries is developing fast, and so are the financial, organizational, and social frameworks. The various groups that are developing digital libraries bring different social conventions and different attitudes to money. Publishers and libraries have a long tradition of managing physical objects—notably books, but also maps, photographs, sound recordings, and other artifacts. They evolved economic and legal frameworks that are based on buying and selling these objects. Their natural instinct is to transfer to digital libraries the concepts that have served them well for physical artifacts. Computer scientists and scientific users, such as physicists, have a different tradition. Their interest in digital information began in the days when computers were very expensive. Only a few well-funded researchers had computers on the first networks. They exchanged information informally and openly with colleagues, without payment. The networks have grown, but the tradition of open information remains. The economic framework that is developing for digital libraries shows a mixture of these two approaches. Some digital libraries mimic traditional publishing by requiring a form of payment before users may access the collections and use the services. Other digital libraries use a different economic model. Access to their material is open to all. The costs of creating and distributing the information are borne by the producer, not the user of the information. This book describes many examples of both models and attempts to analyze the balance between them. Almost certainly, both have a long-term future, but the final balance is impossible to forecast.

Why Digital Libraries?

The fundamental reason for building digital libraries is a belief that they will provide better delivery of information than was possible in the past. Traditional libraries are a fundamental part of society, but they are not perfect. Can we do better? Enthusiasts for digital libraries point out that computers and networks have already changed the ways in which people communicate with each other. In some disciplines, they argue, a professional or a scholar is better served by sitting at a personal computer connected to a communications network than by making a visit to a library. Information once available only to the professional is now directly available to all. From a personal computer, the user is able to consult materials that are stored on computers around the world. Conversely, all but the most diehard enthusiasts recognize that printed documents are so much a part of civilization that their dominant role in storing and conveying information cannot change except gradually. Though some important uses of printing may be replaced by electronic information, not everybody considers a large-scale movement to electronic information desirable, even if it is technically, economically, and legally feasible. Here are some of the potential benefits of digital libraries.

The Digital Library Brings the Library to the User
To use a traditional library, a reader must go there. At a university this may take only a few minutes, but most people are not at universities and do not have a library nearby. Many engineers and many physicians have depressingly poor access to the latest information.

A digital library brings the information to the user's desk, either at work or at home. With a digital library on the desk top, the reader need never visit a library building. There is a library wherever there is a personal computer with a network connection.

Computer Power Is Used for Searching and Browsing

Paper documents are convenient to read, but finding information that is stored on paper can be difficult. Despite the myriad of secondary tools and the skill of reference librarians, using a large library can be a tough challenge. A claim that used to be made for traditional libraries is that they stimulate serendipity, because readers stumble across unexpected items of value. The truth is that libraries are full of useful materials that readers discover only by accident.

In most aspects, computer systems are already better than manual methods for finding information. They are not as good as everybody would like, but they are good and improving steadily. Computers are particularly useful for reference work that involves repeated leaps from one source of information to another.

Information Can Be Shared

Libraries and archives contain much information that is unique. Placing digital information on a network makes it available to everybody. Many digital libraries or electronic publications are maintained at a single central site, perhaps with a few duplicate copies strategically placed around the world. This is a vast improvement over expensive physical duplication of little used material, or the inconvenience of unique material that is unobtainable without traveling to the location where it is stored.

Information Is Easier to Keep Current

Much important information needs to be updated continually. Printed materials are awkward to update, since the entire document must be reprinted and all copies of the old version must be tracked down and replaced. Keeping information current is less laborious when the definitive version is in digital format and stored on a central computer.

Many libraries maintain online versions of directories, encyclopedias, and other reference works. Whenever revisions are received from the publisher, they are installed on the library's computer. The Library of

Congress has an online collection, called Thomas, that contains the latest drafts of all legislation currently before Congress.

The Information Is Always Available

The doors of the digital library never close; a recent study at a British university found that about half the use of a library's digital collections was at hours when the library buildings were closed. Materials are never checked out to other readers, mis-shelved, or stolen; they are never in an off-campus warehouse. The scope of the collections expands beyond the walls of the library. Private papers in an office or in a library on the other side of the world are as easy to use as materials in the local library.

This does not imply that digital libraries are perfect. Computer systems can fail, and networks may be slow or unreliable. But, compared with a traditional library, information is much more likely to be available when and where the user wants it.

New Forms of Information Become Possible

Print is not always the best way to record and disseminate information. A database may be the best way to store census data, so that it can be analyzed by computer. Satellite data can be rendered in many different ways. A mathematics library can store mathematical expressions as computer symbols that can be manipulated by means of a program such as Mathematica or Maple.

Even when the formats are similar, materials created explicitly for the digital world are not the same as materials originally designed for paper or other media. Words that are spoken have a different impact from words that are written, and online textual materials are subtly different from either the spoken or the printed word. Good authors use words differently when they write for different media and users find new ways to use the information. Materials created for the digital world can have a vitality that is lacking in material that has been mechanically converted to digital formats, just as a feature film never looks quite right when shown on television.

Each of the benefits described above can be seen in existing digital libraries. Another group of potential benefits, which have not yet been demonstrated, hold out tantalizing prospects. The hope is that digital libraries will develop from static repositories of immutable objects to provide a wide range of services that will allow collaboration and exchange of ideas. The technology of digital libraries is closely related to the technology used in electronic mail and teleconferencing, which have historically had little relationship to libraries. The potential for convergence between these fields is exciting.

The Cost of Digital Libraries

A final potential benefit is that digital libraries may save money. There has been a notable lack of hard data on the cost of digital libraries, but some of the underlying facts are clear.

Conventional libraries are expensive. They occupy expensive buildings on prime sites. Big libraries employ hundreds of people—well educated, though poorly paid. Libraries never have enough money to acquire and process all the materials they desire. Publishing is also expensive. Converting to electronic publishing adds new expenses. To recover the costs of developing new products, publishers sometimes charge more for a digital version than for the printed equivalent.

Today's digital libraries are also expensive—initially, more expensive than conventional ones. However, the components of digital libraries are declining rapidly in price. As the cost of the underlying technology continues to fall, digital libraries become steadily less expensive. In particular, the costs of distributing and of storing digital information decline. The reduction in cost will not be uniform. Some things are already cheaper by computer than by traditional methods. Other costs will not decline at the same rate and may even increase. Overall, however, there is a great opportunity to lower the costs of publishing and libraries.

Lower long-term costs are not necessarily good news for existing libraries and publishers. In the short term, the pressure to support traditional media alongside new digital collections is a heavy burden on budgets. Because people and organizations appreciate the benefits of online access and online publishing, they are prepared to spend an increasing amount of their money on computing, networks, and digital information. Most of this money, however, is going not to traditional libraries but to new areas: computers, networks, web sites, webmasters.

Publishers face difficulties because the normal pricing model of selling individual items does not fit the cost structure of electronic publishing. Much of the cost of conventional publishing is in the production and distribution of individual copies of books, photographs, video tapes, or other artifacts. Digital information is different. The fixed cost of creating the information and mounting it on a computer may be substantial, but the cost of using it is almost zero. Because the marginal cost is negligible, much of the information on the networks has been made openly available, with no restrictions on access. Not everything on the world's networks is freely available; however, a great deal is open to everybody, and this undermines revenue for the publishers. These pressures are inevitably changing the economic decisions of authors, users, publishers, and libraries.

Technical Developments

The first serious attempts to store library information on computers, in the late 1960s, faced serious technical barriers, including the high cost of computers, terse user interfaces, and the lack of networks. Because storage was expensive, the first applications were in areas where financial benefits could be gained from storing comparatively small volumes of data online. One early success was the Library of Congress's development of MARC, a format for machine-readable cataloging. The use of MARC by the Online Computer Library Center (OCLC) to share catalog records among many libraries resulted in large savings for libraries.

Early information services, such as shared cataloging, legal information systems, and the National Library of Medicine's Medline service, used the technology that existed when they were developed. Small quantities of information were mounted on a large central computer. Users sat at a dedicated terminal connected to the central computer by a low-speed communications link, either a telephone line or a special-purpose network. These systems required a trained user who would accept a cryptic user interface in exchange for faster searching than could be carried out manually and for access to information that was not available locally.

Such systems were no threat to the printed document. All that could be displayed was unformatted text, usually in a fixed-space font, without diagrams, mathematics, or the graphic quality that is essential for easy

Panel 1.1
Two Pioneers of Digital Libraries

The vision of the digital library is not new. This is a field in which progress has been achieved by the incremental efforts of numerous people over a long period of time. However, a few authors stand out because their writings have inspired future generations. Two of them are Vannevar Bush and J. C. R. Licklider.

In July of 1945, Bush, then director of the U.S. Office of Scientific Research and Development, published an article titled "As We May Think" in the *Atlantic Monthly*. This article is an elegantly written exposition of the potential that technology offers the scientist to gather, store, find, and retrieve information. Much of his analysis rings as true today as it did 50 years ago.

Bush commented that "our methods of transmitting and reviewing the results of research are generations old and by now are totally inadequate for their purpose." He discussed recent technological advances and how they might conceivably be applied at some distant time in the future. He provided an outline of one possible technical approach, which he called Memex. An interesting historical footnote is that the Memex design used photography to store information. For many years, microfilm was the technology perceived as the most suitable for storing information cheaply.

Bush is often cited as the first person to articulate the new vision of a library, but that is incorrect. His article built on earlier work, much of it carried out in Germany before World War II. The importance of his article lies in its wonderful exposition of the relationship between information and scientific research, and in the latent potential of technology.

The *Atlantic Monthly* has placed a copy of "As We May Think" on its web site. Anyone interested in libraries or in scientific information should read it.

In the 1960s Licklider was one of several people at the Massachusetts Institute of Technology who studied how digital computing could transform libraries. Like Bush, Licklider was most interested in the literature of science; however, he foresaw many developments that have occurred in modern computing.

In a 1965 book titled *Libraries of the Future*, Licklider described the research and development needed to build a truly usable digital library. When he wrote, time-shared computing was still in the research laboratory, and computer memory cost a dollar a byte, but he made a bold attempt to predict what a digital library might be like 30 years later, in 1994. His predictions proved remarkably accurate in their overall vision, though naturally he did not foretell every change that has happened in 30 years. In general, he underestimated how much would be achieved by brute-force methods, using huge amounts of cheap computer power, and overestimated how much progress could be made from artificial intelligence and improvements in computer methods of natural language processing.

Licklider's book is hard to find and less well known than it should be. It is one of the few important documents about digital libraries that are not available on the Internet.

reading. When these weaknesses were added to the inherent defects of early computer screens—poor contrast and low resolution—it is hardly surprising that most people were convinced that users would never willingly read from a screen.

The past thirty years have steadily eroded these technical barriers. During the early 1990s, a series of technical developments took place that removed the last fundamental barriers to building digital libraries. Some of this technology is still rough, but low-cost computing has stimulated an explosion of online information services. Four technical areas stand out as being particularly important to digital libraries.

Electronic Storage Is Becoming Cheaper Than Paper
Large libraries are painfully expensive for even the richest organizations. Buildings account for about a quarter of the total cost of most libraries. Many great libraries have huge old buildings with poor environmental control. Even when money is available, space for expansion is often hard to find in the center of a busy city or on a university campus.

Whereas the costs of constructing new buildings and maintaining old ones to store printed books and other artifacts will only increase with time, the costs of electronic storage decreasing by at least 30 percent per annum. In 1987, when we began work on the Mercury digital library at Carnegie Mellon University, several computers, each with 10 gigabytes of disk storage, were ordered. The list price of one of these computers was about $120,000. In 1997, a much more powerful computer with the same storage capacity cost about $4000. In ten years the price had dropped by about 97 percent. There is every reason to believe that by 2007 it will have dropped by another 97 percent.

In 1987, the cost of storing documents on CD-ROM was already less than the cost of storing books in libraries. Today, storing most forms of information on computers is much cheaper than storing physical artifacts in a library. In 1987, equipment costs were a major barrier to digital libraries. Today they are much lower, although storing large objects such as digitized videos, extensive collections of images, or high-fidelity sound recordings is still expensive. In ten years, equipment that is too expensive to buy today will be so cheap that price will rarely be a factor in decision making.

Personal Computer Displays Are Becoming More Pleasant to Use
Storage cost is not the only factor. (If it were, libraries would have standardized on microfilm years ago.) Until recently, few people were happy to read from a computer. The quality of the representation of documents on the screen was too poor. The usual procedure was to print a paper copy. Recently, however, major advances have been made in the quality of computer displays, in the fonts displayed on them, and in the software used to manipulate and render information. More and more, people are reading directly from computer screens—particularly when viewing materials that were designed for computer display, such as web pages. The best computers displays are still quite expensive, but every year they get cheaper and better. It will be a long time before computers match the convenience of books for general reading, but the high-resolution displays to be seen in research laboratories are very impressive indeed.

High-Speed Networks Are Becoming Widespread
The growth of the Internet during the 1990s has been phenomenal. Telecommunications companies compete to provide local and long-distance Internet service across the United States; international links reach almost every country in the world; every sizable company has its internal network; universities have built campus networks; individuals can purchase low-cost dial-up services for their homes. Even in the United States there are many gaps, and some countries are not yet connected at all. However, in many countries it is easier to receive information over the Internet than to acquire printed books and journals by orthodox methods.

Computers Have Become Portable
Although digital libraries use networks, their utility has been greatly enhanced by the development of portable "laptop" computers. By attaching a laptop computer to a network connection, a user combines the digital library resources of the Internet with the personal work that is stored on the computer. When the user disconnects the computer, copies of selected library materials can be retained for personal use.

During the past few years, laptop computers have increased in power, the quality of their screens has improved immeasurably, and their prices have declined steadily.

Access to Digital Libraries

Traditional libraries usually require that the user be a member of an organization that maintains expensive physical collections. In the United States, universities and some other organizations have excellent libraries, but most people do not belong to such an organization. Much of the Library of Congress is open to anybody over the age of 18, and a few cities have excellent public libraries, but most people are restricted to the small collections held by their local public library. Even scientists often have poor library facilities. Doctors in large medical centers have excellent libraries, but those in remote locations typically have nothing. One of the motives that led the Institute of Electrical and Electronics Engineers (IEEE) to take an early interest in electronic publishing was the fact that most engineers do not have access to an engineering library.

Use of a digital library requires a computer attached to the Internet. In the United States, many organizations provide all their staff members with computers. Some have done so for many years. Across the nation, there are programs to bring computers into schools and pubic libraries. For individuals who must provide their own computing, adequate access to the Internet requires less than $2000 worth of equipment, perhaps $20 per month for a dial-up connection, and a modicum of skill. For a little more money, a powerful computer and a higher-speed dedicated connection can be obtained. These are small investments for a prosperous professional, but can be a barrier for others. In 1998 it was estimated that 95 percent of people in the United States lived in areas where there was reasonably easy access to the Internet. This percentage is growing rapidly.

Outside the United States, the situation varies. Few countries' library services are as good as those in the United States. For example, universities in Mexico report that reliable delivery of scholarly journals is impossible, even when funds are available. Some nations are well supplied with computers and networks, but in most places equipment costs are higher than in the United States, people are less wealthy, monopolies keep communications costs high, and the support infrastructure is lacking. Digital libraries do bring information to many people who lack traditional libraries, but the Internet is far from being conveniently accessible from everywhere.

A factor that must be considered in planning digital libraries is that the quality of the technology available to users varies greatly. A favored few have the latest personal computers on their desks, with high-speed connections to the Internet and the most recent release of software; they are supported by skilled staff who can configure and tune the equipment, solve problems, and keep the software up to date. Most people, however, make do with less. Their equipment may be old, their software out of date, their Internet connection troublesome, and the members of their technical support staff undertrained and overworked. One of the great challenges in developing digital libraries is to build systems that take advantage of modern technology yet perform adequately in less-than-perfect situations.

Basic Concepts and Terminology

Terminology often proves to be a barrier in discussing digital libraries. The people who build digital libraries come from many disciplines and bring the terminologies of those disciplines with them. Some words have such strong social, professional, legal, or technical connotations that they obstruct discussion between people of varying backgrounds. Simple words mean different things to different people. For example, the words "copy" and "publish" have different meanings to computing professionals, to publishers, and to lawyers. Common English usage is not the same as professional usage, the dialects of English used around the world have subtle variations of meaning, and discussions of digital libraries are not restricted to the English language.

Some words cause such misunderstandings that it is tempting to ban them from any discussion of digital libraries. In addition to "copy" and "publish," the list includes "document," "object," and "work." Such words must be used carefully, and their exact meaning must be made clear whenever they are used. And some other words, though not quite so troublesome, have distinctly different meanings in different contexts. For example, in certain contexts the distinction must be made between "photograph" (an image on paper), and "digitized photograph" (a set of bits in a computer). Most of the time, however, such precision is mere pedantry. In this book, I follow the majority of the practitioners in the field of digital libraries and use terms informally where the meaning is clear from the context.

Collections

Digital libraries can hold any information that can be encoded as sequences of bits. Sometimes these are digitized versions of conventional media, such as text, images, music, sound recordings, specifications and designs, and many, many more. As digital libraries expand, the contents are less often the digital equivalents of physical items and more often items that have no equivalent, such as data from scientific instruments, computer programs, video games, and databases.

Data and metadata

The information stored in a digital library can be divided into data and metadata. *Data* is a general term used to describe information that is encoded in digital form. (Whether this word is singular or plural is a source of contention. In this book, following the custom in computing, I treat it as a singular collective noun.)

Metadata is data about other data. Many people dislike this word, but it is widely used. Common categories of metadata include *descriptive metadata* (e.g., bibliographic information), *structural metadata* (information about formats and structures), and *administrative metadata* (which includes, rights, permissions, and other information used to manage access). One item of metadata is the *identifier,* which identifies an item to the outside world.

The distinction between data and metadata often depends on the context. Catalog records and abstracts are usually considered to be metadata (because they describe other data), but in an online catalog or a database of abstracts they are the data.

Items in a digital library

No generic term has yet been established for the items stored in a digital library. In this book, several terms are used. The most general is *material,* which pertains to anything that might be stored in a library. The word *item* is essentially synonymous with *material.* Neither of these words implies anything about the content, the structure, or the user's view of the information.

The word *material* can be used to describe physical objects or information in digital formats. The term *digital material* is used when *digital* is needed for emphasis. The more precise term *digital object* is used to describe an item as it is stored in a digital library. Typically, a digital object consists of data, associated metadata, and an identifier.

Some people call every item in a digital library a *document*. This book reserves that term for a digitized text, or for a digital object whose data is the digital equivalent of a physical document.

Library objects

The term *library object* is useful in that it expresses the user's view of what is stored in a library. For example, an article in an online periodical is probably stored on a computer as several separate objects (pages of digitized text, graphics, and perhaps even computer programs or linked items stored on remote computers). From the user's viewpoint, this is one library object made up of several digital objects.

Library objects have internal structure. They usually include both data and associated metadata. Structural metadata is used to describe the formats and the relationship of the parts.

Presentations, disseminations, and the stored form of a digital object

The form in which information is stored in a digital library may be very different from the form in which it is used. A simulator used to train airplane pilots might be stored as several computer programs, data structures, digitized images, and other data. This is the *stored form* of the object, but the user perceives a series of images, synthesized sound, and control sequences. Some people use the term *presentation* for what is presented to the user, and in many contexts this term is appropriate. A more general term is *dissemination*, which emphasizes that the transformation from the stored form to the user requires the execution of some computer program.

When digital information is received by a user's computer, it must be converted into the form that is provided to the user—typically a display on a computer screen, perhaps augmented by a soundtrack or some other presentation. The conversion is called *rendering*.

Works and content

Finding terms to describe content is especially difficult. The English language is very flexible, and words have varying meanings depending on the context. Consider, the example, "the song Simple Gifts." Depending on the context, that phrase could refer to the song as a work with words and music, to the score of the song, to a performance of somebody singing it, to a recording of the performance, to an edition of music on compact disk, to a specific compact disc, to the act of playing the music from the recording, to the performance encoded in a digital library, or to various other aspects of the song. Such distinctions are important to the music industry, because they determine who receives money that is paid for a musical performance or recording.

Several digital library researchers have attempted to define a general hierarchy of terms that can be applied to all works and library objects. This is a bold and useful objective, but it is fraught with difficulties. Library materials vary so much that a classification may match some types of material well but fail to describe others adequately.

Nonetheless, *work* and *content* are useful words. Most people use the word *content* loosely, and this book does the same. The word is used in any context where the emphasis is on library materials not as bits and bytes to be processed by a computer but as information that is of interest to a user. We cannot define content, but we know it when we see it.

Whereas *content* is used as a loosely defined, general term, *work* is used more specifically. In U.S. copyright law, *literary work* is carefully defined as abstract content (e.g., a sequence of words or musical notes) independent of any particular stored representation, presentation, or performance. This book usually uses the word *work* roughly with this meaning, though not always with legal precision.

People

A variety of words are used to describe the people who are associated with digital libraries.

The *creators* of information in a library include authors, composers, photographers, mapmakers, designers, and anybody else who creates intellectual works. Some are professionals, some amateurs. Some work individually, others in teams. They have many different reasons for creating information.

Another group consists of the *users* of the digital library. Depending on the context, users may be described by different terms. In libraries, they are often called *readers* or *patrons;* at other times they may be called the *audience* or the *customers.* As is true of traditional libraries, the creators and the users of digital libraries are sometimes the same people. In academia, scholars and researchers use libraries as resources for their research, and publish their findings in forms that become part of library collections.

The final group of people is a broad one that includes everybody whose role is to support the creators and the users: computer specialists, librarians, publishers, editors, and many others. They can be called *information managers*. The World Wide Web has created a new profession: webmaster. A single individual may be creator, user, and information manager.

Computers and Networks

A digital library consists of many computers united by a communications network. The dominant network is the Internet, the emergence of which as a flexible, low-cost, worldwide network has been a major factor in the growth of digital libraries.

Figure 1.1 shows some of the computers that are used in digital libraries. They have three main function: to help users interact with the library, to store collections of materials, and to provide services.

In the terminology of computing, anybody who interacts with a computer is a *computer user* or simply a *user*. This broad term covers creators, library users, information professionals, and anybody else who accesses the computer. A computer used to access a digital library is called a *client*.

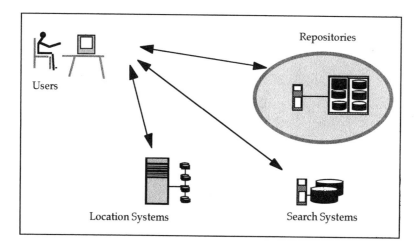

Figure 1.1

Sometimes, clients may interact with a digital library without the involvement of a human user. Among the clients that do this are robots that automatically index library collections and sensors that gather data about the weather and supply it to digital libraries.

Repositories are computers that store collections of information and provide access to them. An *archive* is a repository that is organized for long-term preservation of materials.

Two typical *services* provided by digital libraries are *search services* and *location services*. Search services provide catalogs, indexes, and other services to help users find information. Location services are used to identify and locate information.

In some circumstances there may be other computers between clients and the computers that store information. *Mirrors* and *caches* store duplicate copies of information, for faster performance and reliability. Mirrors replicate large sets of information; caches store recently used information only. *Proxies* and *gateways* provide bridges between different types of computer systems and are particularly useful in reconciling systems that have conflicting technical specifications.

The generic term *server* is used to describe any computer other than a client. A single server may provide several of the functions listed above, perhaps acting as a repository, a search service, and a location service. Conversely, individual functions can be distributed across many servers. For example, the domain-name system, a locator service for computers on the Internet, is a single, integrated service that runs on thousands of separate servers.

A *distributed system* is a group of computers that work as a team to provide services to users. Digital libraries are among the most complex and ambitious distributed systems ever built. Users' personal computers, which have to exchange messages with the server computers, are of every known type, managed by thousands of different organizations, and running software that ranges from state-of-the-art to antiquated. The term *interoperability* refers to the task of building coherent services for users when the individual components are technically different and managed by different organizations. Some people argue that all technical problems in digital libraries are aspects of interoperability. This is probably an overstatement, but it is certainly true that interoperability is a fundamental challenge in all aspects of digital libraries.

The Challenge of Change

If digital technology is so splendid, what is stopping every library immediately becoming entirely digital? Part of the answer is that the technology of digital libraries is still immature, but the challenge is much more than technology. An equal challenge is the ability of individuals and organizations to devise ways to use technology effectively, to absorb the inevitable changes, and to create the required social frameworks. The world of information has many participants, each contributing experience, expertise, and resources. To make fundamental changes in the system requires interrelated shifts in the economic, social, and legal relationships among these parties.

Digital libraries depend on people and cannot be introduced faster than people and organizations can adapt. This applies equally to the creators, the users, and the professionals who support them. The relationships among these groups are changing. With digital libraries, readers frequently go directly to information, without visiting a library building or having any contact with a professional intermediary. Authors may carry out more of the preparation of a manuscript. Professionals need new skills and new training to support these new relationships. Some of these skills are absorbed through experience; others can be taught. Schools of librarianship are adapting their curricula, but it will be many years before the changes work through the system. The traditions of hundreds of years go deep.

The general wisdom is that, except in a few specialized areas, digital libraries and conventional collections will continue to coexist—that institutional libraries will maintain large collections of traditional materials in parallel with their digital services, and publishers will continue to have large markets for their traditional products. However, the spectacular and continuing decline in the cost of computing and the corresponding increase in capabilities sometimes leads to complete substitution. Word processors supplanted typewriters in barely ten years. Card catalogs in libraries are on the same track. In 1980, only a handful of libraries could afford online catalogs. Twenty years later, card catalogs are becoming historic curiosities in American libraries. In some specialized areas, digital libraries may completely replace conventional library materials.

Many exciting developments in digital libraries have been introduced by new organizations. New organizations can begin afresh, whereas older organizations often must maintain current services while introducing new services. One likely effect of digital libraries will be a massive transfer of money from traditional suppliers of information to new information entrepreneurs and to the computing industry. Naturally, existing organizations will try hard to discourage any change that diminishes their importance, but the economic relationships among the parties are already changing. Some important organizations will undoubtedly shrink in size or even go out of business. Predicting these changes is made particularly difficult by uncertainties about the finances of digital libraries and electronic publishing, and by the need for the legal system to adapt. Eventually, the pressures of the marketplace will establish a new order. At some point, the market will have settled down sufficiently for the legal rules to be clarified. Until then, economic and legal uncertainties are annoying, though they have not proved to be serious barriers to progress.

In the long run, there appear to be no barriers to digital libraries and electronic publishing. Technical, economic, social, and legal challenges abound, but they are being overcome steadily. We cannot be sure exactly what form digital libraries will take, but it is clear that they are here to stay.

2

The Internet and the World Wide Web

The Internet

As its name suggest, the Internet is an interconnected group of independently managed networks. Each network supports the technical standards needed for interconnection—the TCP/IP family of protocols and a common method for identifying computers—but in many ways the separate networks are very different. The various sections of the Internet use almost every kind of communications channel that can transmit data. They range from fast and reliable to slow and erratic. They are privately owned or operated as public utilities. They are paid for in different ways. The Internet is sometimes called an "information highway." A better comparison would be to the international transportation system, which includes everything from airlines to dirt tracks.

The networks that make up the Internet originated in two ways. One line of development was the local-area networks that were created to link computers and terminals within a department or an organization. Many of the original concepts came from the Xerox Corporation's Palo Alto Research Center (PARC). In the United States, universities were pioneers in expanding small local networks into campus-wide networks. The second source of network developments were the national wide-area networks. The best known of these was the ARPAnet, which by the mid 1980s linked about 150 computer science research organizations. Other major networks, such as Bitnet, have been almost forgotten. Their former users are now served by the Internet.

Since the early networks used differing technical approaches, linking them together was hard. During the late 1980s, the universities and the research communities converged on using TCP/IP, the protocols of the ARPAnet, to create the Internet that we know today. A key event was the 1986 decision by the National Science Foundation to build a high-speed network backbone for the United States and to support the development of regional networks connected to it. To create this backbone, the foundation decided to build on the ARPAnet's technical achievements. This set the standards for the Internet. Meanwhile, campus networks were using the same standards. Carnegie Mellon University's high-speed network, completed in 1986, is a good example of an early network. It accommodated several methods of data transmission, and supported competing network protocols from Digital, Apple, and IBM, but the unifying theme was the use of TCP/IP.

Future historians can argue over the combination of financial, organizational, and technical factors that led to the acceptance of the ARPAnet technical standards. Several companies made major contributions to the development and expansion of the Internet, but the leadership came from two U.S. government organizations: the Defense Advanced Research Projects Agency (DARPA) and the National Science Foundation.

The technology of the Internet is the subject of whole books. Most of the details are unimportant to users, but a basic understanding of the technology is useful to the designers and the users of digital libraries. TCP/IP and the numeric addresses known as IP addresses are introduced in panel 2.1. Another way to identify a computer on the Internet is to give it a name, such as tulip.mercury.cmu.edu. Names of this form are known as *domain names*, and the system that relates them to IP addresses is known as the *domain-name system* (DNS). Computers that supports the TCP/IP protocols usually provide a standard set of basic applications. These applications are known as the *TCP/IP suite*. Some of the most commonly used are listed in panel 2.2.

The Internet Community
The Internet pioneered the concept of open standards. In 1997, Vinton Cerf and Robert Kahn received the National Medal of Technology for their contributions to the Internet. The citation praised their work on the TCP/IP protocols, but it also noted that they had "pioneered not just a technology, but also an economical and efficient way to transfer that technology," and that they had "steadfastly maintained that their internetworking protocols

Panel 2.1
TCP/IP

The two basic protocols that form the Internet are TCP and IP. One sees them mentioned together (TCP/IP) so often that it is easy to forget that these abbreviations represent two separate protocols.

The *Internet Protocol* (IP) interconnects the separate network segments that constitute the Internet. Every computer on the Internet has a unique address, known as an *IP address*. The address (for example, 132.151.3.90) consists of four numbers, each in the range 0–255. Within a computer these are stored as four bytes. When printed, the convention is to separate them with periods as in this example. The Internet Protocol enables any computer on the Internet to dispatch a message to any other. The various parts of the Internet are connected by specialized computers known as *routers*. As their name implies, routers use the IP address to route each message on the next stage of the journey to its destination.

On the Internet, messages are transmitted as short packets, typically a few hundred bytes in length. A router simply receives a packet from one segment of the network and dispatches it on its way. An IP router has no way of knowing whether the packet ever reaches its ultimate destination. Users of the network are rarely interested in individual packets or network segments. They need reliable delivery of complete messages from one computer to another. This is the function of the *Transport Control Protocol* (TCP). An application program at the sending computer passes a message to the local TCP software. TCP takes the message, divides it into packets, labels each with the destination IP address and a sequence number, and sends them out on the network. At the receiving computer, each packet is acknowledged when received. The packets are reassembled into a single message and handed over to an application program.

TCP should be invisible to the user of a digital library, but the responsiveness of the network is greatly influenced by the protocol and this often affects the performance that users see. Not all packets arrive successfully. A router that is overloaded may simply ignore ("drop") some packets. If this happens, the sending computer never receives an acknowledgment. Eventually it gets tired of waiting and sends the packet again. This is known as a "time-out." It is perceived by the user as an annoying delay.

TCP guarantees error-free delivery of messages, but it does not guarantee that they will be delivered punctually. For some applications, punctuality is more important than complete accuracy. Suppose one computer is transmitting a stream of audio that another is playing immediately on arrival. If an occasional packet fails to arrive on time, the human ear would much prefer to lose tiny sections of the sound track rather than wait for a missing packet to be retransmitted, which would be horribly jerky. Since TCP is unsuitable for such applications, they use an alternate protocol, named UDP, which also runs over IP. With UDP, the sending computer sends out a sequence of packets, hoping that they will arrive. The protocol does its best, but makes no guarantee that any packets ever arrive.

Panel 2.2
The TCP/IP suite

The *TCP/IP suite* is a group of computer programs (based on TCP/IP) that are provided by most modern computers. They include the following.

Terminal emulation   A program known as Telnet allows a personal computer to emulate an old-fashioned computer terminal that has no processing power of its own and relies on a remote computer for processing. Since it provides a lowest-common-denominator user interface, Telnet is often used for system administration.

File transfer   The protocol for moving files from one computer to another across the Internet is the file transfer protocol (FTP). Since FTP was designed to make use of TCP, it is effective for moving large files across the Internet.

Electronic mail   Internet mail uses the Simple Mail Transport Protocol (SMTP). This is the protocol that turned electronic mail from a collection of local services to a single world-wide service. It provides a basic mechanism for delivering mail. In recent years, a series of extensions have been made to allow messages to include wider character sets, permit multi-media mail, and support the attachment of files to mail messages.

Panel 2.3
NetNews

The NetNews bulletin boards (also known as Usenet) are an important and revealing examples of the Internet community's approach to the open distribution of information. Thousands of bulletin boards, called *newsgroups*, are organized in a series of hierarchies. The highest-level groupings include comp, rec, the notorious alt, and many more. For example, rec.arts.theatre.musicals is a bulletin board for discussing musicals.

The NetNews system is so decentralized that no one has a comprehensive list of all the newsgroups. An individual who wishes to post a message to a group sends it to the local news host. This passes it to its neighbors, who pass it to their neighbors, and so on.

NetNews is the exact opposite of a digital library in the sense that NetNews information is entirely unmanaged. There are essentially no restrictions on who can post or what one can post. At its worst the system distributes libel, hate, pornography, and simply wrong information, but many newsgroups work remarkably well. For example, people around the world who use the Python programming language have a newsgroup (comp.lang.python) in which they exchange technical information, pose queries, and communicate with the language's developer.

would be freely available to anyone." TCP/IP, the citation continued, "was deliberately designed to be vendor-independent to support networking across all lines of computers and all forms of transmission."

The Internet tradition continues to emphasize collaboration on technical matters, and the continuing development of the Internet remains firmly in the hands of engineers. Some people seem unable to accept that the U.S. government is capable of anything worthwhile, but the creation of the Internet was led by government agencies, often against strong resistance by companies who now profit from its success. Recently, attempts have been made to rewrite the history of the Internet to advance vested interests, and individuals have claimed responsibility for achievements that many shared. There is a striking contrast between the coherence of the Internet—coordinated by far-sighted government officials—and the mess of incompatible standards in areas left to commercial competition, such as mobile telephones.

An important characteristic of the Internet is that the engineers and computer scientists who develop and operate it are heavy users of their own technology. They communicate by email, dismissing conventional mail as "snail mail." When they write a paper, they compose it at their own computer. If it is a web page, they insert the markup tags themselves rather than use a formatting program. Senior computer scientists may spend more time preparing public presentations than writing computer programs, but programming is the basic skill that everybody is expected to have.

Scientific Publishing on the Internet

The publishing of serious academic materials on the Internet goes back many years. Panels 2.4 and 2.5 describe two important examples: the Internet RFC series and the Physics E-Print Archives at the Los Alamos National Laboratory. Both are poorly named. "RFC" once stood for "Request for Comment," but the RFC series is now the definitive technical series for the Internet. It includes a variety of technical information and the formal Internet standards. The Los Alamos service is not an archive in the usual sense. Its primary function is as a "preprint server"—a site where researchers can publish research as soon as it is complete, without the delays of conventional journal publishing.

Panel 2.4
The Internet Engineering Task Force and the RFC Series

The Internet Engineering Task Force is the body that coordinates technical aspects of the Internet. Its methods of working are unique, yet it has proved extraordinarily good at getting large numbers of people, many from competing companies, to work together. The first unusual feature is that the IETF is open to all. Anyone can go to meetings, join working groups, and vote.

The IETF's basic principle of operation is "rough consensus and working code." Anyone who wishes to propose a new protocol or some other technical advance is encouraged to provide a technical paper (called an *Internet Draft*) and a reference implementation of the concept. The reference implementation should be in the form of openly available software. At meetings of working groups, the Internet Drafts are discussed. If there is a consensus in favor of going ahead, a draft may be put on the *RFC standards* track. No draft standard can become a formal standard until implementations of the specification (usually computer programs) are available for everybody to use.

The IETF began in the United States but is now international. Every year, one meeting is held outside the United States. Participants, including the leaders of working group, come from around the world. The IETF, originally funded by U.S. government grants, is now self-sufficient. The costs are covered by meeting fees.

The processes of the IETF are open to all who wish to contribute. Unlike some other standards bodies, whose working drafts are hard to obtain and whose final standards are complex and expensive, all Internet Drafts and RFCs are available online. Because of the emphasis on working software, the first of two rival technical approaches to be demonstrated with software that actually works has a high chance of acceptance. As a result, the Internet's core standards are remarkably simple.

Recent IETF meetings have attracted more than 2000 people; however, because they divide into working groups addressing specific topics, a feeling of intimacy remains. Almost everyone is a practicing engineer or computer scientist. The managers stay home. The formal meetings are short and informal, the informal meetings long and intense. Many an important specification has come out of a late-night session at the IETF, with people from competing organizations working together.

Because of its rapid growth, the Internet is always in some danger of breaking down technically. The IETF is the fundamental reason that it shows so much resilience. If a single company controlled the Internet, the technology would be as good as the company's senior engineering staff. Because the IETF looks after the Internet technology, the world's best engineers work together to deal with anticipated problems.

The Internet Drafts are a remarkable series of technical publications. In science and engineering, most information goes out of date rapidly, but journals sit on library shelves for ever. Internet Drafts are the opposite. Each begins with a fixed statement that includes this wording: "Internet-Drafts are draft documents valid for a maximum of six months and may be updated, replaced, or obsoleted by other documents at any time. It is inappropriate to use Internet-Drafts as reference material or to cite them other than as work in progress."

The IETF posts online every Internet Draft that is submitted, and it notifies interested people through mailing lists. Then the review begins. Individuals post their comments on the relevant mailing list. Comments range from detailed suggestions to biting criticisms. By the time the working group comes together to discuss it, a proposal has been subjected to public review by the experts in the field.

The RFCs are the official publications of the IETF. These few thousand publications form a series that goes back to 1969. They are the heart of the documentation of the Internet. The best known RFCs are those that form the *standards track*. They include the formal specification of each version of the IP protocol, Internet mail, components of the World Wide Web, and many more. Other types of RFC include informational RFCs, which publish technical information relevant to the Internet.

Discussions of scientific publishing rarely mention the RFC series, yet it is hard to find another set of scientific or engineering publications that are so heavily reviewed before publication or so widely read by the experts in the field. RFCs have never been published on paper. Originally available over the Internet by FTP, they are now available (still in a basic text-only format) on the web.

Whatever the merits of their names, these two services are of fundamental importance for the publishing of research in their respective fields. They are important also because they demonstrate that the digital libraries find new ways of doing things. One of the articles of faith within scholarly publishing is that quality can be achieved only by peer review, the process by which every article is read by other specialists before publication. The process by which Internet Drafts become RFCs is an intense form of peer review, but it takes place after a draft of the paper has been officially posted. The Los Alamos service has no review process. Yet both have proved to be highly effective methods of scientific communication.

They are also interesting economically. Both services are completely open to the user. They are run professionally, with substantial budgets, but no charges are made to authors who provide information to the service or to readers who use the information.

Panel 2.5
The Los Alamos E-print Archives

The Physics E-print Archives provide an illuminating example of practicing scientists' taking advantage of the Internet technology to create a new form of scientific communication by extending the custom of circulating preprints of research papers. The first archive was established in 1991 by Paul Ginsparg of the Los Alamos National Laboratory to serve the needs of a group of high-energy physicists. Later, archives were created for other branches of physics, mathematics, and related disciplines. In a 1996 UNESCO talk in Paris, Ginsparg reported: "These archives now serve over 35,000 users worldwide from over 70 countries, and process more than 70,000 electronic transactions per day. In some fields of physics, they have already supplanted traditional research journals as conveyers of both topical and archival research information."

The primary function of the E-print Archives is to present the results of research, often in a preliminary version of a paper that will later be published in a traditional journal. Papers are prepared for the archives in the usual manner. Many physicists use the TeX format, but PostScript and HTML are also used. Graphs and data are sometimes embedded in text, sometimes provided as separate files.

A paper may be submitted to an archive by electronic mail, by file transfer (using the FTP protocol), or via the web. The author is expected to provide a short abstract and a standard set of indexing metadata. The processing is entirely automatic. The archives provide an electronic-mail-based search service, a web-based search system, and an email notification service to subscribers. Search options include searching one archive, searching many archives, searching by author and title, and searching the full text of abstracts.

The technology of the archives is straightforward. They use the standard formats, protocols, and networking tools that researchers know and understand. The user interfaces have been designed to minimize the effort required to maintain the archive. Authors and readers are expected to assist by installing appropriate software on their own computers and by following procedures.

This is an open-access system, funded through annual grants from the National Science Foundation and the Department of Energy. Authors retain copyright in their papers. (About the only mention of copyright in the archive instructions is buried in a page of disclaimers and acknowledgments.)

As Ginsparg writes, "many of the lessons learned from these systems should carry over to other fields of scholarly publication, i.e. those wherein authors are writing not for direct financial remuneration in the form of royalties, but rather primarily to communicate information (for the advancement of knowledge, with attendant benefits to their careers and professional reputations)."

Both of the aforementioned services were well established before the emergence of the web. The web has been so successful that many people forget that there are other effective ways to distribute information on the Internet. Both the Los Alamos archives and the RFC series now use web methods, but they were originally based on electronic mail and file transfer.

The World Wide Web

The World Wide Web (colloquially "the web") has been one of the great successes in the history of computing. It ranks with the development of word processors and spreadsheets as a definitive application of computing. The web and its associated technology have been crucial to the rapid growth of digital libraries. This section gives a basic overview of the web and its underlying technology. Details of specific aspects are spread throughout the book.

The web is a linked collection of information on many computers on the Internet around the world. These computers are called *web servers*. Some of the web servers and the information on them are maintained by individuals and some by small groups, including university departments and research centers; others are large corporate information services. Some sites are consciously organized as digital libraries; others (some of them excellent) are managed by individuals who would not consider themselves librarians or publishers. Some web servers have substantial collections of high-quality information; others are used for short-term or private purposes, are informally managed, or are used for purposes (such as marketing) that are outside the scope of libraries.

The web technology was developed around 1990 by Tim Berners-Lee and colleagues at the Centre Européenne pour la Recherche Nucléaire (CERN), in Switzerland. It was made popular by Mosaic, a user interface developed by Marc Andreessen and others at the University of Illinois at Urbana-Champaign. Mosaic was released in 1993. Within a few years, numerous commercial versions of it followed. Of those, the most widely used are the Netscape Navigator and Microsoft's Internet Explorer. These user interfaces are called *web browsers*, or simply *browsers*.

The basic reason for the success of the web can be summarized succinctly: It provides a convenient way to distribute information over the

Internet. Individuals can publish information, and they can access that information by themselves, with no training and no help from outsiders. A small amount of computer knowledge is needed to establish a web site; next to none is needed to use a browser.

The introduction of the web was a grassroots phenomenon. Not only is the technology simple; the manner in which it was released to the public removed almost all barriers to its use. What happened at Carnegie Mellon University was typical: Individuals copied web software over the Internet onto private computers. They then loaded information that interested them and made it available to others. Their computers were already connected to the campus network and hence to the Internet. Within six months of the first release of Mosaic, three individuals had established major collections of academic information on statistics, English language and literature, and the environment. Since the Internet covers the world, huge numbers of people had immediate access to this information. Eventually the university adopted the web officially, with a carefully designed home page providing information about the university, but only after individuals had shown the way.

One reason that individuals have been able to experiment with the web is that web software has always been available at no charge over the Internet. CERN and the University of Illinois set the tradition with open distribution of their software for web servers and user interfaces. Today's most widely used web server is Apache, a no-cost version of the Illinois web server. The open distribution of software over the Internet provides a great stimulus for acceptance of new technology. Most technical people enjoy experimentation but dislike bureaucracy. The joy goes out of an experiment if they must issue a purchase order or ask a manager to sign a software license.

Another reason for the instant success of the web was that the technology provided gateways to information that had not been created specifically for the web. The browsers are designed around the web protocol called Hypertext Transfer Protocol (HTTP), but the browsers also support other Internet protocols, such as the File Transfer Protocol (FTP), Net News, and electronic mail. Support for the Gopher and WAIS protocols (now almost obsolete) allowed earlier collections of information to coexist with the first web sites. Another mechanism, the Common Gateway Interface (CGI), allowed browsers to bridge the gap between the web and any other system for storing online information. In this way, large amounts of information were available as soon as Mosaic became available.

From the first release of Mosaic, the leading browsers have been available for the most common operating systems—the various versions of Windows, Macintosh, and Unix—and browsers are now provided for all standard computers. The administrator of a web site can be confident that users around the world will see the information provided on the site in roughly the same format, whatever computers they have.

The Technology of the Web

Technically, the web is based on four simple techniques: the Hypertext Markup Language (HTML), the Hypertext Transfer Protocol (HTTP), MIME data types, and Uniform Resource Locators (URLs). Each of these concepts has importance that goes beyond the web into the general field of interoperability of digital libraries.

HTML

HTML is a language for describing the structure and the appearance of text documents. Panel 2.6 shows a simple HTML file and how a typical browser might display, or render, it.

As the example shows, an HTML file contains both the text to be rendered and codes, known as *tags*, that describe the format or structure. HTML tags can always be recognized by the delimiters < and >. Most HTML tags are in pairs, with a slash identifying the second of a pair. For example, <title> and </title> enclose text that is interpreted as a title. Some of the HTML tags specify format: <i> and </i> enclose text to be rendered in italic, and <br> indicates a line break. Other tags specify structure: <p> and </p> delimit a paragraph, and <h1> and </h1> bracket a first-level heading. Structural tags do not specify the format, which is left to the browser. For example, many browsers show the beginning of a paragraph by inserting a blank line, but this is a stylistic convention determined by the browser.

The example in panel 2.6 also shows two features are special to HTML that have been vital to the success of the web. The first special feature is the ease of including color image in web pages. The tag <img src = "logo.gif">

Panel 2.6
An Example of HTML

Here is an example of how a simple text file in HTML format is stored in a computer, with tags used to define structure and format:

```
<html>
<head>
<title>HTML Example</title>
</head>

<body>
<h1>An Example of HTML</h1>
<img src = "logo.gif">

<p>Since the first issue appeared in July 1995, <a href =
"http://www.dlib.org/dlib.html">D-Lib Magazine</a> has appeared
monthly as a compendium of research, news, and progress in digital
libraries.</p>
<p><i>William Y. Arms
<br>January 1, 1999</i></p>

</body>
</html>
```

When displayed by a browser, this document might be rendered as shown below. The exact format depends on the browser, the computer, and the choice of options.

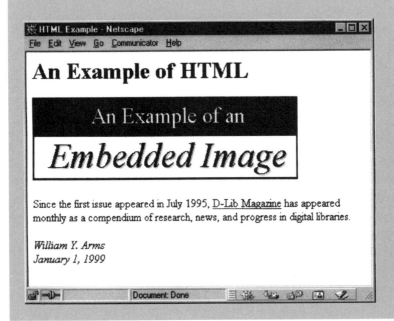

is an instruction to insert an image that is stored in a separate file; img stands for *image* and src for *source*. The string that follows is the name of the file in which the image is stored. With the introduction of this simple command, Mosaic brought color images to the Internet. Before the web, Internet applications were drab. Common applications used unformatted text with no images. The web was the first widely used system to combine formatted text and color images. Suddenly the Internet came alive. The second and even more important special feature is the use of *hyperlinks*. Web pages do not stand alone. They can link to other pages anywhere on the Internet. The example in panel 2.6 contains one hyperlink: the tag <a href = "http://www.dlib.org/dlib.html">. This tag is followed by a string of text terminated by </a>. When displayed by a browser, the text string is highlighted; usually it appears in blue and is underlined. The convention is simple. If something is underlined in blue, the user can click on it and the hyperlink will be executed. This convention is easy for the both the user and the creator of the web page. (In this example, the link is to an HTML page on another computer: the home page of *D-Lib Magazine*.)

The basic concepts of HTML can be described in a short tutorial and absorbed quickly, but even simple tagging can create an attractive document. In the early days of the web, everybody was self-taught. A useful characteristic of HTML is that its syntax is forgiving of small mistakes. Other computing languages have strict syntax. Omit a semicolon in a computer program and the program fails or gives the wrong result. With HTML, if the markup is more or less right, most browsers will usually accept it. The simplicity has the added benefit that computer programs to interpret HTML and display web pages are straightforward to write.

Uniform Resource Locators (URLs)

The second key component of the web is the Uniform Resource Locator (URL). URLs are ugly to look at, but they are flexible. They provide a simple addressing mechanism that allows the web to link information on computers all over the world. A simple URL, found in the HTML example in panel 2.6, is http://www.dlib.org/dlib.html, where http is the name of a protocol, www.dlib.org is the domain name of a computer, and dlib.html is the name of a file on that computer. This URL can be interpreted informally as follows: "Using the HTTP protocol, connect to the computer with the Internet address www.dlib.org, and get the file dlib.html."

HTTP

In computing, a protocol is a set of rules that are used to send messages between computer systems. A typical protocol includes descriptions of the formats to be used, the various messages, the sequences in which they should be sent, appropriate responses, error conditions, and so on. HTTP is the protocol that is used to send messages between web browsers and web servers.

The basic message type in HTTP is *get*. For example, clicking on the hyperlink with the URL http://www.dlib.org/dlib.html specifies an HTTP *get* command. This command can be interpreted informally as follows: "Open a connection between the browser and the web server that has the domain name 'www.dlib.org.' Copy the file 'dlib.html' from the web server to the browser. Close the connection."

MIME types

A file of data in a computer is simply a set of bits. To be useful, the bits must be interpreted. In the example above, in order to display the file "dlib.html" correctly the browser must know that it is in the HTML format. The interpretation depends on the *data type* of the file. Two common data types are html (for a file of text that is marked up in HTML format) and jpeg (for a file that represents an image encoded in the jpeg format).

In the web, and in a wide variety of Internet applications, the data type is specified by a scheme called *MIME*. (The official name is Internet Media Types.) MIME was originally developed to describe information sent by electronic mail. It uses two-part encoding, with a generic part and a specific part. For example, text/ascii is the MIME type for text encoded in ASCII, image/jpeg is the type for an image in the jpeg format, and text/html is text marked up with HTML tags. There is a standard set of MIME types that are used by numerous computer programs, and additional data types can be described using experimental tags.

The importance of MIME types in the web is that the data transmitted by an HTTP get command has a MIME type associated with it. For example, the file "dlib.html" has the MIME type text/html. When the browser receives a file of this type, it knows that the appropriate way to handle this file is to render it as HTML text and display it on the screen.

Many computer systems use file names as a crude method of recording data types. For example, some Windows programs use file names that end in .htm for files of HTML data. Unix computers use .html for the same purpose. MIME types are a more flexible and systematic method to record and transmit typed data.

Information on the Web

The simple components described above can be used to create many applications, only some of which can be considered digital libraries (i.e., managed collections of diverse information). Here are some examples of other applications: Many a company has a web site that describes the company and provides information about its products and services. Airline tickets can be purchased from web servers. Associations maintain web sites that provide information to their members. Private individuals have their own web sites, or personal home pages. Research results may be reported first on the web. Many web sites meet the definition of junk. In aggregate, however, the various sites are important to the development of digital libraries. They are responsible for technical developments beyond the simple building blocks described above, for experimentation, for the establishment of conventions for organizing materials, for the increasingly high quality of graphical design, and for the large number of skilled creators, users, and webmasters. The size of the web has stimulated numerous companies to develop products, many of which are now being used to build digital libraries. Less fortunately, the success of all these web sites often overloads sections of the Internet, and has generated social and legal concerns about abusive behavior on the Internet.

Conventions of the Web

The first web sites were created by individuals, who used whatever arrangement of the information they considered appropriate. Soon, however, conventions about how to organize materials began to emerge.

Hyperlinks permit an indefinite variety of arrangements of information on web sites. Users, however, navigate most effectively through familiar structures. Therefore, conventions are of great importance in the design of

Panel 2.7
The World Wide Web Consortium

Although no central organization controls the web, there must be agreement on the basic protocols, formats, and practices so that the independent computer systems can interoperate. In 1994, recognizing this need, the Massachusetts Institute of Technology created the World Wide Web Consortium ("W3C") and hired Tim Berners-Lee, the creator of the web, as its director. Later, MIT added international partners at the Institut National de Recherche en Informatique et en Automatique in France and at Keio University's Shonan Fujisawa campus in Japan. W3C is funded by member organizations who include most of the larger companies who develop web browsers, servers, and related products.

W3C is a neutral forum in which organizations work together on common specifications for the web through a series of conferences, workshops, and design processes. It provides a collection of information about the web for developers and users, including samples of code that help to promote standards. It works closely with the Internet Engineering Task Force to promulgate standards for basic web technology, such as HTTP, HTML, and URLs.

Because W3C acts as a neutral body in a field dominated by fiercely competing companies, its power depends on its influence. One of its greatest successes was the rapid development of PICS, an industry standard for the rating of content, which was created in response to political worries in the United States about the ability of minors to access pornography and other undesirable content. More recently, W3C has been active in the development of the XML markup language.

Although Microsoft, Netscape, and other companies sometimes seem to believe that they gain by supplying products that have non-standard features, such features are detrimental to the homogeneity of the web. W3C deserves much of the credit for the reasonably coherent way in which the web technology continues to be developed.

digital libraries that are built on the web. The conventions that have developed never went through any standardization body, but their widespread adoption adds a coherence to the web that is not inherent in the basic technology.

Web sites

A web site is a collection of information that the user perceives to be a single unit. Often a web site corresponds to a single web server; however, a large site may be physically held on several servers, and one server may host many web sites.

Home pages

A home page is the introductory page to a collection of web information. Almost every web site has a home page. If the address in a URL does not specify a file name, the server conventionally supplies a page called index.html. Thus, for example, the URL http://www.loc.gov/ is interpreted as http://www.loc.gov/index.html.

Every designer has slightly different ideas about how to arrange a home page. However, just as the title pages of books usually follow certain conventions, a home page usually provides an overview of the web site (typically in combination with an introduction to the site, a table of contents, and some help in finding information).

Small sets of information within a web site also can be called home pages. It is common for information relevant to a specific department, project, or service to have its own home page within the web site of a company or an institution.

Buttons

Most web pages have buttons labeled as "home," "next," and "previous" to help users navigate the web site. These buttons provide hyperlinks to other parts of the site.

Hierarchical organization

From the viewpoint of the user, many web sites are organized hierarchically. From the home page, links lead to a few major sections; these lead to more specific information, and so on. Often, buttons on each page allow the user to go back to the next higher level of the hierarchy or to move to the next page at the same level.

The Web as a Digital Library

Some people talk about the web technology as though it were an inferior stopgap until proper digital libraries are created. One reason for this attitude is that members of other professions have difficulty in accepting that definitive work in digital libraries was carried out by physicists at a laboratory in Switzerland, rather than by well-known librarians or computer scientists. But the web is not a detour to follow until the real digital libraries come along. It is central to the development of digital libraries.

In addition, some who are not familiar with online collections make derogatory statements about the information on the web. The two most common complaints are that the information is of poor quality and that finding it is impossible. These two complaints have some validity, but they are far from the full truth. There is an enormous amount of material on the web; much of the content is indeed of little value, but many of the web servers are maintained conscientiously and contain information of the highest quality. Finding information on the web can be difficult, but tools and services exist that enable a user, with a little ingenuity, to discover most of the information that is out there.

Today's web, however, is a beginning, not the end. The simplifying assumptions behind the technology are brilliant, but these same simplifications are also limitations. Although the web of today provides a basis for the building of digital libraries with better collections, better services, and better underlying technology, much of the current research in the field of digital libraries can be seen as extending the basic building blocks of the web. We can expect that 25 years from now digital libraries will be very different, and the early days of the web will be hard to recall. The names "Internet" and "web" may be history, or they may be applied to systems that are unrecognizable as descendants of the originals. Digital libraries will absorb materials and technology from many places. For the next few years, however, we can expect to see the Internet and the web as the basis on which the libraries of the future are being built. Just as the crude software on early personal computers has developed into modern operating systems, the web can become the foundation for many generations of digital libraries.

3

Libraries and Publishers

Libraries have a proud tradition as early adopters of new technologies, including microfilm, online information services, and CD-ROMs. (The second typewriter imported into Brazil was for the National Library of Brazil to type library catalog cards.) The Internet and the web are the latest examples of libraries' embracing new technologies and adapting it to their needs.

Mainstream commercial products do not always fit the needs of libraries. The computing industry aims its products at the large markets provided by commercial businesses, science, medicine, and the military. In the United States, much of the basic research behind these products has been funded by the Department of Defense or by companies such as IBM. Until recently, these large markets had little interest in the management of the kinds of information that are found in digital libraries, and the products sold by the computing industry did not address important needs in information management. Therefore, libraries are accustomed to taking core technologies from other fields and tailoring them to their needs.

Resource Sharing and Online Catalogs

In libraries, the word *networking* has two meanings. Before modern computer networks, libraries had a wide variety of arrangements to share resources. These included interlibrary lending, reciprocal reading privileges between institutions, and the exchange of photocopies. The term used for these arrangements was *networking* or *resource sharing*. Resource-sharing services, such as the photocopying and document delivery provided by the British Library, enhanced the availability of information around the world.

However, nothing in resource sharing has had an impact to rival that of computer networking.

Almost every library has a catalog with records of the materials in the collections. The catalog helps users find material in the library, provides bibliographic information about the items, and is an important tool in managing the collections.

Cataloging is a area in which librarians use precise terminology, some of which may be unfamiliar to outsiders. Whereas a non-specialist may use the term *catalog* as a generic term, in a library it has a specific meaning: a collection of bibliographic records created according to strict rules. Rather than the everyday word *book*, librarians use the term *monograph*. Over the years, the information that is included in a monograph catalog record has been codified into cataloging rules. English-speaking countries use the Anglo-American Cataloging Rules (AACR), the current version of which is known as AACR2.

The task of cataloging each monograph takes considerable time and requires considerable expertise. To save costs, libraries share catalog records. Major libraries that catalog large numbers of monographs, such as the Library of Congress and the major university libraries, make their catalog records available to others free of charge. Rather than create duplicate records, most libraries look for an existing catalog record and create their own records only when they cannot find another to copy.

Since the late 1960s, this sharing of catalog records has been computer based. Technically, the fundamental tool for representing catalog records in computers is the MARC (Machine-Readable Cataloging) format. MARC was developed by Henriette Avram and her colleagues at the Library of Congress, initially as a format for distributing catalog records on magnetic tape. In practice, the term *MARC cataloging* is often used in a general sense to cover both the catalog records and the computer format in which they are stored. MARC cataloging has been expanded far beyond monographs and is now used for most categories of library materials, including serials, archives, and manuscripts. Panel 3.1 shows an example of a MARC record.

The development of MARC led to two important types of computer-based system. The first was *shared cataloging*, pioneered by Fred Kilgour (who founded OCLC in 1967). The OCLC has a large computer system

Panel 3.1
A MARC record

Consider a monograph for which the bibliographic citation might be written as follows:

Caroline R. Arms, editor, *Campus strategies for libraries and electronic information*. Bedford, Mass.: Digital Press, 1990.

A search of the Library of Congress catalog, done with a terminal-based interface, displays the entry for the aforementioned work in a form that shows the information in the underlying MARC record:

&001 89-16879 r93
&050 Z675.U5C16 1990
&082 027.7/0973 20
&245 Campus strategies for libraries and electronic
      information/Caroline Arms, editor.
&260 {Bedford, Mass.} : Digital Press, c1990.
&300 xi, 404 p. : ill. ; 24 cm.
&440 EDUCOM strategies series on information technology
&504 Includes bibliographical references (p. {373}-381).
&020 ISBN 1-55558-036-X : $34.95
&650 Academic libraries--United States--Automation.
&650 Libraries and electronic publishing--United States.
&650 Library information networks--United States.
&650 Information technology--United States.
&700 Arms, Caroline R. (Caroline Ruth)
&040 DLC DLC DLC
&043 n-us---
&955 CIP ver. br02 to SL 02-26-90
&985 APIF/MIG

The information is divided into fields, each with a three-digit code. For example, the 440 field is the title of a monograph series, and the 650 fields are Library of Congress subject headings. Complex rules tell the cataloger which fields should be used and how relationships of elements should be interpreted.

The actual coding is more complex than what is shown here. The full MARC format consists of a pre-defined set of fields, each identified by a tag. Subfields are permitted. Fields are identified by three-digit numeric tags, subfields by single letters. To get a glimpse of how information is encoded in this format, consider the 260 field, which begins with &260. In an actual MARC record, this is encoded as follows, where the string "abc" indicates that there are three subfields.

&2600#abc#{Bedford, Mass.} :#Digital Press,#c1990.%

The first subfield, indicated by the tag a, gives the place of publication; the next, indicated by the tag b, gives the publisher; the third, indicated by the tag c, gives the date.

which has grown to more 35 million catalog records in MARC format, including records received from the Library of Congress. When an OCLC member library acquires a book that it wishes to catalog, it begins by searching the OCLC database. If it finds a MARC record, it downloads the record to its own computer system and records the holding in the OCLC database. This is called *copy cataloging*. If the OCLC database does not contain the record, the library is encouraged to create a record and contribute it to the OCLC. With copy cataloging, each item is cataloged once, and the intellectual effort is shared among all libraries. MARC cataloging and the OCLC's success in sharing catalog records have been emulated by similar services around the world.

The availability of MARC records stimulated a second development: Individual libraries began to create online catalogs of their holdings. In most cases, the bulk of the records were obtained from copy cataloging. Today, almost every substantial library in the United States has an online catalog. In library jargon, such a catalog is an *online public access catalog* (OPAC). Many libraries have gone to great efforts to convert their old card catalogs to MARC format, so that the online catalog is the record of their entire holdings; this avoids having an online catalog for recent acquisitions and a separate card catalog for older materials. In Harvard University's recently completed conversion, 5 million cards were converted at a cost approaching $15 million.

MARC was an innovative format at a time when most computer systems represented text as fixed-length fields with capital letters only. It remains a vital format for libraries, but it is showing its age. Speculation on its future is complicated by the enormous investment that libraries have made in it. Whatever its future, MARC was a pioneering achievement in the history of both computing and libraries. It is a key format that must be accommodated by digital libraries.

Linking Online Catalogs and Z39.50

During the 1980s, universities libraries began to connect their online catalogs to networks. By 1984 there was a comprehensive campus network at Dartmouth College, and, since the computer that held the library catalog was connected to the network, anyone on the Dartmouth campus with a terminal or a personal computer connected to the network could search the catalog. Members of the university could use their own computers to search the catalogs of other universities. When the campus network was connected to the Internet, people all over the world could search the catalog. The sharing of library catalogs was one of the first instances of large-scale cooperative sharing of information over the Internet.

In the late 1970s, several bibliographic utilities, including the Library of Congress, the Research Libraries Group, and the Washington Libraries Information Network, began a project known as the Linked Systems Project, which developed the protocol now known by the name of Z39.50. This protocol allows one computer to search for information on another. It is used primarily for searching records in MARC format, but the protocol is flexible and is not restricted to MARC. Technically, Z39.50 specifies rules that allow one computer to search a database on another and retrieve the records that are found. Z39.50 is widely used for interoperation among diverse computer systems.

Abstracts and Indexes

Library catalogs are the primary source of information about monographs, but they are less useful for journals. Catalogs provide a single, brief record for an entire run of a journal. Because this is of little value to somebody who wants to look up individual articles, abstracting and indexing services developed to help researchers to find individual articles. Some typical examples are Medline (for the biomedical literature), Chemical Abstracts (for the literature of chemistry), and Inspec (for the literature of the physical sciences, including computing). These services differ in many details, but they are similar in basic structure. Professionals who are knowledgeable about a certain subject area read each article in a large number of journals and assign index terms or write abstracts. Some of these services use index terms that are drawn from a carefully controlled vocabulary, such as the MeSH headings that the National Library of Medicine uses for its Medline service. Others services are less strict. Some generate all their own abstracts. Others, such as Inspec, will use an abstract supplied by the publisher.

Most of these services began by producing printed volumes for sale to libraries, but today almost all of the searching is done by computer.

(Computer searching of indexes goes back to the days of batch processing and magnetic tape.) Some indexing services run computer systems on which users can search for a fee; others license their data to third parties who provide online services. Many large libraries license the data and mount it on their own computers. In addition, much of the data is available on CD-ROM.

Once their catalogs were online, libraries began to mount other data, such as abstracts of articles, indexes, and reference works. These sources of information can be stored in a central computer, and the retrieved records can be displayed on terminals or personal computers. Reference works consisting of short entries are particularly well suited to this form of distribution, since users move rapidly from one entry to another and will accept a display that has text characters with simple formatting. Quick retrieval and flexible searching are more important than the aesthetics of the output on the computer screen. As a typical example, here are some of the many information sources that the library at Carnegie Mellon University provided online during 1998:

Carnegie Mellon library catalog
Carnegie Mellon journal list
Bibliographic records of architectural pictures and drawings
Who's who at CMU
American Heritage Dictionary
Periodical Abstracts
ABI/Inform (business periodicals)
Inspec (physics, electronics, and computer science)
Research directory (Carnegie Mellon University)

Several of these online collections provide local information, such as *Who's Who at CMU* (the university's directory of faculty, students, and staff). Libraries' patrons are not interested only in formally published or academic materials. Public libraries, in particular, offer many kinds of information, from tax forms to bus timetables. Full-text indexes and web browsers allow traditional and non-traditional library materials to be combined in a single system with a single user interface. This approach has become so standard that it is hard to realize that only a few years ago the merging of information from diverse sources was rare.

Mounting large amounts of information online and keeping it current is expensive. Although the costs hardware fall continually, they are still noticeable. The big costs are associated with the licensing of data and the people who handle both the business aspects and the large data files. To reduce these costs, libraries have formed consortia so that one set of online data serves many libraries.

Information Retrieval

Information retrieval is a central topic for libraries. A user—perhaps a scientist, a doctor, or a lawyer—is interested in information on some topic and wishes to find the objects in a collection that cover the topic. This requires specialized software. During the mid 1980s, libraries began to install computers with software that allowed full-text searching of large collections. Usually the MARC records of a library's holdings were the first data to be loaded onto this computer, followed by standard reference works. Full-text searching meant that a user could search using any words that appeared in the record; the user did not have to be knowledgeable about the structures of the records or the rules used to create them.

Research in this field is at least 30 years old, but the basic approach has changed little. A user expresses a request as a *query*. This may be a single word (such as *cauliflower*), a phrase (such as *digital libraries*), or a longer query (such as "In what year did Darwin travel on the Beagle?"). The task of information retrieval is to find objects in the collection that match the query. Since a computer does not have the time to go through the entire collection for each search, looking at every object separately, the computer must have an index of some sort that enables it to retrieve information by looking up entries in indexes.

As computers have grown more powerful and as the price of storage has declined, methods of information retrieval have moved from carefully controlled searching of short records (such as catalog records or those used by abstracting and indexing services) to searching the full text of every word in large collections. In the early days, the expense of computer storage and processing power stimulated the development of compact storage methods and efficient algorithms. More recently, web search programs have intensified research into methods for searching large amounts of information distributed across many computers.

Markup Languages

Libraries and publishers share an interest in using computers to represent the full richness of textual materials. Textual documents are more than simple sequences of letters; they may contain, for example, mathematical or musical notation, characters from any language, a variety of fonts, and structural elements such as headings, footnotes, and indexes. A desirable way to store a document in a computer is to encode these features and store them with the text, the figures, the tables, and other content. Such encoding is accomplished by means of a *markup language.*

For several years, organizations seriously interested in text have been developing a markup scheme known as SGML (Standard Generalized Markup Language). HTML, the format for text that is used by the web, is a simple derivative of SGML.

Since the representation of a document in SGML is independent of how it will be used, the same text, defined by its SGML markup, can be displayed in many forms and formats: paper, CD-ROM, online text, hypertext, and so on. This makes SGML attractive for publishers who may wish to produce several versions of the same underlying work. A pioneer application in which SGML was used in this way was the preparation of the new Oxford English Dictionary. SGML has also been heavily used by scholars in the humanities, who find in it a method of encoding the structure of text that is independent of any specific computer system or method of display.

Digital Libraries of Scientific Journals

Early Experiments
During the late 1980s several publishers and libraries became interested in building online collections of scientific journals. The technical barriers that had made such projects impossible earlier were disappearing, though still present to some extent. The cost of online storage was coming down, personal computers and networks were being deployed, and good database software was available. The major obstacles to building digital libraries were that academic literature was on paper, not in electronic formats, and that institutions were organized around physical media, not around computer networks.

One of the first attempts to create a campus digital library was the Mercury Electronic Library project (Carnegie Mellon University, 1987–1993). This project availed itself of the advanced computing infrastructure at Carnegie Mellon, which included a high-performance network and a fine computer science department; in addition, the university's libraries had a tradition of innovation. A slightly later effort was the CORE project at Cornell University, which involved the mounting of images from chemistry journals. Both of these projects worked with scientific publishers to scan journals and establish collections of online page images. Whereas Mercury set out to build a production system, CORE also emphasized research into user interfaces and other aspects of the system by chemists. Although both Mercury project and CORE converted existing journal articles from print to bit-mapped images, such conversion was not seen as the long-term future of scientific libraries. It simply reflected the fact that none of the journal publishers was in a position to provide other formats. Printers had used computer typesetting for many years, but their systems were organized entirely for the production of printed materials. The printers' files were in a wide variety of formats. Often proof corrections were held separately rather than merged with the master files, so that they could not be used in a digital library without enormous effort.

Mercury and CORE were followed by a number of other projects that explored the use of scanned images of journal articles. One of the best known was Elsevier Science Publishing's Tulip project. For three years, Elsevier provided a group of universities (including Carnegie Mellon and Cornell) with images from 43 journals in the field of materials science. Each university mounted these images on its own computers and made them available locally.

Mercury, CORE, and Tulip were not long-term production systems. Each had rough edges technically and suffered from the small size of the collection provided to researchers. But they demonstrated that the potential benefits of a digital library could be realized in practice.

The next generation of developments in electronic publishing were able to take advantage of much cheaper computer storage, which allowed large collections of images to be held online. The emergence of the web and the widespread availability of web browsers went a long way toward simplifying the development of user interfaces. Web browsers are not ideal for a

Panel 3.2
Mercury and CORE

Mercury was a five-year project whose goal was to build a prototype digital library at Carnegie Mellon University. Begun in 1988, it went live in 1991 with a dozen textual databases and a small number of page images of journal articles in computer science. It provides a good example of the state of the art before the arrival of the web.

One of Mercury's objectives was to mount page images of journal articles licensed from their publishers. Four publishers were identified as publishing 16 of the 20 computer science journals most heavily used at the university: the Association for Computing Machinery, the Institute of Electrical and Electronics Engineers, Elsevier, and Pergamon. During the project, Pergamon was taken over by Elsevier. None of the publishers had machine-readable versions of their journals, but they gave permission to convert printed materials for use in the library. Thus, an important part of the work was the conversion, storage, and delivery of page images over the campus network.

The fundamental paradigm of Mercury was searching a text database in order to identify the information to be displayed. An early version of Z39.50 was chosen as the protocol for sending queries between the client computers and the servers on which the indexes were stored. Mercury introduced the concept of the *reference server*, which keeps information about information stored on other servers, fields that may be searched, indexes, and restrictions on access. To display bit-mapped images, the project developed a new algorithm to take page images stored in compressed format, transmit them across the network, decompress them, and display them, with an overall response time of 1–2 seconds per page.

Since Mercury was attached to the Internet and most materials were licensed from publishers, security was important. The university already had a mature set of network services, known as Andrew. Mercury was able to use standard Andrew services for authentication and printing. Information was dispatched to other computers by email.

CORE was a joint project of Bellcore, Cornell University, OCLC, and the American Chemical Society that ran from 1991 to 1995. It converted about 400,000 pages, representing 4 years' articles in 20 journals published by the American Chemical Society.

The CORE project used a number of ideas that have since become popular in conversion projects. There were two versions of every article: a scanned image and a text version marked up in SGML. The scanned images ensured that when a page was displayed or printed it had the same design and layout as the original paper version; the SGML text was used to build a full-text index for information retrieval and for rapid display on computer screens. Two scanned images were stored for each page: one for printing and the other for screen display. The printing version was black and white, with 300 dots per inch; the display version was grayscale, with 100 dots per inch.

CORE was one of the first projects to articulate several results that have since been confirmed by numerous studies. One of the conclusions was that the technical problems of representing, storing, and storing complex scientific materials are substantial, particularly if they were originally designed to be printed and digitization was an afterthought. CORE also highlighted the impacts of scale. The CORE collections, comprising only 20 journals, occupied about 80 gigabytes of storage. All the early digitization projects found that the operational problems of managing large collections were greater than had been predicted.

Despite such annoyances, CORE's user-interface studies showed considerable promise. Chemists liked the collections. Though they may have preferred the print versions when reading articles in detail, they found the online versions easier to search and the screen displays more than adequate. CORE was one of the first studies to emphasize the importance of browsing as an alternative to searching—a conclusion that the web has amply confirmed.

digital library, though they are a good start; however, they have the great advantage that they exist for all standard computers and operating systems. No longer does every project have to develop its own user interface programs for every type of computer.

Electronic Journals

Until the mid 1990s, established publishers of scientific journals hesitated about online publishing. Although commercial publishing on CD-ROM had developed into an important part of the industry, few journals were available online. Publishers could not make a business case for online publishing, and they feared that if materials were available online then sales of the same materials in print would suffer. By about 1995, however, it was clear that big changes were occurring in how people were using information. Libraries and individuals were expanding their use of online information services and other forms of electronic information much more rapidly than their use of printed materials. Print publications were competing for a declining portion of essentially static library budgets.

As circulations remain flat or decline, journal publishing is in a price spiral. In the past, publishers used new technology to reduce production costs, thus mitigating some of the effects of declining circulation, but now the potential for such savings is becoming exhausted. Publishers realize that to grow their business or even sustain its current level they must have products

Panel 3.3
HighWire Press

HighWire Press, a venture of the Stanford University Libraries, has brought some of the best scientific and medical journals online by building partnerships with the scientific and professional societies that publish them. Its success can be credited to the amount of attention it paid to the interests of senior researchers, to its focus on the most important journals, and to its technical excellence.

HighWire Press began in 1995 with an online version of the *Journal of Biological Chemistry*, several members of whose editorial board were on Stanford's faculty. Each week's issue of this journal has about 800 pages, and no one reads it from cover to cover. Therefore, the HighWire Press interface treats articles as separate documents. It provides two ways to find them: by browsing the contents issue by issues, and by searching. The search options include searching for authors, searching for words in titles, full-text searching of abstracts, and full-text searching of entire articles. The search screen and the displays of articles were designed to emphasize that this is indeed the *Journal of Biological Chemistry* and not a publication of HighWire Press. Great efforts were made to display Greek letters, mathematical symbols, and other special characters.

In three years, HighWire Press went from an experiment to a major operation with almost a hundred journals online, including *Science*. Despite its resources, the American Association for the Advancement of Science—the publisher of *Science*—experienced a fear that is faced by every society that publishes only a few journals: that an in-house effort to bring *Science* online might overextend the staff and lower the overall quality of their work. A partnership with HighWire Press enabled the AAAS to share the development costs with other society journals and to collaborate with specialists at Stanford University. The AAAS has been delighted by the number of people who visit their site every week, most of whom were not regular readers of *Science*.

for the expanding online market. Electronic information is seen as a promising growth market.

Most of the major publishers of scientific journals have moved rapidly to electronic publishing. Panel 3.4 details the approach taken by the Association for Computing Machinery. With only minor variations, the same strategy is being followed by Elsevier, Wiley, Academic Press, and other large commercial publishers, by the American Chemical Society, and by The MIT Press and other university presses.

Panel 3.4
The Association for Computing Machinery's Digital Library

The Association for Computing Machinery is a professional society that publishes seventeen research journals in computer science. In addition, its 38 special-interest groups run a wide variety of conferences, many of which publish proceedings. Its members are practicing computer scientists, including many of the individuals who built the Internet and the web. They were among the first people to become accustomed to communicating online, and they expected their society to be a leader in the move to online journals.

Traditionally, the definitive version of a journal has been a printed version. In 1993, the ACM decided that its future production process would use a computer system that creates a database of journal articles, conference proceedings, magazines, and newsletters, all marked up in SGML. Later the ACM also decided to convert large numbers of its older journals to build a digital library covering its publications from 1985 on.

The SGML files were to be used in the production of printed journals. However, the ACM planned for the day when members would retrieve articles directly from the online database, sometimes reading them on the screen of a computer and sometimes downloading them to a local printer. A library would be able to license parts of the database or to take out a general subscription for its patrons.

The collection, which went online in 1997, uses a web interface that offers readers the opportunity to browse the contents pages of the ACM's journals and to search by author and keyword. When an article has been identified, a subscriber can read its full text. Other readers must pay for access to full texts but may read abstracts without paying.

The ACM needed revenue to cover the substantial costs of the library but did not want to restrain authors and readers unduly. The initial, experimental business arrangements fall into two categories: those having to do with authors and those having to do with readers.

In 1994 the ACM published an interim copyright policy that describes the relationship between the society (as a publisher) and the authors. It attempts to balance the interest of the authors against the association's need to generate revenue from its publications. In a sign of the times, the ACM first published the new policy on its web server. One of the key features of this policy is the explicit acknowledgment that many of the journal articles are first distributed via the web.

To generate revenue, the ACM charges for access to the full text of an article. Members and libraries may subscribe to the electronic versions of the association's journals, which are priced about 20 percent below the prices of printed versions. Alternatively, individuals may pay for single articles. The price structure aims to encourage subscribers to sign up for the full set of publications rather than to read only individual journals.

The term *electronic journal* is commonly used to describe a publication that maintains many of the characteristics of printed journals but is produced and distributed online. Rather confusingly, this term is used both for a journal that is purely digital and exists only online and for the digital version of a journal that is primarily a print publication (e.g., the ACM journals mentioned in panel 3.4).

Many established publishers have introduced a small number of purely online periodicals, and there have been many similar efforts by other groups. Some of these online periodicals have set out to mimic the processes and procedures of traditional journals. Perhaps the most ambitious publication to use this approach was the *On-line Journal of Current Clinical Trials*, developed by the American Association for the Advancement of Science in conjunction with OCLC. Unlike other electronic publications, whose online versions were secondary to printed ones, this new journal was planned as a high-quality refereed journal for which the definitive version would be the electronic version. (There was no printed version.) Since the publisher had complete control over the journal, it was able to design it and store it in a form that was tailored to electronic delivery and display, but the journal was never accepted by researchers or physicians. The *On-line Journal of Current Clinical Trials* first appeared in 1992 and but never attracted the numbers of good papers that were planned for. Such is the fate of many pioneers.

More recent electronic periodicals combine features of traditional journals with formats or services that take advantage of online publishing. One of these is *D-Lib Magazine*, which we introduced in 1995 as an online magazine about digital libraries research and innovation. Printed publications are constrained to follow strict design standards, but online publications can allow authors to be creative in their use of technology. Conventional journals appear in issues, each containing several articles. Some electronic journals publish each article as soon as it has is ready, but *D-Lib Magazine* publishes a monthly issue with strong emphasis on punctuality and rapid publication. It is a sign of the changing times that *D-Lib Magazine*, which is entirely online and does not use peer review, has emerged as an important periodical about digital libraries research.

Conversion Projects and the Humanities

One of the fundamental tasks of research libraries is to save today's materials as the long-term memory for tomorrow. The great libraries have wonderful collections that form the raw material of history and of the humanities. These collections consist primarily of printed materials and other physical artifacts. The development of digital libraries has created great enthusiasm for digitizing some of these collections. One reason for this is that older materials are often in poor physical condition. Making a digital copy preserves the content of the materials as well as making them available to the whole world.

Many digital library projects convert existing paper documents into bit-mapped images. Printed documents are scanned one page at a time. In early experiments, the page was recorded as an array of black and white dots (often 300 dots per inch). More recently, higher resolution and full-color scanning have become common. Good bit-mapped images are crisp enough that they can be displayed on large computer screens or printed on paper with good legibility. Since high-resolution scanning generates a huge number of dots per page, various methods are used to compress the images so as to reduce the number of bits to be stored and the size of files to be transmitted across the network. But even the simplest images are tens of thousands of bytes per page.

Since scientific and technical fields have been the driving force in electronic libraries and information services, rather basic needs of other disciplines, such as character sets beyond English, have often been ignored. The humanities have been in danger of being left behind, but a new generation of humanities scholars is embracing computing. Fortunately, they have friends. Panel 3.6 describes JSTOR, a project of the Andrew W. Mellon Foundation that is saving costs for libraries and bringing important journal literature to a wider audience than would ever be possible without digital libraries.

Libraries and Innovation

Libraries, by their nature, are conservative organizations. Their collections and their catalogs have developed over decades or even centuries.

Panel 3.5
American Memory and the National Digital Library Program

The Library of Congress, the world's biggest library, has magnificent special collections of unique or unpublished materials. Among its treasures are the papers of 23 presidents. Rare books, pamphlets, and papers provide valuable material for the study of historic events, periods, and movements. Millions of photographs, prints, maps, musical scores, sound recordings, and moving images in various formats reflect trends and represent people and places. Until recently, anyone who wanted to use these materials had to travel to the library's buildings on Capitol Hill.

American Memory was a pilot program that, from 1989 to 1994, reproduced selected collections for national dissemination in computerized form. Collections were selected for their value for the study of American history and culture and for the purpose of exploring the problems of working with materials of various kinds, such as prints, negatives, early motion pictures, recorded sound, and textual documents. At first American Memory used a combination of digitized representations on CD-ROM and analog forms on videodisk, but in June of 1994 three collections of photographs were made available on the web.

The National Digital Library Program builds on the success of American Memory. Its objective is to convert millions of items to digital form and make them available over the Internet. The focus is on materials that are important in American history, such as Walt Whitman's notebooks and documents from the Continental Congress and the Constitutional Convention.

Some of the collections that are being converted are coherent archives, such as the papers or the photograph collection of a particular individual or organization. Some are collections of items in certain original forms, such as daguerreotypes and paper prints of early films. Others are thematic compilations by curators or scholars, selected either from within an archival collection or from all the library's resources.

American Memory discovered that schoolteachers were enthusiastic about having access to these primary source materials, and the National Digital Library Program views education as its primary mission. The most comprehensive means of access to the collections is searching an index. However, many of the archival collections being converted do not have catalog records for each individual item; instead, they have *finding aids*—structured documents that describe the collection, and groups of items within it, without describing each item. Hence, access to material in American Memory is a combination of methods, including searching bibliographic records for individual items where such records exist, browsing subject terms, searching full text, and, in the future, searching the finding aids.

This program is technically important because of its scale and its visibility. Conscious of the long-term problems of maintaining large collections, the Library of Congress has placed great emphasis on how it organizes the items within its collections. The National Digital Library Program takes seriously the process of converting these older materials to digital formats, selecting the most appropriate format to represent the content, and exercising careful quality control. Textual material is usually converted twice: to a scanned page image and to a text with SGML markup. Several images are made from each photograph, ranging from a small thumbnail to a high-resolution image for archival purposes.

Many of the materials selected for conversion are free from copyright or other restrictions on distribution, but others are not. In addition to copyright, there may be conditions required by the donors of original materials. In the case of older materials (especially unpublished items), it is often impossible to discover all the restrictions that might conceivably apply and prohibitively expensive to conduct an exhaustive search for every single item. Therefore, the library's legal staff has to develop policies and procedures that balance the value of making materials available against the risk of inadvertently infringing some right.

Other libraries look to the Library of Congress for leadership. The library is an active member of several collaborations, it has overseen an important grant program, and it is becoming a sponsor of digital library research. The expertise that the library has developed and its partnerships with leading technical groups enable it to help the entire library community move forward.

Panel 3.6
JSTOR

JSTOR is a project that was initiated by the Andrew W. Mellon Foundation to provide academic libraries with back runs of important journals. It combines both academic and economic objectives. The academic objective is to build a reliable archive of important scholarly journals and provide widespread access to them. The economic objective is to save libraries money by eliminating the need for every library to store and preserve the same materials.

The JSTOR collections are organized by field—economics, history, philosophy, and so on. The first phase is expected to involve about a hundred journals from some fifteen fields. For each journal, the collection usually consists of all issues from the first up to about five years before the current date.

JSTOR was established in August of 1995 as an independent not-for-profit organization. It aims to become self-sustaining by charging libraries for access to its database. The fees are set lower than the comparable costs of storing paper copies of the journals.

The organization has three offices. Its administrative, legal, and financial activities are managed and coordinated from the main office in New York, as are its relations with publishers and libraries. In addition, offices at the University of Michigan and at Princeton University maintain two synchronized copies of the database, maintain and develop JSTOR's technical infrastructure, provide support to users, and oversee conversion from paper to computer formats. (The actual scanning and keying are done by outside vendors.) JSTOR has recently established a third database mirror site at the University of Manchester in the United Kingdom.

JSTOR has straightforward licenses with publishers and with subscribing institutions. By emphasizing back runs, JSTOR strives to avoid competing with publishers, whose principal revenues come from current issues. So far, access to the collections has been provided only to academic libraries who subscribe to the entire collection. The fee each library pays is based on the library's size. In the best Internet tradition, the fee schedule and the license are openly available online.

All pages in each issue of each archived journal are scanned at high resolution (600 bits per inch), with particular emphasis on quality control. In contrast with some other projects, only one version of each image is stored. Other versions, such as low-resolution thumbnails, are computed when required but are not stored. Text conversion is done by optical character recognition, with intensive proofreading. The converted text is used only for indexing. In addition, a table-of-contents file is created for each article. This includes bibliographic citation information with keywords and abstracts if available.

New services are introduced cautiously, because they are expected to last for a long time. However, in technical fields, libraries have frequently been adventurous. MARC, OCLC, the Linked Systems Project, Mercury, CORE, and the recent conversion projects may not have invented all the technology they used, but the deployment as large-scale, practical systems was pioneering.

Chapter 2 discussed the community that has grown up around the Internet and the web. Many members of this community discovered online information very recently, and are unaware that libraries and publishers developed many of the concepts that are the basis for digital libraries, years before the web.

4

Innovation and Research

Innovation is a theme that runs throughout the fields of digital libraries and electronic publishing. Some of the innovation comes from the market's demand for information, some from systematic research at universities or corporations. This chapter looks at the process of research and provides an overview of current research. Most of the topics introduced here are discussed in greater detail in later chapters.

Until recently, innovation by libraries and publishers was far from systematic. Most lacked budgets for research and development. The National Library of Medicine and the OCLC's Office of Research were notable exceptions, performing research in the true sense of exploring new ideas without preconceptions of how the ideas will eventually be deployed. Other libraries and publishers have an approach to innovation that is motivated by practical considerations of how to enhance their services and products in the near term. The rate of innovation is controlled by the state of technology and the availability of funds, but also by an interpretation of the current demand for services.

Publishers, although they are well organized to bring new ideas to the market, do not carry out much research. Large publishers have the resources to undertake substantial investments in new ventures, but they see advanced projects as business development rather than as research. The move to make scientific journals available online cannot be called research, although changing the entire publishing process so that journals can be produced in both print and online forms is certainly a complex task.

Libraries tend to be more innovative than publishers, though they often appear poorly organized in their approach to change. Typically, they spend almost their entire budget on current activities. Innovation is often treated as an extra, not as the key to the future. Large libraries have large budgets, yet their budget systems are so inflexible that research and innovation are grossly understaffed.

The Library of Congress's National Digital Library Program may be the most important library project in the United States. It is a showcase of how a library can expand beyond its traditional role by managing its collections differently, handling new types of material, and providing wider access to its collections. Yet the Library of Congress provides little financial support to the program. It raises most of its funds from private foundations and other gifts, and is staffed by people on short-term contracts. The Library of Congress does support technical developments, such as Z39.50 and MARC; however, its most visionary project has no long-term funding.

Despite such apparent conservatism, libraries are moving ahead on a broad front, particularly at universities. The structure of university libraries inhibits radical change, but university librarians know that computing is fundamental to the future of scholarly communication. Computer scientists can be seen as the hares of digital libraries, leaping ahead, trying out new fields, then jumping somewhere else. The large libraries are the tortoises. They move more slowly, but each step is a preparation for the next. The steps often take the form of focused projects, sometimes in partnership with other organizations and often with grants from foundations. The individual projects may not have the visibility of big government-funded research initiatives, but their collective impact may well be equally great in the long term.

Many notable projects have their origins in university libraries. Some university libraries are converting materials to digital formats; others are working with publishers to make materials available online. HighWire Press at Stanford University is putting scientific journals online. University libraries collaborated with Elsevier Science in the Tulip project to explore digitized version of scientific journals. The University of Michigan and Princeton University are contributing to the JSTOR project to convert historic back-runs of important journals. Rutgers University and Princeton jointly created the Center for Electronic Texts in the Humanities.

Most of the projects are made possible by funds from foundations, industry, or the federal government. For example, the Mercury project at Carnegie Mellon University received major grants from the Pew Charitable

Trusts, from Digital Equipment Corporation, and from the Defense Advanced Research Projects Agency, and smaller but welcome support from other donors. Several private foundations have been strong supporters of digital libraries for the humanities, notably the Andrew W. Mellon Foundation and the J. Paul Getty Trust. Finally, although its budget is small compared with those of the National Science Foundation and DARPA, the National Endowment for the Humanities devotes a significant proportion of its funds to digital libraries.

Computer scientists take research seriously. They are accustomed to long-term projects the end results of which are not products or services but new concepts or a deeper understanding of the field. In the United States, much of the money for research comes from federal agencies. The world's biggest sponsor of computer science research is the Defense Advanced Research Projects Agency (which has changed its name from ARPA to DARPA, then back to ARPA, then back again to DARPA). The second-largest is the National Science Foundation. DARPA is a branch of the U.S. Department of Defense. Although ultimately its mission is to support the military, DARPA has always taken a broad view. It encourages fundamental research in almost every aspect of computer science, and it is particularly noted for its emphasis on research projects that build large experimental systems. The NSF has a general responsibility for promoting science and engineering in the United States. Its programs spend more than $3.3 billion per year to support almost 20,000 research and education projects. It supports research in computer science and in applications of computing to almost every scientific discipline.

Many engineering and computer companies have large budgets for computing research and development—often as much as 10 percent of the total budget for operations. Most industrial research is aimed at developing new products in the short term, but fundamental advances in computing have come from industrial laboratories, such as Xerox PARC, Bell Laboratories, and the labs of IBM. More recently, the Microsoft Corporation has established an impressive research team.

Much of the underlying technology that makes digital libraries feasible was created by people whose primary interests were in other fields. The Internet, without which digital libraries would be very different, was originally developed by ARPA and the NSF. The web was developed at

Panel 4.1
The Coalition for Networked Information

A focal point for innovation among libraries and publishers in the United States is the Coalition for Networked Information. Most of the people who attend its semiannual meetings are from university libraries or computing centers, but the meetings also attract individuals from publishers, computer companies, national libraries, and the U.S. government. In recent years, there have been many attendees from outside the United States.

The CNI is a partnership of the Association of Research Libraries and Educause (an association of university computer centers). It was founded in March of 1990 to help realize the promise of high-performance networks and computers for the advancement of scholarship and the enrichment of intellectual productivity. Among the 200 institutional members of this coalition are institutions of higher education; publishers; network service providers; computer hardware, software, and systems companies; library networks and organizations; and public and state libraries.

In 1991, several years before web browsers were introduced, the CNI was one of the first organizations to create a well-managed information service on the Internet. The following list of its activities is taken from its web site:

- access to networked government information via the Internet
- federal information for higher education
- evaluation of how networks have affected academic institutions
- authentication, authorization, and access management
- cost centers and measures in the networked information value chain
- consortium for university printing and information distribution
- capture and storage of electronic theses and dissertations
- electronic billboards on the digital superhighway
- 51 reasons to invest in the national information infrastructure
- the Government Printing Office wide information network data on-line act
- humanities and arts on the information highway
- institution-wide information policies
- CNI/OCLC metadata workshop
- national initiative for networked cultural heritage
- networked information discovery and retrieval
- creating new learning communities via the network
- technology, scholarship and the humanities
- rights for electronic access to and dissemination of information
- regional conferences
- scholarship from California on the net
- teaching and learning via the network
- protecting intellectual property in the networked multimedia environment
- the transformation of the public library
- planning retreat for library and information technology professionals
- Z39.50 resources.

This list illustrates CNI's broad-ranging interests, which emphasize practical applications of digital libraries, collections, relationships between libraries and publishers, and policy issues of access to intellectual property. What the list does not show is the human side of CNI, established by its founding director, the late Paul Evan Peters, and continued by his successor, Clifford Lynch. CNI meetings are noted for the warmth with which people from different fields meet together. People whose professional interests may sometimes appear in conflict have learned to respect each other and come to work together. Progress over the past few years has been so rapid that it is easy to forget the vacuum that CNI filled by bringing people together to discuss their mutual interests in networked information.

CERN, a European physics laboratory that receives substantial funding from the NSF. The first web browser, Mosaic, was developed at the NSF-funded supercomputing center at the University of Illinois. Several areas of computer science—networking, distributed computer systems, multimedia, natural language processing, databases, information retrieval, human-computer interactions—are important to information management; most research in those areas has roots that predate the current interest in digital libraries.

In addition to funding specific research, the federal agencies assist in the development of research communities and often coordinate the deployment of new technology. The NSF supported the early years of the Internet Engineering Task Force. The World Wide Web Consortium, based at the Massachusetts Institute of Technology, is funded primarily by industrial associates but also has received money from DARPA.

Digital libraries were not an explicit subject of federal research until the 1990s. In 1992, DARPA funded the Computer Science Technical Reports project, which was coordinated by the Corporation for National Research Initiatives and which involved five universities: Carnegie Mellon, Cornell, MIT, Stanford, and the University of California at Berkeley. The project encouraged those universities' strong computer science departments to develop research programs in digital libraries. However, the initiative that really established digital libraries as a distinct field of research came in 1994, when the NSF, DARPA, and the National Aeronautic and Space Agency created the Digital Libraries Initiative.

The Digital Libraries Initiative focused international attention on research in the field of digital libraries. Beyond the specific work that it funded, the program gave shape to an emerging discipline. Research in digital libraries was not new, but previously it had been fragmented. Even the name "digital libraries" was uncertain. The Digital Libraries Initiative highlighted digital libraries as a challenging and rewarding field of research. It led to conferences, to publications, and to the appointment to academic departments of individuals who were explicitly interested in doing research in the field of digital libraries. This establishment of a new field was important because it created the confidence that a commitment to long-term research requires.

In addition, the Digital Libraries Initiative has clarified the distinction between research and the implementation of digital libraries. When the initiative was announced, some people thought that the federal government was providing a new source of money with which to build digital libraries. However, the projects that ensued were true research projects. Some of the work has already migrated into practical applications; some anticipates hardware and software developments; some is truly experimental.

The emergence of digital libraries as a research discipline raises the danger that researchers may concentrate on fascinating theoretical problems in computer science, economics, sociology, or law, forgetting that this is a practical field in which research should be justified by its utility. The field is fortunate that the federal funding agencies are aware of this dangers and appear determined to maintain a focus on the real needs.

DARPA, NASA, and the NSF are granted budgets by Congress to carry out specific objectives, and each operates within well-defined boundaries. None of these agencies has libraries as a primary mission; the money for the Digital Libraries Initiative came from funds that Congress had voted for computer science research. As a result, the first phase of research emphasized the computer science aspects of the field. However, the agencies know that digital libraries are more than a branch of computer science. In 1998, when they created a second phase of the initiative, they sought partners interested in supporting a broader range of activities. The new partners include the National Library of Medicine, the National Endowment for the Humanities, the Library of Congress, and the NSF's Division of Undergraduate Education. This book was written before these new grants

Panel 4.2
The Digital Libraries Initiative

In 1994, the computer science divisions of the NSF, DARPA, and NASA provided funds for six four-year research projects having to do with digital libraries. The total government funding was $24 million; the funding provided by numerous external partners exceeded that amount. Each of these projects was expected to implement a test-bed digital library and to carry out associated research. The six projects are listed below, along with some highlights of the work.

• The University of California at Berkeley built a large collection of documents on California's environment, including maps, pictures, and government reports. Notable research included work with multivalent documents (a conceptual method for expressing documents as layers of information), Cheshire II (a search system that combines the strengths of SGML formats with the information in MARC records), and research into image recognition (so that features such as dams and animals can be recognized in pictures).

• The University of California at Santa Barbara concentrated on maps and other geospatial information. Its collection is called the Alexandria Digital Library. Research topics included metadata for geospatial information, user interfaces for overlapping maps, wavelets for compressing and transmitting images, and novel methods for analyzing how people use libraries.

• Carnegie Mellon University built a library of segments of video, called Informedia. The research emphasized automatic processing for information discovery and display. Work was done on multi-modal searching (in which information gleaned from many sources is combined), speech recognition, image recognition, and video skimming (to provide a brief summary of a longer video segment).

• The University of Illinois worked with publishers to build a federated library of journals in science and engineering. Much of this effort concentrated on the manipulation of documents in SGML. This project also used supercomputing to study the problems of semantic information in very large collections of documents.

• The University of Michigan project built on the digital library collections being developed by the university's libraries. In addition to investigating educational applications, the researchers have experimented with economic models and with an agent-based approach to interoperability.

• Stanford University concentrated on the literature of computer science. At the center of the project was the InfoBus, a method of combining services from many sources into a coherent set of digital library services. Other topics included modeling digital libraries' economic processes and demonstrations of novel user interfaces.

were announced, but everybody expects to see funding for a broad range of projects that reflect the missions of all these agencies.

To shape the agenda, the funding agencies have sponsored a series of workshops. Some of these workshops have been on specific research topics, such as managing access to information. Others have had the broader objectives of developing a unified view of the field and identifying key research topics. The small amounts of federal funding used for coordination of research on digital libraries have been crucial in shaping the field. The important word is *coordination*, not *standardization*. Although these efforts sometimes produce standards, their fundamental role is to stimulate research and maximize its impact.

As digital libraries have established themselves as a field of serious research, certain research topics have emerged as fundamental, and a body of people now work on them. The central part of this chapter is a quick overview of the principal areas of research in digital libraries.

Object Models

One important research topic is how to understand the objects that are in digital libraries. Digital libraries store and disseminate any information that can be represented in digital form. As a result, the research problems in representing and manipulating information are varied and subtle.

What a user of a digital library sees as a single work may be represented in a computer as an assembly of files and data structures in many formats. The relationship between these components and the user's view of the object is sometimes called an *object model*

To the user, a journal article stored on a web server may appear to be a single continuous text with a few graphics; however, it may be stored as several text files, several images, and perhaps some executable programs. A single image may be stored several times: once as a high-quality archival image, once as a medium-resolution version for normal use, and once as a small "thumbnail" that gives an impression of the image but omits many details. The image may be referenced by a single bibliographic identifier, but to the computer it is a group of distinct files. Many versions of the same object might exist. And digital libraries often have private versions of materials that are being prepared for release to the public. After their release, new versions may be required to correct errors, or the materials may be reorganized or moved to different computers, or new formats may be added as technology advances.

The ability of user interfaces and other computer programs to present a work to a user depends on the program's being able to understand how the various components relate to form a single library object. Structural metadata is used to describe the relationships. Markup languages are one method of representing structure in text. For example, in an HTML page, the <img> tag is structural metadata that indicates the location of an image.

Much of the early work on structural metadata has been carried out with libraries of digitized pictures, music, video clips, and other objects converted from physical media. Maps are another subject of current research. Beyond the realm of conventional library materials, there is research interest in real-time data (e.g., data obtained from remote sensors), in mobile agents that travel on networks, and in other categories of digital objects that have no physical counterparts. Each type of object presents questions: how to create it, how to store it, how to describe it, how to find the information that it contains, and how to deliver it. These questions are tough individually and even tougher in combination. The challenge is to devise object models that will support library materials that combine many formats and that will enable independent digital libraries to interoperate.

User Interfaces and Human-Computer Interaction

Improving how users interact with information on computers might be thought to be so complex as to be an art rather than a topic of systematic research. Fortunately, such pessimism has been shown to be unfounded. The development of web browsers has accelerated creative research in areas such as visualization of complex sets of information, layering of information contained in documents, and automatic skimming to extract a summary or to generate links.

To a user at a personal computer, digital libraries are just part of the working environment. Some user-interface research looks at the whole environment, which is likely to include electronic mail, word processing, and applications specific to the individual's field of interest. In addition, the environment will probably include a wide range of information that is not in digital form, such as books, papers, video tapes, maps, and photographs. The ability of users to annotate digital objects, to manipulate them, and to add them to their own personal collections is proving to be a fertile area of research.

Information Discovery

Finding and retrieving information is central to libraries, and searching for specific information in large collections of text—known as *information retrieval*—has long been of interest to computer scientists. Until the development of the web, browsing received less research effort, despite its importance. Digital libraries bring information retrieval and browsing together in the general problem of *information discovery*—how to find information. Enormous amounts of research are being carried out in this area; only a few topics will be mentioned here.

Descriptive Metadata: Cataloging and Indexing

Most of the best systems for information discovery use cataloging or indexing metadata produced by individuals who have expert knowledge, such as library catalogers and the staff members of abstracting and indexing services. Unfortunately, indexing performed by humans is slow and expensive. The huge volumes of fast-changing material that can be expected to appear in digital libraries will require different approaches. Some metadata will be generated automatically, some by trained professionals, and some by less experienced people and some by asking the creator of each digital object to provide small amounts of descriptive metadata. The metadata can then be fed into an automatic indexing program.

Research in automatic indexing uses computer programs to scan digital objects, extract indexing information, and build searchable indexes. Web search programs such as AltaVista, Lycos, and Infoseek are the products of such research, much of which was carried out long before digital libraries became an established field.

Natural-Language Processing

Searching of text is greatly enhanced if the search program understands some of the structure of language. Relevant research in computational linguistics includes automatic parsing (to identify grammatical constructs), work on morphology (to associate variants of the same word), and the compilation of lexicons and thesauruses. Some research goes even further, attempting to bring knowledge of subject matter to bear on information retrieval.

Non-Textual Material

Most methods of information discovery use text, but researchers are slowly making progress on ways to search for specific content in other formats. Speech recognition is just beginning to be usable for indexing radio programs and the audio tracks of videos. Image recognition—automatic extraction of features from pictures—is an active area of research but is not ready for deployment.

Managing and Preserving Collections

Collection management is a research topic that is just beginning to receive the attention than it deserves. Over the years, traditional libraries have developed methods that allow relatively small teams of people to manage vast collections of material. Early digital libraries, in contrast, have often been highly labor intensive. In the excitement of creating digital collections, the needs of organizing and preserving the materials over long periods of time were neglected. These needs are now being recognized.

Organization

Organizing large collections of online materials is a complex task. Many of the issues are the same whether the material is an electronic journal, a large web site, a software library, an online map collection, or a large information service. Two important issue are how to load information in varying formats and how to organize it for storage and retrieval.

The difficulty of organizing collections is compounded by the fact that digital information changes. In the early days of printing, corrections were made continually, so that every copy of a book might be slightly different from the last. Online information can also change continually. Keeping track of minor changes is never easy, and large collections must be reorganized often. Many of the research topics that are important for interoperability between collections are equally important for organizing collections. In particular, current research on identifiers, metadata, and authentication applies both to management of individual collections and to interoperation among collections.

Archiving and Preservation

The long-term preservation of digital materials has recently emerged as a major topic of research in collection management. Whereas physical materials (such as books) can be neglected for decades and still be readable, the media on which digital data is stored have quite short life expectancies—often frighteningly short. Periodically, the bits must be copied onto new media. To complicate matters, the formats in which information is stored are frequently replaced by new versions. Formats for word processor and image storage that were in common use ten years ago are already obsolete and hard to use. To interpret archived information, future users will need to be able to recognize the formats and display them successfully.

Conversion

Conversion of physical materials into digital formats illustrates the difference between small-scale and large-scale efforts. What is the best way to convert huge collections to digital format? What is the tradeoff between cost and quality? What is the likelihood that today's efforts will be useful in the long term? In a small project requiring a few thousand items to be used for research, the conversion is perceived as a temporary annoyance that is necessary before beginning the real research. Members of the research team will pass the materials through a digital scanner, check the results for obvious mistakes, and create the metadata required for a specific project. But libraries and publishers convert millions of items, and those who do the work are unlikely to be as motivated as researchers working on a small project. Furthermore, in a large-scale conversion effort, metadata must be generated without knowledge of the long-term uses of the information, and quality control is paramount.

Some organizations have developed effective processes for converting large volumes of material. (Often, part of the work is shipped to countries where labor costs are low.) However, each of these organizations has its own private method. There is duplication of tools and little sharing of experience. For converting text, optical character recognition, which uses a computer to identify the characters and words on a page, has reached a tantalizing level of being almost good enough. Several teams have developed considerable expertise, but little of this expertise is systematic or shared.

Interoperability

From a computing viewpoint, many of the most difficult problems facing digital libraries are aspects of a single challenge: how to achieve *interoperability*—that is, how to get a wide variety of computing systems to work together. Interoperability ranges from the syntactic level (where there is superficial uniformity in access and in navigation but near-complete reliance on human intelligence for coherence) to a deeper level where separate computer systems share an understanding of the information.

Around the world, many independently managed digital libraries are being created. These libraries have different management policies and different computing systems. Some are modern, state-of-the-art computer systems; others are elderly, long past retirement age. The term *legacy system* is often used to describe old systems, but every system is built on the past. As soon as a commitment is made to build a computer system or to create a new service or product, that commitment is a factor in all future decisions. Thus, every computer system is a legacy system, even before it is fully deployed.

Interoperability and standardization are interrelated. Unfortunately, the formal process of creating international standards is often the opposite of what is required for interoperability in digital libraries. Not only is the official process of standardization much too slow for the fast-moving world of digital libraries; it also encourages standards that are unduly complex. Many international standards have never been tested in real life. In practice, the only standards that matter are those that are widely used. Sometimes a de facto standard emerges because a prominent group of researchers uses it; the use of TCP/IP for the Internet is an example. Some standards become accepted because the leaders of the community decide to follow certain conventions; the MARC format for catalog records is an example of this. Sometimes, generally accepted standards are created through a formal standards process; MPEG, the compression format used for video, is a good example. Other de facto standards are proprietary products from prominent corporations; Adobe's Portable Document Format is a recent example. (TCP/IP and MARC were created by the communities that use them, then became official standards and were enhanced through a formal process.)

The following are among the many aspects of interoperability.

User interfaces   A user will typically use many collections from many digital libraries. Interoperability aims at presenting the materials from those collections in a coherent manner, though it is not necessary to hide all the differences. Although a collection of maps is not the same as a collection of music, a user should be able to move smoothly between them, search across them, and be protected from idiosyncrasies of computer systems or peculiarities of how the collections are managed.

Naming and identification   Some way is needed to identify the materials in a digital library. Every computer on the Internet has an IP address and a domain name. The web's Uniform Resource Locators extend these names to individual files. However, neither domain names nor URLs are fully satisfactory. Library materials need identifiers that identify the material, not the location where an instance of the material is stored at a given moment of time. Location-independent identifiers are sometimes called Uniform Resource Names (URNs).

Formats   Materials in every known digital format are stored in digital libraries. The web has created de facto standards for a few formats—notably HTML for simple text and GIF and JPEG for images. Beyond these basic formats, there is little agreement. Text provides a particular challenge for interoperability. ASCII, which emerged in the 1980s as the standard character set for computers, has few characters beyond those used in English. Unicode now appears to be emerging as an extended character set that supports a very wide range of scripts, but it is not yet supported by many computer systems. Although the widely advocated SGML is used in some digital library systems as a markup language for both text and metadata, it is so complex and so flexible that it makes full interoperability hard to achieve. XML, a simplified version of SGML that has recently become popular, may succeed in bridging the gap between the simplicity of HTML and the full generality of SGML.

Metadata   Metadata is important to many aspects of digital libraries, but is especially important for interoperability. As has already been mentioned, metadata is often divided into three categories: descriptive metadata (used for bibliographic purposes and for searching and retrieval), structural metadata (which relates different objects and parts of objects to each other), and administrative metadata (which is used to manage collections and to control access to them). For interoperability, some of this metadata must be exchanged between computers. This requires agreement on the names given to the metadata fields and on the format used to encode them, and at least some agreement on semantics. (A trivial example of the importance of semantics is the fact that there is little value in having a metadata field called "date" if one collection uses the field for the date when an object was created and another uses it for the date when it was added to the collection.)

Distributed searching   Users often wish to find information that is scattered across many independent collections. Each collection may be organized in a coherent way, but the descriptive metadata will vary, as will the capabilities provided for searching. The traditional approach to finding information by searching across collections is to insist that all the collections agree on a standard set of metadata and support the same search protocols. Increasingly, digital library researchers are recognizing that this is unrealistic. It must be possible to search sensibly across collections even if their materials are organized differently.

Network protocols   Moving information from one computer to another requires interoperability at the network level. The near-universal adoption of the Internet protocols has largely solved this problem, but there are gaps. For example, the Internet protocols are not good at delivering continuous streams of data, such audio or video materials, which must arrive in a steady stream at predictable time intervals.

Retrieval protocols   In one of the fundamental operations of digital libraries, a computer sends a message to another in order to retrieve certain items. This message must be transmitted in some protocol. The protocol can be a simple one, such as HTTP, or a much more complex one. The ideal protocol would support secure authentication of both computers, high-level queries to discover what resources each provides, a variety of search and retrieval capabilities, methods of storing and modifying intermediate results, and interfaces to many formats and procedures. The most ambitious attempt to achieve these goals, the Z39.50 protocol, is in danger of collapsing under its own complexity while still not meeting all the needs.

Authentication and security   Several of the biggest obstacles to interoperability among digital libraries involve authentication. Three categories of authentication are needed. The first is authentication of users. Since few methods of authentication have been widely adopted, digital libraries are often forced to provide every user with a "user ID" and a password. The second category is authentication of computers. Systems that handle valuable information, especially financial transactions or confidential information, need to know which computer they are connecting to. One crude approach is to rely on the Internet IP address of each computer, but this is open to abuse. Third, there is authentication of library materials. People need to be confident that they have received the authentic version of an item, not one that has been modified (either accidentally or deliberately). Some good methods of authentication exist, but they have not been deployed widely enough to permit full interoperability.

Semantic interoperability   Semantic interoperability is a broad term for the need of computers to share a semantic interpretation of the information in the messages they pass. Semantic interoperability deals with the user's ability to access similar classes of digital objects, distributed across heterogeneous collections, with compensation for site-by-site variations. Full semantic interoperability embraces a family of deep research problems, some of them extraordinarily difficult.

The web provides a base level of interoperability, but the simplicity of the underlying technology that has led to its wide acceptance also brings weaknesses: URLs make poor names for the long term. HTML is restricted in the variety of information that it can represent. MIME, which identifies the type of each item, is good as far as it goes, but library information is far richer than the MIME view of data types. User interfaces are constrained by the simplicity of the HTTP protocol. Developing extensions to the web technology has become big business. Some extensions are driven by genuine needs, but others are driven by competition between companies. One notable success has been the programming language Java, which has made a great contribution to user interfaces, overcoming many of the constraints of HTTP.

Paradoxically, the web's success is also a barrier to the next generation of digital libraries. The web has become a legacy system. If researchers want their work to gain acceptance, they must provide a path for migration from the web of today to its successor. (The need for such a path is illustrated by the fact that the leading web browsers do not support URNs; this has been a barrier to using URNs to identify materials within digital libraries.)

Interoperability is easy to describe but hard to achieve. Researchers must develop new concepts that offer great improvements yet are easy to introduce. The new methods will have to be highly functional (in order to overcome the inertia of the installed base) and inexpensive to adopt. Careful design of extensibility in digital library systems will allow continued progress with the least disruption to the installed base.

Scale

Interoperability and collection management grow more difficult as the scale of a library increases. A user may find it more difficulty to use a monograph catalog in a very large library, such as the library of Harvard University, than to use one in a small college library where there are only a few entries under each main heading. Many would agree that, as the web has grown, indexing programs such as Infoseek have become less useful—they often respond to simple queries with hundreds of similar hits, and valuable results are hard to find among the duplicates and the rubbish. It is difficult to do research on the scale of digital libraries without building large ones. The current research in this area focuses on technical aspects, particularly reliability and performance.

Reliability and Robustness

Questions of reliability and robustness of service pervade the field of digital libraries. The complexity of large computer systems exceeds our ability to understand fully how all the parts interact. In a sufficiently large system, some components inevitably will be out of service at any given moment. One general approach is to duplicate data. *Mirroring*—the installation of duplicate copies of a collection at several sites—is often used. Unfortunately, mirror sites are rarely exact duplicates, because of the necessary delays in replicating data from one place to another. What are the consequences for distributed retrieval if some part of the collections cannot be searched today, or if a backup version containing slightly out-of-date information is used?

Research in performance is a branch of research in computer networking, not a topic peculiar to digital libraries. The Internet now reaches almost every country in the world, but it is far from providing uniformly high performance everywhere at all times. *Caching*—storing temporary copies of recently used information, either on the user's computer or on a nearby server—helps achieve decent performance across the worldwide Internet, but it brings complexity. For example, what happens if the temporary copies are out of date? Every aspect of security and every aspect of access control is complicated by the knowledge that information is likely to be stored in insecure caches around the world.

Some interesting research on performance has been based on locality, a concept by which selected information is replicated and stored at a location that has been chosen because it has good Internet connections. For example, the Networked Computer Science Technical Reference Library uses a series of zones, each of which stores everything needed to search and identify information. Messages are sent outside a zone only to retrieve actual digital objects from their home repositories.

Economic, Social, and Legal Issues

Digital libraries exist within a complex social, economic, and legal framework. The legal issues are both national and international. They range across several branches of law, including copyright, communications, privacy, obscenity, libel, national security, and even taxation. The social context includes authorship, ownership, the act of publication, authenticity, and integrity. These are not easy areas for research.

Some of the most difficult questions to study are economic. If digital libraries are managed collections of information, skilled professionals are needed to manage them. Who pays these people? The conventional wisdom assumes that the users of the collections, or their institutions, will pay subscriptions or make a payment for each use of the collections. Therefore, research is being done on payment methods, on authentication, and on methods of controlling the use of collections. Meanwhile, the high quality of many open-access web sites has shown that there are other financial models. Researchers have developed some interesting economic theories, but the real advances in understanding the economic forces are coming from the people who are actually creating, managing, or using digital information. Pricing models cease to be academic when mistakes cause individuals to lose their jobs or an organization to go out of business.

Libraries and publishers sometimes wish to control access to their materials, perhaps in order to ensure payment, or to fulfill requirements set by copyright owners or conditions laid down by donors, or in response to concerns about privacy, libel, or obscenity. Such methods are sometimes called *rights management*; however, a better term is *access management*, since issues of access are much broader than simply copyright control or the generation of revenue. Some of the methods of access management involve encryption. Encryption is a highly complex field where technology, law, and public policy have become hopelessly entangled.

Evaluating the impact made by digital libraries proves to be very difficult. Can the value of digital libraries, and the value of research in the field, be measured? Unfortunately, despite some noble efforts, it is not clear how much useful information can be acquired. Systematic results are few and far between. The problem is well known in market research. Techniques such as focus groups and surveys are quite effective in predicting how incremental changes will affect existing products but are much less effective in anticipating the effects of fundamental changes. This does not imply that measurements are not needed. It is impossible to develop any large system without good management data. How many people use each service? How satisfied are they? What is the unit cost of the service? What is the cost of adding material to the collections? What are the delays? Ensuring that systems provide such data is essential, but this is good computing practice, not research.

Economic, social, and legal issues were left to the end of this survey not because they are unimportant but because they are so difficult. In selecting research topics, two criteria are important: the topic must be worthwhile and the research must be feasible. The value of libraries to education, to scholarship, and to the public good is almost impossible to measure quantitatively. Attempts to measure the early impact of digital libraries are heavily constrained by incomplete collections, rapidly changing technology, and users who are adapting to new opportunities. Measurements of dramatically new computer systems are inevitably a record of history, interesting in hindsight but of limited utility in planning for the future. Determining the value of digital libraries may continue to be a matter for informed judgment, not research.

Research around the World

Digital libraries are a worldwide phenomenon. The Internet allows researchers from around the world to collaborate on a day-to-day basis. Researchers in Australia and New Zealand have benefited greatly and are important contributors. The World Wide Web was developed in Switzerland. The British e-lib project provided added stimuli to a variety of library initiatives having to do with electronic publication and with distribution of material in digital forms. Recently, the European Union and the (U.S.) National Science Foundation have sponsored a series of joint planning meetings. A notable international effort has been the series of Dublin Core metadata workshops, described in chapter 10. The stories on digital libraries research published in *D-Lib Magazine* each month illustrate that this is indeed a worldwide field; during the first three years of publication, articles came from authors in more than ten countries. The big, well-funded American projects are important, but they are far from being the whole story.

5

People, Organizations, and Change

The story of digital libraries is one of change. Authors, readers, librarians, publishers and information services are adopting new technology with remarkable speed, and this is altering relationships among people.

Every organization has some members who wish to use the most advanced systems (even when not appropriate) and others who demand the traditional ways of doing things (even when the new ones are superior). This is sometimes called a "generation gap," but that is a misnomer—people of all ages can be receptive to new ideas.

Aside from the preferences of individuals, the pace of change varies widely among organizations and disciplines. Some corporate libraries, such as those of drug companies, already spend more than half of their acquisition funds on electronic materials and services. In contrast, printed materials, manuscripts, and other tangible items will be central to humanities libraries for the foreseeable future.

Perhaps the most fundamental change is that online computing is altering the behavior of the creators and users of information. Tools on personal computers allow individuals with a modicum of skill to carry out processes that once required skilled craftsmen. Word processing and desktop publishing have made office correspondence almost as elegant as professionally designed books. Diagrams, graphs, and other illustrations can be created in color. Not everyone wishes to learn these techniques, and some miserable-looking materials are still being produced; however, many people create elegant and effective materials without professional assistance, and their ability to do so affects all information professionals, including publishers, librarians, archivists, indexers, catalogers, and webmasters.

A few people argue that the new technology eliminates the need for professional management of information. That is naive. Publishers and libraries perform functions that go far beyond the management of physical items. Services such as refereeing, editing, abstracting, and indexing are not tied to any particular technology. Although the web permits users to mount their own information, most people are pleased to have support from a professional webmaster. The overall need for information professionals will continue, and may grow, as their specific practices change with the technology, but the new forms of organizations and the new types of professionals that will emerge are open to speculation.

Digital Libraries Created by Users

Some of the most successful digital libraries were created by researchers or groups of professionals for themselves and their colleagues, with minimal support from publishers or librarians. Two of these, the Physics E-Print Archives at the Los Alamos National Laboratory and the Internet RFC series, were described in chapter 2. The panels in this section describe three more: the Netlib library of mathematical software, the data archives of the International Consortium for Political Science Research, and the Perseus collections of classical texts. These digital libraries are well established and heavily used. They employ professionals, but the leadership and most of the staff come from the respective disciplines: physics, computing, applied mathematics, the social sciences, and classics.

Digital libraries created by user communities are particularly interesting because their services were constructed to meet the needs of the disciplines, without preconceived notions of how collections are conventionally managed. When creators and users develop systems that they want for their own work, they encounter the usual questions about organizing and retrieving information, quality control, standards, and services that are the lifeblood of publishing and libraries. Sometimes they find new and creative answers to these old questions.

Libraries and museums play a special role for users in the humanities, because they provide the raw material on which the humanities are based. Digital libraries can provide much wider access to these materials than could ever be provided by physical collections. A university with a fine

Panel 5.1
Netlib

Netlib is a digital library of high-quality mathematical software. Founded in 1985 by Jack Dongarra and Eric Grosse (who remain its editors-in-chief), it is now maintained by a consortium of AT&T Bell Laboratories, the University of Tennessee, and the Oak Ridge National Laboratory. It has mirror sites around the world. Hundreds of thousands of software programs are downloaded per year, and they are used in almost every branch of scientific research.

At first, Netlib specialized in software produced from research in numerical analysis, especially software for supercomputers with vector or parallel architectures. However, its collections now include other software tools, technical reports and papers, benchmark performance data, and information about professional conferences and meetings. Though most of the materials are available openly and for free, payment is sometimes required for commercial use.

The technical history of Netlib spans a period of rapid development of the Internet. Netlib began as an electronic mail service. At various times, it has provided an X-Windows interface, anonymous FTP, CD-ROMs, and Gopher services. At present, it uses web technology. The Netlib team continues to be among the leaders in developing advanced architectures for organizing and storing materials in digital libraries.

The organization of the Netlib collections is highly pragmatic. It assumes that the users are mathematicians and scientists who are familiar with the field and will incorporate the software into their own computer programs. The collections are arranged in a hierarchy, with software grouped by discipline, application, or source. Each collection has its own editor, and the editors use their knowledge of the specific field to decide the method of organization. Netlib has developed a form of indexing record that is tailored to its specialized needs. The collections are also classified under the Guide to Available Mathematical Software, which is a cross-index provided by the National Institute of Standards and Technology.

library will always have an advantage in serving humanities teaching and research, but it need not have exclusive use of unique items. The British Library is beginning to digitize and mount on the web treasures such as the Magna Carta and the manuscript of *Beowulf*. In the past, access to such documents was restricted to scholars who visited the library and to purchasers of expensive facsimile editions. In the future, everybody will be able to see excellent reproductions.

Panel 5.2
The Inter-university Consortium for Political and Social Research

The Inter-university Consortium for Political and Social Research (ICPSR), a not-for-profit organization based at the University of Michigan, has been in operation since 1962. Its digital library allows social scientists to store data that they have gathered for others to use. Data that was expensive to gather will lose its usefulness unless it is organized, documented, and made available to researchers. The data collected spans a broad range of disciplines, including political science, sociology, demography, economics, history, education, gerontology, criminal justice, public health, foreign policy, and law.

ICPSR is a not-for-profit consortium. Hundreds of colleges and universities in the United States and around the world are members. Their annual subscriptions provide access to the collections to their faculty and students. People whose organizations do not belong to ICPSR can pay for the use of individual data sets.

About 200 data sets (several thousand files) are added to the archive in a year. Some of the data sets are very large. The archive also stores documentation about the data and codebooks explaining designs of studies, decisions made by the original researchers, how data was gathered, adjustments made, and technical information needed to use the data in further research. The collection is organized hierarchically by discipline, so browsing is easy. Each data set is described by a short record containing basic cataloging information and an abstract.

The archive has been in existence through many generations of computer systems. The ICPSR's current web-based user interface can be used for browsing or for searching the catalog records. Data sets are delivered over the Internet by FTP, and selected data is available on CD-ROM.

Panel 5.3
Perseus

Some of the major projects in the field of electronic information have been led by established members of humanities faculties, but many others have been maverick projects with little institutional support. Sometimes junior faculty members have pursued new ideas against the opposition of senior members of their departments. At Harvard University in the mid 1980s, Gregory Crane, a junior faculty member in classics, initiated the Perseus project, which uses hyperlinks to relate sources such as texts and maps to tools such as dictionaries. In particular, Crane aimed to give the general student an appreciation of the poems of the Greek poet Pindar. From this early work has emerged one of the most important digital libraries in the humanities.

The Perseus collections now cover the classical Greek period comprehensively and are extending steadily into other periods of Greek history, into the Roman period, and beyond. The source materials include texts (in the original language and in translation) and images of objects (e.g. vases) and architectural sites. However, perhaps the greatest resource is the effort that has been made in structuring the materials and the database of links between items.

The emphasis on content has enabled the Perseus collections to migrate through several generations of computer systems. Classical texts are fairly stable, though new editions may have small changes, and the supporting works, such as lexicons and atlases, have long lives. Therefore, the effort put into acquiring accurate versions of texts, marking them up with SGML, and linking them to related works is a long-term investment that will outlive any computer system. Perseus, which has never had more than one programmer on its staff, relies on the most appropriate computer technology available. It was an early adopter of Apple's Hypercard system, it published a high-quality CD-ROM, and it quickly moved to the web when that technology emerged. The only elaborate programs that the project has developed are rule-based systems for analyzing the morphology of inflected Greek and Latin words.

The long-term impact of Perseus is difficult to predict, but the goals are ambitious. In recent years, academic studies in the humanities have become increasingly esoteric and detached. It is typical of the field that Crane was unable to continue his work at Harvard, because it was not considered serious scholarship; he moved to Tufts University. Perseus may not be Harvard's idea of scholarship, but it is certainly not lightweight. The 4 million words of Greek source texts include most of the commonly cited texts. When there are no suitable images of a vase, Perseus has been know to take a hundred new photographs; the user interface helps the reader with easy access to translations and dictionaries but maintains a strong focus on the original materials. Perseus, a treasure trove for the layman, is increasingly being used by researchers as an excellent resource for traditional studies. Perseus's greatest achievement may be to show the general public the fascination of the humanities and to show the humanities scholar that popularity and scholarship can go hand in hand.

The Motives of Creators and Users

Creators

To understand how libraries and publishing are changing requires an appreciation of the varied motives that lead some people to create materials and others to use them.

One common misconception is that people create materials primarily for the fees and royalties that they generate. Though many people make their livelihood from works they create, others have different objectives. Darwin's *Origin of Species* was written to promulgate ideas; so were Paine's *Rights of Man,* Marx's *Kapital,* and Saint Paul's Epistle to the Romans. From classical times, some books, manuscripts, pictures, musical works, and poems were commissioned for the aggrandizement of patrons. Many of the world's great buildings, including the Egyptian pyramids and the Bibliothèque de France, were created because of an individual's wish to be remembered. Photographs, diaries, poems, and letters may be created simply for the private pleasure of the creator, yet subsequently they become important library items. Few activities generate so many fine materials— fine writing, art, music, and architecture—as religion; conversely, few activities create as much of dubious merit. And the web includes large amounts of advertising and promotional materials, some of which will eventually be incorporated in digital libraries.

The act of creation can be incidental to another activity. A judge who delivers a legal opinion is creating material that will be incorporated in digital libraries. So is a museum curator preparing an exhibition catalog, or a drug researcher filing a patent claim. Government agencies create materials for public use: navigational charts, weather forecasts, official statistics, treaties, trade agreements, and so on. Many materials now preserved in libraries and archives were created to provide records of events or decisions: law reports, parish records, government records, official histories, wartime photographs.

People who convert materials from other media to digital formats can also be considered creators. Such conversion activities range from an individual's efforts to transcribe a favorite story and mount it on the web to projects that convert millions of items. The actual act of creation can even be carried out by a machine, as when images are captured by a satellite circling the earth.

Another misconception is that creators and the organizations they work for have the same motives. For one thing, some works are created by teams and others by individuals. A feature film must be a team effort, but nobody would want a poem written by a committee. Hence, whereas some creators (freelance writers, photographers, composers) are individuals, others belong to an organization, and the materials that the latter create are part of the organization's activities. When somebody is employed by an organization, the employer often directs the act of creation and owns the results. In the case of such "work for hire," the motivations of the individual and those of the organization may be different. A corporation that makes a feature film may be motivated by profit, but the director might see an opportunity to advocate a political opinion and the leading actress may have artistic goals.

Creators whose immediate motive is not financial usually benefit from the widest possible exposure of their work. This creates a tension with their publishers, whose business model is usually to allow access only after payment. Academic journals are an important category of materials in which authors' interests (recording their research and enhancing their reputations, both of which benefit from broad dissemination) may be in direct conflict with the publisher's desire for revenue.

Users
Libraries' users vary as much as the creators of material in their interests and in their levels of expertise. Urban public libraries serve a particularly diverse group of users. The library is a source of recreational reading, an employment center providing information about job openings, or a source of bus timetables. A library may provide Internet connections that people use as a source of medical or legal information. It may have audio tapes of children's stories. It may have reference materials that are used by local historians, by casual visitors, and by experts.

Aside from the variations among individuals, an individual may have different needs at different times. And even two users who have similar needs may use a library differently. One may use catalogs and indexes extensively; another may rely more on links and citations. Designers of digital libraries must resist the temptation to assume a uniform, specific pattern of use and to create a system specifically for that pattern.

Some broad categories of users can be distinguished, however, and most such characterizations apply to both digital libraries and to conventional libraries. One category consists of people who use libraries for recreation; in digital libraries this sometimes takes the form of unstructured browsing, colloquially known as *surfing*. Another consists of those who use a library to find an introductory description of some subject—for example, an engineer beginning the study of some technical area by reading a survey article, or a tourist looking for information about countries to be visited. Sometimes a user wants to know a simple fact: What is the wording of the First Amendment to the U.S. Constitution? What is the melting point of lead? Who won yesterday's football game? Some of these facts are provided by reference materials, such as maps, encyclopedias, and dictionaries; others lie buried deep within the collections. Occasionally a user wants comprehensive information about some topic—a medical researcher may wish to find a citation for every published paper that contains information about the effects of a certain drug, or a lawyer may wish to know every precedent that might apply to a current case.

In many of these situations, the user's requirements can be satisfied from a variety of sources. For example, many maps and atlases will contain information relevant to a question about geography. Comprehensive study of a topic, however, requires access to specific sources. These distinctions are important when one is considering the economics of information (since alternative sources of information lead to price competition) and when one is studying information retrieval (where comprehensive searching has long been given special importance).

The Information Professions and Change

As digital information augments and sometimes replaces conventional forms, the information professions are changing. Librarians and publishers, in particular, have different traditions, and it is not surprising that their reactions to change differ.

Librarians

To examine how change affects librarians, it is useful to examine four aspects separately: library directors, mid-career librarians, the education of young librarians, and the increasing importance in libraries of specialists from other fields, notably computing.

Library directors are under pressure. Directing a major library used to be a job that provided pleasant work, prestige, and a good salary for life. The prestige and the good salary remain, but the work has changed dramatically. Digital libraries offer long-term potential but short-term headaches. Libraries are being squeezed by rising prices across the board. Conservative users demand that none of the conventional services be diminished; other users want every digital service immediately. Many directors do not receive the support they deserve from the people to whom they report, whose understanding of the changes in libraries is often weak. Every year a number of prominent directors decide not to spend their working lives being buffeted by administrative confusion and resign to find areas of work in which they have more control over their own destiny.

Mid-career librarians find that digital libraries are both an opportunity and a challenge. The serious shortage of senior librarians who are comfortable with modern technology offers opportunities to energetic and creative individuals who are more at ease with it. Conversely, mid-career librarians who are not at ease with technology may get left behind. Adapting to technical change is more than a matter of retraining. Training is important, but it fails if it merely replaces one set of static skills with another. Libraries need people who are aware of the changes that are happening around them and who are inquisitive and open to new ideas.

The education of young librarians revolves around library schools. Librarianship is a profession. In the United States, a master's degree from a library school is required for many library jobs. For years, library schools' curricula were rather pedestrian, focusing on the basic skills needed by mid-level librarians, and in many a university the library school was one of the weaker schools academically. In recent years, however, some universities have realized that digital libraries provide opportunities for a new type of library school, with a new curriculum and a vigorous program of research.

Digital libraries require some experts who are not professional librarians, such as computer specialists and lawyers. Fitting such people into the highly structured world of libraries is problematic. Librarians are hesitant to recruit talent from outside their ranks, and they restrict their choices needlessly when they require candidates for one of the new positions to have

Panel 5.4
The Ticer Summer School

In 1996, Tilburg University in the Netherlands introduced a two-week summer school intended to educate senior librarians about digital libraries. The program, called Ticer, was an immediate success and has been fully subscribed every year. Most of the students are from northern Europe, but in 1998 there were participants from Malaysia, Japan, India, South Korea, and many other countries. Most are senior staff members of academic or special libraries.

Tilburg University has been a leader in the implementation of digital library for many years, and the course reflects the combination of strategic planning and practical implementation that has marked the university's efforts. Many of the lecturers at the summer school are members of the university's libraries or its computing services. In addition, a range of visiting experts provide breadth and visibility for the program. The fat book of lecture notes that every student receives is a major resource.

Other features, too, have figured in the success of the Ticer summer school. The costs have been kept reasonably low, yet a high standard of facilities is provided. A pleasant social program enhances the value of 50 people from around the world living and working together. Ticer has a close relationship with Elsevier Science, a large Dutch publisher. Elsevier staffers from around the world attend as students, and senior Elsevier personnel give lectures.

Ticer demonstrates how international the field of digital libraries has become and the privileged position of the English language. The Ticer program is so thoroughly English that the publicity materials do not even mention that fact, yet few of the students come from English-speaking countries.

Panel 5.5
The School of Information Management and Systems at Berkeley

In the early 1990s, several leading universities questioned the quality of their library schools. While their professional schools of law and business were attracting the nation's brightest students and faculty, contributing outstanding research, and making a hefty profit, their library schools were drifting. Faculty members were underpaid and unproductive. Worst of all, the educational programs were not creating the leaders that the new digital libraries and electronic publishing would require.

Columbia University simply closed down its library school; the programs were considered less valuable than the buildings that the school occupied. The University of Chicago also closed its library school. The University of

California at Berkeley and the University of Michigan went the other way and completely refurbished their schools. Perhaps the most dramatic change was at Berkeley.

Many universities claim that academic decisions are made by the faculty. At most universities this is pretense, but at Berkeley the academic community has great power. Berkeley's first instinct was to follow Columbia and to close down its library school, but there was enough opposition that the university changed its mind and set up a high-level planning group. The report of this group, titled Proposal for a School of Information Management and Systems, was released in December of 1993. In classic bureaucratic doublespeak, its fundamental recommendation was to "disestablish" the existing school and "reconstitute" a new school from its ashes.

In creating new academic programs, good universities look at two factors. The first is academic content: Does the area have deep intellectual content that will attract first-rate faculty members whose scholarship will be a credit to the university? The second is education: Will the program attract able students who will later go out and become leaders? The Berkeley planning group's report answered these questions affirmatively subject to the fulfilment of certain criteria.

As a starting point, the report explicitly rejected the traditional library school curriculum and the Master of Library Science degree. With remarkable frankness, the report stated "The degree to be awarded by this program . . . is not designed to meet American Library Association requirements; rather, it will serve as a model for the development of accreditation criteria for the emerging discipline upon which the School is focused."

The report was accepted, and the school set out to recruit faculty and students. From the start the emphasis was on interdisciplinary studies. The planning report is full of references to joint programs with other schools and departments. The program announcement for the new master's degree program mentioned "aspects of computer science, cognitive science, psychology and sociology, economics, business, law, library/information studies, and communications." Students were required only to have significant computer skills.

The appointment of faculty was equally diverse. The first dean, Hal Varian, is an economist. Other faculty members include a prominent scholar in copyright law and a former chair of university's computer scientist department. Many of the faculty members have joint appointments and teach and do research across traditional department boundaries.

It is too early to claim success for this new school or for the similar effort at the University of Michigan, but the first signs are good. The school has met the basic requirements of high-quality faculty and students. The research programs have grown fast, with large external grants for research on interesting topics. A few years from now the first graduates should be emerging as the leaders of the next generation of information professionals.

library science degrees. Few of the young people who are creating digital libraries see library school on their career path.

Compared with other professions, librarianship is notable for how badly mid-level professionals are paid. Top-class work requires top-class people, and in the case of digital libraries the best people have high market value. It is troubling to pay a programmer more than a department head, but it is even more troubling to see a good library deteriorate because of a poor computing staff. Part of the success of the Mercury project at Carnegie Mellon University was due to the fact that the members of the technical staff were administratively considered employees of the university's computing center. Their offices were in the library, and their allegiance was to the digital library; however, they were supervised by technical managers, they worked their usual irregular hours, they had excellent equipment, and they were paid the same salary as other computing professionals. Few libraries are so flexible.

Publishers

The changes that are happening in publishing are as dramatic as those happening in libraries. Since the fifteenth century, when printing was introduced in Europe, publishing has been a slow-moving field. Traditionally, a publisher's task has been to create and distribute printed documents. Today, the publishing industry still draws most of its revenue from sales of physical products—books, journals, magazines, and more recently videos and compact disks. However, many publishers see their future growth in electronic publishing.

Publishing is a mixture of cottage industry and big business. Large publishers, such as Time Warner, Reed Elsevier, and the Thomson group, rank among the biggest and most profitable corporations in the world, yet most of the 50,000 publishers in the United States publish fewer than ten items per year. Academic publishing has the strange feature that some publishers are commercial organizations, in business to make profits for their shareholders, while others are not-for-profit societies and university presses whose primary function is to support scholarship.

The success of a publishing house depends on the editors who select the materials to be published, work with the creators, and sometimes oversee each work as it goes through production. Publishing may be a business, but many of the people who go to work in it are not looking for a business career. They enter the field because they are interested in the content of the materials that they publish.

Publishers use contractors extensively. A few, such as West Publishing (a large legal publisher), run their own printing presses, but most printing is done by specialist printers. The detailed editing of manuscripts is often done by freelancers. Books are sold through booksellers, and journals through subscription agents. This use of contractors gives publishers flexibility that they would not have if everything were carried out in house. When Elsevier moved to producing journals in SGML markup, they could withdraw contracts from those printers who were not prepared to change to SGML.

A recent wave of corporate takeovers in the publishing industry has created a few huge companies with the wealth to support large-scale computing projects. Whether size is necessarily a benefit in electronic publishing remains to be seen, however. Web technology means that small companies can move rapidly into new fields, and small companies sometimes have an advantage in developing close relationships between editors and authors. Some observers thought that the sale of West Publishing, which had been privately held, was driven by fear that electronic publishing might weaken the firm's dominance of the legal market.

A few university presses, including the Oxford University Press and the University of Chicago Press, have much in common with commercial publishers of academic materials. They publish large numbers of general-interest, reference, and scholarly books. These presses operate on a sound financial footing and give no priority to authors from their own universities. Other university presses have a different role: supporting scholarship by publishing scholarly works (e.g., monographs in the humanities), many of which have such narrow appeal that only a few hundred copies are sold. Such books would never be considered by commercial publishers. These university presses operate on extremely tight budgets. In recent years, as universities have tightened their belts, their subsidies to their presses have been decreasing or disappearing.

Computing Professionals and Webmasters

Computing professionals are as much a part of digital libraries as librarians and publishers, but the cultural differences and the barriers to cooperation are great. Many members of the Internet community grew up immersed in computing and have unorthodox styles of working. As in every discipline, some are so knowledgeable about technological details that they see nothing else, and they often have genuine difficulty in describing technological matters to non-specialists. A few are deliberately obscure, apparently defining merit as knowledge of the arcane. Fortunately, deliberate obscurity is rare. Most people would like others to know what they do, but technical people often have genuine difficulty describing technology to non-specialists.

The Internet community has its foundation in the generation of computer scientists who grew up on the Unix operating system. Much of the success of Unix was due to a tradition of openness. The Unix, Internet, and World Wide Web communities share their efforts with one another. They have discovered that this makes everybody more productive. An appreciation of this spirit of openness is fundamental to understanding how computer scientists view the development of digital libraries. Their attitude can become a utopian dream, and a few idealists advocate a completely uncontrolled information society, but this is an extreme viewpoint. Most members of the Internet community have a healthy liking for money; entrepreneurship is part of the tradition, and new companies are being formed continually.

Even in the rapidly changing world of computing, the emergence of the profession of webmaster has had few parallels. At the beginning of 1994 the web was hardly known; yet in the summer of 1995 more than a thousand people attended the first meeting of the Federal Webmasters, an informal group of people who maintain web sites for the U.S. government. The title *webmaster* appeared overnight and immediately became so firmly entrenched that attempts to find an alternative (on the notion that *master* is excessively masculine) failed. *Webmaster* must be understood as applying to both men and women.

A webmaster is a publisher, a librarian, a computer administrator, and a designer. The job requires a range of expertise that includes, in addition to the traditional publishing skills of selection and editing, skills in user-interface design and in operating a high-performance computer system. A web site is the face that an organization presents to the world. The quality of its graphics and the way it presents the material on the site are as important as any public-relations material that the organization issues. (At CNRI, the webmaster refers to herself, half-jokingly, as "the Art Department." A professional librarian who is highly skilled technically, she spends much of her time doing work that in other contexts would be called graphic design.)

In some organizations, the webmaster selects or even creates the materials that appear on a web site. More commonly, the materials are generated by individuals or groups within the organization. The webmaster's task is to edit and format individual items, and to organize them within the web site. Thus, the overall shape of the site is created by the webmaster, but not the individual items. For example, CNRI manages the web site of the Internet Engineering Task Force. The content is firmly controlled by the IETF secretariat, but the webmaster contributed the design of the home page and set up the links from that page to other items on the web site.

Webmasters' computing skills vary, as do the size and the complexity web sites. Some user-interface methods, such as the Java programming language, require skilled programmers. Some web sites are very large, replicating information on many powerful computers which are distributed around the world. A really popular site, such as that of the Cable News Network, has more than 100 million hits per day. Designing and monitoring these large systems and their network connections is a skilled computing job. If a web site handles commercial transactions, the webmaster must also have expertise in network security.

Many of the organizations that contribute to digital libraries have computing departments. The webmasters can rely on them for occasional technical tasks, such as setting up a web server or a searchable index to the site. In other organizations, the webmaster must be a jack of all trades. Many web sites serve organizations that have no computing staff. A plethora of companies provide web services for such organizations, designing web pages, running server computers, and performing administrative tasks such as registering domain names.

New Forms of Organizations

Consortia

Managing large online collections is expensive and labor intensive. Libraries can save effort by working together in consortia to acquire and mount shared collections. This also saves effort for publishers, since they then have fewer customers to negotiate with and support. In the United States, library consortia have been organized by states (e.g., Ohio) and by

Panel 5.6
Melvyl and the California Digital Library

The nine campuses of the University of California often act as though they were nine independent universities. Campuses such as UC Berkeley and UC Los Angeles rank as major universities in their own right, but organizationally they are parts of a single huge university. For many years, they have shared a digital library system called Melvyl. For much of its life, Melvyl was under the vigorous leadership of Clifford Lynch.

At the center of Melvyl is a computer-based catalog of holdings of all libraries at the nine campuses, the California State Library in Sacramento, and the California Academy of Sciences. This catalog has records of more than 8.5 million monograph titles, representing 13 million items. In addition to book holdings, it includes maps, films, musical scores, data files, and sound recordings. The periodicals database has about 800,000 unique titles of newspapers, journals, proceedings, etc., including the holdings of other major California libraries. Melvyl also provides access to numerous abstracting and indexing files, including the entire Medline and Inspec databases. In 1995, Melvyl added bit-mapped images of the publications of the Institute of Electrical and Electronics Engineers. The images are linked through the Inspec database. For users who access the Inspec database, the message "Image available" indicates that records are linked to IEEE bit-mapped images. The user can then request the server to open a window on the user's workstation to display the bit-mapped images. Use of the books and periodicals files is open to all, though use of the article databases is limited to members of the University of California.

Melvyl has consistently been an early adopter of new digital library technology. Much of the development of Z39.50 has been associated with it. The Melvyl team was also responsible for creating the communications network that links the University of California's campuses.

The success of Melvyl influenced the University of California's organization of its digital library services. Each of the university's nine campuses has its own library. In 1997, after two years of planning, the university created the California Digital Library, which provides digital library services to the entire university. Organizationally it is intended to be equal to each of the others. Its director, Richard Lucier, ranks equally with the nine other directors. Its budget, initially about $10 million a year, is expected to rise sharply.

The university could easily have justified central digital library services through arguments of economies of scale, a focus for licensing negotiations, and leveraged purchasing power. For these reasons, the campuses have historically shared some library services through Melvyl, which is incorporated in the new digital library. The California Digital Library is much more ambitious, however. It is explicitly charged with being an active part in the changes that are transforming scholarly communication. It is expected to have a vigorous research program and to work with organizations everywhere to enhance the role of libraries in supporting teaching and research. At the very least, the University of California will receive excellent digital library services; at best, the California Digital Library will change academic life.

academic partnerships. In Europe, where most universities are state run, there are well-established national consortia that provide digital library services for the entire academic community. One good example of a collaborative effort is Melvyl, which was established by the University of California before the days of the web (originally to share catalog and indexing records).

Secondary Information Services and Aggregators

The term *secondary information* covers a wide range of services, including catalogs, indexes, and abstracting, that help users find information. Some of these services (such as Chemical Abstracts) grew out of professional societies; others (such as ISI, which publishes *Current Contents* and *Science Citation Index*, and Bowker, which publishes *Books in Print*) have always been commercial. OCLC has a special niche; it is a membership organization that grew up around shared cataloging.

These organizations are simultaneously vulnerable to change and well placed to expand their services into digital libraries. Their advantages are years of computing experience, good marketing, and large collections of valuable data. Many have strong financial reserves or are subsidiaries of conglomerates with the money to support new ventures. Almost every one of these organizations sees its future in the integration of secondary and primary information. Therefore, there are many joint projects between publishers and secondary information services.

Aggregators are services that assemble publications from many publishers and provide them to users as a single package, usually through sales to libraries. Some had their roots in the early online information systems, such as Dialog and BRS. These services licensed indexes and other databases, mounted them on central computers with a specialized search interface, and sold access. Nowadays, a large aggregator may negotiate licenses with 5000 or more publishers and offer a customer a single license.

Universities and Their Libraries

Changes in University Libraries

Like most organizations, universities have difficulty handling change. Universities are large, conservative organizations with caste distinctions that inhibit teamwork. The cultural divide between the humanities and the sciences is well known, but similar divides separate scholars, librarians, and computing professionals. Faculty members treat non-faculty colleagues with disdain, librarians have a jargon of their own, and computing professionals consider technical knowledge the only measure of worth.

Academic departments, which are dominated by tenured faculty members, are powerful forces for retaining the status quo. To close a department, no matter how moribund, is seen as an act of academic vandalism. When a corporation closes a factory, its stock price usually goes up. When Columbia University closed its library school, nobody's stock went up. There are few obvious incentives to change and much vocal opposition to it.

Yet, universities are a source of continual innovation. Chapters 2 and 3 gave numerous examples of universities developing new technologies and deploying them long before the commercial sector. The flow of high-technology companies that fuels the American economy is driven by a small number of research universities, including Stanford, Berkeley, Harvard, MIT, Cornell, and Carnegie Mellon.

Innovation in a large organization requires strategic reallocation of resources. New initiatives require new funding. Resources can be found only by making hard choices. The process by which resources are allocated at a research university appears arcane. Moving resources from one area to build up another is fraught with difficulties. The director of the Ashmolean Museum in Oxford once mused that the best strategy for the museum might be to sell part of its collection to provide funds to look after the rest; he doubted that he would retain his position if he carried out such a strategy. Few deans would advocate cutting the faculty to provide resources that would make the remaining faculty more productive. Yet funds are reallocated. Year by year, the portion of the budget that goes into computers, networks, and support staff increases, perhaps 1 percent each time.

It is not clear whether, in the long term, such reallocations will bring more resources to existing library organizations, or whether universities will develop new information services outside their libraries. The signals are mixed. Paradoxically, good information has never been more important than it is today, yet the university library is declining in importance relative to other information sources. The university library, with its collections of journals and monographs, is only one component in the exchange of academic information. Fifty years ago, faculty and students had few sources of information. Today they have dozens of methods of communication. Desktop computing, the Internet, and video conferencing allow individual scholars to exchange large amounts of information. The technology has become so simple that scholars are able to create and distribute information with less help from professionals, and to do it outside the formal structure of libraries.

If libraries are to be the center for new information services, they have to reallocate resources internally. Discussions of library budgets usually focus on the rising costs of materials, on overcrowding in the buildings, and on the cost of computing, but the biggest cost is that of the staff. Few universities make an honest effort to estimate the costs of their libraries, but a true accounting of a typical research library would assign about 25 percent of the costs to acquisitions, about 50 percent to the staff, and the rest to the building and the equipment. If libraries are to respond to the opportunities presented by electronic information while increasing salaries to attract excellent employees, they will have to reorganize their staffs. It is not merely a question of urging people to work harder or of streamlining internal processes; what is needed is fundamental restructuring.

Buildings for Digital Libraries

An area of change that is difficult for all libraries, but particularly for universities, is how to plan for library buildings. While digital libraries are the focus of research and development around the world, for many libraries the biggest problem is seen as the perennial lack of space. For example, in December of 1993 the funding councils for higher education in the United Kingdom released a report on university libraries, known as the Follett Report. In terms of money, the biggest recommendation from the Follett Committee was the need for a major building program. This need was especially acute in Britain, because the numbers of students at universities had grown sharply and much of the space was required to provide study space on campus.

The expense of a new building to house rarely used paper is hard to justify, but old habits are slow to change. Imposing libraries are being built in many places, including new national libraries in London and Paris. Many a library retains a card catalog in elegant oak cabinets to satisfy the demands of a few senior users, even though the catalog is online and no new cards have been filed for years.

To use a traditional library, the user almost invariably goes to the library. Some libraries will deliver books or photocopies to privileged users, but even those users must be near the library and known to the library staff. In contrast, users of a digital library have no incentive to visit any particular location. The librarians, webmasters, and other professionals who manage the collections have offices where they work, but there is no reason why they should ever see a user. The New York Public Library must be in New York, but the New York digital library could store its collections in Bermuda.

It is difficult to know what will make a good library building in future years. The trials and tribulations of the new British Library building in London show what can happen without good planning. Library buildings typically last at least 50 years, but nobody can anticipate what an academic library will look like even a few years from now. Therefore, the emphasis in designing new library buildings must be on flexibility. Since the designers of library buildings must anticipate communications needs that are only glimpsed today, all spaces must be provided with general-purpose network wiring and generous electrical supplies. Yet the same structures must be suitable for traditional stacks.

Panel 5.7
The Renovation of the Harvard Law Library

Langdell Hall, the main library of Harvard Law School, is not only the working library of a large law school but also one of the great collections of the history of law. During 1996 and 1997, the library was fully renovated at the cost of $35 million. The project illustrates the challenges of building for the long term during a period of rapid change.

When the renovations were being planned, Harvard made two bold proposals: that the library provide no public computers and that every working space support laptop computers. Since it was assumed that visitors to the library would bring their own computers, every place where users might work was provided with a power outlet and a network connection. There are 540 Ethernet ports at tables, carrels, lounges, and study rooms throughout the building. A total of 1158 network connections are installed within the building, and almost all of them were activated immediately (the rest were kept in reserve). Relaxing the "no public computers" decision slightly, Harvard installed about a hundred public computers, including one computer classroom and two small training labs.

Even for Harvard Law School, the cost of this project, $35 million, is a great deal of money. The school has effectively gambled on its assumptions that all users will have laptop computers and that the network installation has enough flexibility to adapt to changes with time. However, the biggest gamble was probably never stated explicitly. The school actually increased the amount of space devoted to library users. The assumption is that people will continue to come to the library to study. Law school faculty are known to prefer working in their offices rather than walk to the library. Many years ago, the librarian, Harry S. Martin III, stated: "Our aim is to keep the faculty out of the library." This witticism describes a commitment to provide faculty with service in their offices, including both online information and an excellent courier service. However, the attention given to reading spaces in Langdell implies a belief that legal scholars and law school students will come to the library to do serious work for many years.

Not all of the money went to technology. Langdell is an elegant old building, with historic books and valuable art. Much of the budget went into elevators, heating, air conditioning, and plumbing. The dignity of the library was not forgotten. Old tables were restored, chandeliers replaced an elderly and ineffective dropped ceiling, Latin inscriptions were relocated, and bas-relief symbols of the law were highlighted. This vision of a great law library combines the traditional view of a library with access to modern technology.

6

Economic and Legal Issues

This chapter, more than any of the others, is a quick review of an extremely complex area. No attempt has been made to describe all the issues. The discussion reflects my own viewpoint, which will probably need revision in time. However, I hope that the basic ideas will stand.

Digital libraries are being developed in a world in which issues of users, content, and technology are interwoven with their economic, social, and legal context. These topics have to be studied together and cannot be understood in isolation. Publishing and libraries follow operating rules and conventions that have evolved over many years. As electronic publication and digital libraries expand, business practices and the legal framework are changing quickly.

Because digital libraries are based on technology, some people hope for technical solutions to all problems. Other people believe that everything can be achieved by passing new laws. Both approaches are flawed. Technology can contribute to the solutions, but it cannot resolve economic or social issues. Changes in laws may be helpful, but bad laws are worse than no laws. Laws are effective only when they codify a framework that people understand and are willing to accept. In the same manner, business models for electronic information will fail unless they appeal to the interests of all interested parties. The underlying challenge is to establish social customs for using information that are widely understood and generally followed. If those customs allow reasonable people to carry out their work, reasonable people will observe them. The economic and legal frameworks will follow.

Economic Issues

Libraries and publishing are big businesses. Huge industries create information or entertainment for financial gain: feature films, newspapers, commercial photographs, novels, textbooks, computer software, musical recordings, and so on. Some estimates suggest that these industries are 5 percent of the economy of the United States. In 1997, Harvard University's libraries had a budget well over $50 million and employed 1000 people. The Library of Congress employs about 4500. Time Warner and other publishing companies are major forces on the world's stock markets. In 1996 the Thomson Corporation paid more than $3 billion for West Publishing. The stock-market valuation of the Internet search firm Yahoo is even higher, though its profits are tiny.

The publishers' concerns about the business and legal framework of online information derive from greed and fear. The greed comes from a belief that publishers stand to make huge sums of money from electronic information if only they can figure out how. The fear is that the changing economic picture will destroy traditional sources of revenue, organizations will wither away, and people will lose their jobs. To computing professionals, this fear is completely reasonable. Most of the companies that have succeeded in one generation of computing have failed in the next. Mainframe companies such as Univac, CDC, Burroughs, and Honeywell were supplanted by minicomputers. Minicomputer companies, such as Prime, Wang, and Data General, did not survive the transition to personal computers. Early personal computer companies have died, as have most of the software pioneers. Even IBM has lost its dominance. Will we see the same pattern with electronic information? The publishers and information services that dominated traditional markets will not necessarily be leaders in the new markets.

Whichever organizations thrive, large or small, commercial or not-for-profit, they have to cover their costs. Every stage in the creation, distribution, and use of digital libraries is expensive. Authors, photographers, composers, designers, and editors need incentives for their efforts in creating information. In many circumstances, but not all, the incentives are financial. Publishers, librarians, archivists, booksellers, subscription agents, and computing specialists all require payment. As yet, there is no consensus on how best to pay for information on the Internet. Almost every conceivable method is being tried. For the sake of brevity, the various models can be divided into those with open access (funds come from the creator or producer of the information) and those with restricted access (the user or the user's library pays for access to the collections).

In chapter 5 it was noted that the various people who are involved in digital libraries and electronic publishing have many motives. In particular, it was noted that creators and publishers often have different financial objectives. When the creators are principally motivated by financial reward, their interests are quite well aligned with those of the publisher. The aim is to generate revenue. The only question is how much should go to the creator and how much to the publisher. If, however, the creator's motive is non-financial while the publisher is concentrating on covering costs or generating profits for shareholders, then they may have conflicting objectives.

A remarkable aspect of the web is that huge amounts of excellent material are openly available, with no requirement for payment by the user. Many people once predicted that open access would limit the web to inferior material; however, today a remarkable amount of high-quality information, paid for and maintained by the producers, is to be found on the networks. In retrospect this is not surprising. Many creators and suppliers of information are eager to have their materials seen; they are prepared to meet the costs out of their own budgets. Among the creators who invest their own resources to make their materials openly available are researchers seeking professional recognition, government agencies, marketers of all sorts, hobbyists, and other recreational groups.

Whenever creators are motivated principally by the wish to have their work widely used, they will prefer open access. But the money to maintain these collections must come from somewhere. Grants are one important source of funds. The Perseus project has relied heavily on grants from foundations. At the Library of Congress, a combination of grants and internal funds pay for American Memory and the National Digital Library Program. Grants are usually short-term, but they can be renewed. The Los Alamos E-Print Archives receive an annual grant from the National Science Foundation, and Netlib has received funding from DARPA since its inception. In essence, grant funding for these digital libraries has become institutionalized.

The web search firms, such as Yahoo, Infoseek, and Lycos, provide open access paid for by advertising. They have rediscovered the financial model used by broadcast television in the United States. The television networks pay to create programs and broadcast them openly. The viewer, sitting at home in front of a television, does not pay directly; the revenue comes from advertisers.

A crucial point in the evolution of digital libraries occurred when web search programs first became available. Some of the services attempted to charge a monthly fee, but the creator of Lycos, Michael Mauldin, was determined to offer open access. He set out to find alternative sources of revenue. Since Lycos was available at no charge, competing services could not charge access fees for comparable products. Today the web search services remain open to all. After a few rocky years, the companies are now profitable, using advertising and revenue from licensing to support open access to their services.

Research teams have a particular interest in having their work widely read. Most research organizations use their own resources to maintain a web sites. Much scientific research is first reported on one of these sites. The Internet Draft series, maintained at CNRI, is paid for by a different method. The conference fees for meetings of the Internet Engineering Task Force pay the salaries of the people who manage the publications. There is open access to all this information.

Government departments are another important source of open-access collections. They provide much information that is short-lived (such as the hurricane tracking data provided by the National Weather Service), but many of their collections (e.g., the collection of international treaties maintained by the Trade Compliance Center of the Department of Commerce) have long-term value.

Private individuals maintain many open-access library collections. There are excellent collections devoted to sports, hobbies, and fan clubs. There is privately published poetry, and there are online novels. Payment by the producer is not new. What in book publishing would be disparaged as vanity is often the source of fine collections on the Internet.

When the publisher of a digital library collection wishes to collect revenue from the user, access to the collection is almost always restricted. Users have access to the materials only after payment has been received. The techniques used to manage such access are a theme of the next chapter. This section looks at the business practices.

Book and journal publishing have traditionally relied on payment by the user. When a copy of a book is sold to a library or to an individual, the proceeds are divided among the bookseller, the publisher, the author, and the other contributors. Feature films follow the same model. The costs of creating and distributing the film are recovered from users through ticket sales at cinemas and through video rentals. Extending this model to online information leads to fees based on use. Most users of the legal information services Lexis and Westlaw pay a rate that is based on the number of hours that they use the services. Alternative methods of charging for online information, sometimes tried, have set a fee that is based on peak use (perhaps the number of computers that could connect to the information, or the maximum number of simultaneous users). With the Internet and web protocols, these methods are rather artificial.

An alternative is to charge for the content transmitted to the user. Several publishers provide access to the text of an article for a fee, perhaps $10. This could be charged to a credit card, but credit-card transactions are awkward for the user and expensive to process. Therefore, there is research interest in automatic payment systems for information delivered over the networks. The aim of these systems is to build an Internet billing service that allows secure, low-cost transactions. The hope is that this would permit small organizations to set up network service without the complexity of developing private billing services. If such systems became established, they would support high volumes of very small transactions. Whereas physical items (such as books) come in fixed units, a market might be established for small units of electronic information.

At present, the concept of automatic payment systems is mainly conjecture. The dominant form of payment for digital library materials is by subscription, consisting of scheduled payments for access to a set of materials. Unlimited use is allowed so long as reasonable conditions are observed. The *Wall Street Journal* has developed a good business selling individual subscriptions to its online editions. Many large scientific publishers now offer electronic journal subscriptions to libraries. Societies such as the Association for Computing Machinery sell subscriptions to libraries and to individual members. Some of the digital libraries described in earlier chapters began with grants and have steadily moved toward self-sufficiency through sub-scriptions. JSTOR and the Inter-university Consortium for Political and Social Research have followed this path.

Television again provides an interesting parallel. In the United States, two alternatives to advertising revenue have been tried by the television industry. The first, pay-per-view, requires viewers to make a separate pay-ment for each program that they watch. This has developed a niche mar-ket, but it has not become widespread. The second alternative, used by the cable companies, is to ask viewers to pay a monthly subscription for a pack-age of programs. This second business model has been highly successful.

It appears that users of digital libraries, like television viewers, welcome regular, predictable charges. Payment by subscription has advantages for both the publisher and the user. Libraries and other subscribers know the costs in advance and are able to budget accurately. Publishers know how much revenue to expect. For the publisher, subscriptions overcome one of the drawbacks of use-based pricing: that popular items make great profits while specialist items with limited demand lose money.

Libraries are attracted by the subscription form of payment because it encourages wide use. Libraries wish to see their collections used heavily, with a minimum of obstacles. Digital libraries have removed many of the barriers inherent in a traditional library. It would be sad to introduce new barriers through use-based pricing.

An economic factor that differentiates electronic information from tra-ditional forms of publishing is that the costs are essentially the same whether or not anybody uses the materials. Many of the tasks associated with creating a publication—including soliciting, reviewing, editing, design-ing, and formatting material—are much the same whether a print product is being created or an electronic one. With digital information, however, the cost of distribution are tiny once the first copy has been mounted. In economic terms, the cost is almost entirely fixed cost; the marginal cost is near zero. As a result, once sales of a digital product reach the level that covers the costs of creation, all additional sales are pure profit. Unless this level is reached, the product is condemned to make a loss.

With physical materials (for example, books, music CDs, or pho-tographs), it is standard to charge for each physical copy. The production of each copy costs money, and the customer feels that in some way this cost is reflected in the price. With digital information, the customer receives no artifact; this is one reason why use-based pricing is not appealing. Subscriptions match a fixed cost for using the materials against the fixed cost of creating them.

A further way in which electronic publishing differs economically from traditional publishing is that in electronic publishing the pricing must absorb the costs of change. Electronic publishing and digital libraries will be cheaper than print in the long term, but today they are expensive. Organizations wishing to enter this field must continue their traditional operations while investing in the new technology at a time when the new systems are expensive and when, in many cases, the volume of use is still comparatively low.

Many electronic publications are versions of materials that are also published in print. When publishers put a price on an electronic publication, they want to know whether sales of electronic information will diminish the sales of corresponding print products. If a dictionary becomes available online, how will sales in bookstores be affected? If a journal becomes available online, how will that affect the number individual subscriptions? After ten years' experience, evidence is beginning to emerge, but is still hard to find firm evidence for any specific publication. At the macroeconomic level, however, it is clear that electronic information is becoming a significant item in libraries' acquisition budgets. Electronic and print products often compete directly for a single pool of money. If one publisher generates extra revenue from electronic information, it is probably at the expense of another's print products. This overall transfer of money from print to electronic products is among the forces that are driving publishers toward electronic publication.

Some dramatic examples come from secondary information services. Products such as *Chemical Abstracts* and *Current Contents* have changed their core content little since the late 1980s, but in those day they were predominantly print products; now the various digital versions predominate. Publishers have cleverly offered users and their libraries many choices: CD-ROMs, magnetic tape, online services, and printed volumes. Any publisher that stays out of the electronic market must anticipate steadily declines in revenue as the electronic market diverts funds from the purchase of paper products.

Fortunately, librarians and publishers do not have to pay for one of the most expensive components of digital libraries: the general-purpose networks of personal computers that are being installed by organizations everywhere. Investments in long-distance communications and in the equipment that makes digital libraries possible are being made from other budgets.

Use-based pricing and subscriptions are not the only ways to recover revenue from users. Consider the fact that cable television redistributes programs created by the television networks. At first, the broadcasters opposed this strenuously. Political lobbying (notably by Ted Turner) led to the present situation, in which the cable companies can redistribute any program but must pay a percentage of their revenue as royalties. When a radio station broadcasts recorded music, the accrual of revenue to composers, performers, recording studios, and other contributors to the music is based on a complex system of sampling. The British football league gains revenue from gambling by exercising copyright on its fixture list.

There is nothing inevitable about any of these approaches. They are pragmatic resolutions of the complex question of how the people who create and distribute various kinds of information can be compensated by the people who benefit from them.

A Case Study: Scientific Journals in Electronic Format

Scientific journals in electronic format provide an interesting case study, since they are one of the pioneering areas where electronic publications are recovering revenue from libraries and users. They highlight the tension between commercial publishers (whose objective is to maximize profits) and authors (who want to see their work distributed widely).

Academic publishers and university libraries are natural partners, but the movement to electronic publication has aggravated some long-standing friction. As is described in panel 6.1, the libraries can make a strong case that the publishers charge too much for their journals, though in many ways the universities have brought the problem on themselves. Many researchers and librarians hope that digital libraries will lead to new ways of scientific publication that will provide wider access to research at lower costs to libraries. Meanwhile, the commercial publishers are under pressure from their shareholders to make higher profits ever year.

Panel 6.1
The Economics of Scientific Journals

The profits made by commercial publishers of scientific journals have come under increasing scrutiny in recent years.

In the United States, the federal government uses money received from taxes to fund research in universities, government laboratories, medical centers, and other research organizations. The conventional way to report the results of such research is for the researcher to write a paper and submit it to a scientific journal.

The first stage in the publication process is that an editor, who may be a volunteer or work for the publisher, sends out the paper for review by other scientists. The reviewers, serving as unpaid volunteers, read the paper critically for quality, check it for mistakes, and recommend whether or not it should be published. This process is known as *peer review*. Once the editor has decided to publish, he or she gives the author an opportunity to make changes based on the reviewers' comments.

Before publication, most publishers place some requirements on the authors. Usually they demand that copyright in the paper be transferred from the author to the publisher. In addition, many publishers prohibit the author from releasing the results of the research publicly before the article is published. As a result, without making any payment, the publisher acquires control of the work.

Although a few journals (typically those published by societies) have individual subscribers, the main market for journals is academic libraries. Many journals have high subscription prices—more than $1000 per year is common, and annual increases have averaged 10–15 percent during the 1990s. Yet the libraries have felt compelled to subscribe to the journals because their faculty and students need access to the research that is reported in them.

The economic system surrounding scientific journals is strange. The researchers, most of the reviewers, and many of the costs of the libraries are funded by taxpayers, but the copyright is given to the publisher. The universities must take much of the blame for allowing this situation to develop. Since their faculty members perform the research and their libraries buy the journals, simple policy changes on the part of the universities could save millions of dollars while still providing reasonable compensation for publishers. Recently, universities have begun to work together to remedy the situation.

The underlying reason for the reluctance of universities to act lies in the fact that scientific articles are published not only to communicate research but also to enhance the authors' professional reputations. Academic reputations are made by the publication of journal articles and monographs. Professional recognition, which is built on publication, translates into appointments, promotion, and research grants. The biggest hurdle in an academic career is achieving tenure, which is based primarily on peer-reviewed publications. Some academics also write textbooks, which are occasionally very lucrative, but *all* successful academics write research papers (in the sciences) or monographs (in the humanities). The standing joke is "Our dean can't read, but he sure can count." What the dean counts is papers in peer-reviewed journals. Publishers are delighted to make profits by providing things for the dean to count. Every member of the faculty is expected to publish several papers every year, whether or not there is important research to report. Because prestige comes from writing many papers, there is an incentive to write several papers reporting slightly different aspects of a single piece of research. Studies have shown that most scientific papers are never cited by other researchers. Many papers are completely unnecessary.

There are signs that this situation is changing. Digital libraries provide researchers with alternative ways to tell the world about their research. Peer review has considerable value in weeding out bad papers and identifying obvious errors, but it is time consuming; the traditional process of review, editing, printing, and distribution often takes more than a year. An article in a journal that is stored on the shelves of a library is available only to those who have access to the library and are prepared to make the effort to retrieve the article; a research report on the Internet is available to everyone. In some disciplines, a new pattern is emerging: research is communicated through the rapid, open-access publishing of online reports or preprints, but traditional journals are used as an archive and for career purposes.

Subscription to online journals
The publishers of research journals in science, technology, and medicine include commercial companies (such as Elsevier, John Wiley and Sons, and Springer-Verlag) and learned societies (such as the American Association for the Advancement of Science). These publishers have moved energetically into electronic publication, and they are among the first organizations to face the economic challenges. So far, their general approach has been to

publish electronic versions in parallel to the print versions. Since 1996, many scientific publishers have provided electronic versions of their printed journals over the Internet. The online versions are similar to but not always identical to the printed versions. Some leave out certain things (such as letters to the editor); some add supplementary data that was too long to include in print.

Many publishers chose variants on the familiar economic model of selling annual subscriptions to individual libraries or to consortia of libraries. Among the publishers that offer subscriptions to parallel print and electronic versions are the Academic Press, the American Chemical Society, the Association for Computing Machinery, Elsevier, the American Physical Society, the Johns Hopkins University Press, Springer-Verlag, and Wiley. HighWire Press offers online services for smaller publishers who publish high-quality print journals but do not wish to invest in expensive computer systems. A common model is for the publisher to provide open access to a searchable index and abstracts but to require payment for access to the full articles. Payment can be by subscription or by a fee per article.

Subscriptions that provide access to an online collection require an agreement between the publisher and the subscriber. If the subscriber is a library, the agreement is usually written as a contract. Although the details of these agreements vary, a number of topics occur in every agreement. Some of the issues are listed below.

Material   When a library subscribes to a print journal for a year, it receives copies of the journal's issues for that year, which it may then store forever. When a library subscribes to an electronic journal for a year, it typically receives a license for access to the publisher's online collection, which contains the current year's journal and those earlier issues that have been converted to digital form. The library is relieved of the burden of storing back issues, but it loses access to everything if it does not renew the subscription the following year, or if the publisher goes out of business.

Users   If a subscription is sold to a library, the users of that library who are permitted access to the information must be identifiable. Some libraries have well-defined communities of users—for example, it is reasonably easy to identify who is authorized to use the materials in a corporate library or in the library of a residential university. But many universities and colleges have large populations of students who take part-time courses and staff members who are affiliated through hospitals or other local organizations, and public libraries are by definition open to the public. Fortunately, most libraries have traditionally had a procedure for issuing library cards. One simple approach is for the subscription agreement to cover everyone who is eligible for a library card and everyone who is physically in the library.

Prices for organizations of different sizes   Should a university with 5000 students pay the same subscription as a college with 500 or a state university system with a population of 100,000? What should be the price for a small research laboratory within a large corporation? Should a liberal arts university pay as much for its occasional use of a medical journal as is paid by a medical school? There are no simple answers to these questions.

Pricing relative to print subscriptions   When material is available in both print and online versions, how should the prices compare? In the long term, electronic publications are cheaper to produce, because of the savings in printing, paper, and distribution. In the short term, however, electronic publications represent a considerable new investment. Initially, a few publishers attempted to charge more for the electronic versions; now, a consensus is emerging for slightly lower prices. Publishers are experimenting with a variety of pricing options to encourage libraries to subscribe to large groups of journals.

Printing   One of the more contentious issues is the boundaries of the use that subscribers make of online journals. Printing is an example. The publisher of an online journal must expect that some readers will print copies for their private use, but would rightfully object to a subscriber's selling such copies. A consensus on how to allow the former while discouraging the latter has not yet been reached.

The model of institutional subscriptions has moved the delivery of scientific journals from print to the Internet without addressing any of the underlying tensions between publishers and their customers. It will be interesting to see how well that model stands the test of time.

Scientific Journals and Their Authors

The difference in goals between authors and publishers is manifest in restrictions that some publishers place on authors. Many publishers demand that authors restrict the distribution of research. Publishers, quite naturally, will not publish papers that have appeared in other journals; however, many even refuse to publish research results that have been announced anywhere else, such as at a conference or on a web site. Others permit placing a version of the paper on a server, such as the Los Alamos E-Print Archives, but require the open-access version to be removed once the edited journal article is published. This sort of assertiveness antagonizes authors, and there is no evidence that it has any effect on revenue. The antagonism is increased by the publishers' insistence that authors transfer copyright to them, which may leave the authors with few rights to the works they have created and the taxpayers (whose money fuels the process) with nothing.

At the Association for Computing Machinery (ACM), we attempted to find a balance between the authors' interest in widespread distribution and the need for revenue. The resulting policy is clearly seen as interim, but hopefully the balance will be acceptable for the next few years. The current version of the policy retains the traditional copyright transfer from author to publisher and affirms that ACM can use material in any format or way that it wishes. At the same time, however, it allows authors great flexibility. In particular, the policy encourages authors to mount their materials on private servers, both before and after publication. In the fast-moving fields covered by the ACM's journals, preprints (which have always been important) are often put online in collections—maintained privately or by research departments—that are freely available over the Internet. This strategy has its risks. Since the preprints are important to its members, the ACM wants to encourage them, yet in the long term they may destroy the journals' market.

The Legal Framework

This is not a legal textbook (though two lawyers have checked this section), but some legal issues are so important that this book would be incomplete if it did not discuss them. Since the legal system provides a framework that permits the orderly development of online services, it should not be surprising that many aspects of the law are relevant to digital libraries. The relevant areas of law include contracts, copyright and other intellectual property, defamation, obscenity, communications law, privacy, tax, and international law.

The legal situation in the United States is complicated by the number of jurisdictions—the Constitution, international treaties, federal and state statutes—and by the precedents set by courts at each level. Many laws, such as those controlling obscenity, are at the state level. People who mounted sexual material on a server in California, where it is legal, were prosecuted in Louisiana, where it was deemed obscene. Some legal areas, such as copyright, are covered by federal statutes, but some important topics within those areas have never been interpreted by the U.S. Supreme Court. When the only legal rulings have been made by lower courts, other courts are not bound by precedent and may interpret the law differently.

Each of the two communities that are now building digital libraries on the Internet—computer scientists and information professionals—has a tradition of responsible use of shared resources. The traditions are different, and merging them poses some problems. But even worse problems are posed by the fact that individuals who have no such traditions have gravitated to the Internet. Some of these people are malicious; others deliberately exploit the informality of the Internet for personal gain; others are thoughtless and unaware of what constitutes reasonable behavior.

Until the late 1980s, the Internet was the province of academics and other researchers. There were policies on who could use it and on what was appropriate use. More important, the users policed themselves. Someone who violated the norms was immediately barraged with complaints and with less subtle forms of peer pressure. The social conventions were somewhat unconventional, but they worked as long as most users were members of a small community and learned the conventions from their colleagues.

The conventions began to fail when the Internet grew larger. At Carnegie Mellon University, we noticed a change when students who had learned their networked computing outside universities became undergraduates.

Many of the legal issues are general to the Internet, not specific to digital libraries. Currently, the Internet community is working on technical methods of controlling junk electronic mail, which is a burden on the network's capacity and an annoyance to users. Pornography and gambling are two areas that pit commercial interests against diverse social norms, and advocates of civil liberties against more conservative groups.

International Questions

Because the Internet is worldwide, any digital library can be accessed from anywhere in the world. Behavior that is considered perfectly normal in one country is often illegal in another. For example, the United States permits the possession of guns but limits the use of encryption software; in most European countries, the opposite holds.

Attitudes toward free speech, too, vary greatly around the world. Every country has some laws that limit freedom of expression and access to information—for example, those that cover slander, libel, obscenity, privacy, hate, racism, and government secrets. In the United States, information is a fundamental democratic principle, enshrined in the First Amendment to the Constitution, and the courts have consistently interpreted the concept of free speech broadly; but there are limits even in the United States. Every jurisdiction expects to be able to control certain activities. Germany has strong laws on Nazism; Arabic countries are strict about blasphemy. Yet the Internet is hard to control. For years, there was a server in Finland that would act as a relay and post messages on the Internet anonymously. Eventually, under great pressure from outside Finland, Finnish courts forced those who ran this server to disclose the names of people who posted particularly disreputable materials anonymously.

The international nature of the Internet creates difficulty with regard to electronic commerce in general, including electronic information. In the United States, consumers and suppliers are already protected by laws that cover interstate commerce, such as financial payments and mail-order sales across state boundaries. The situation is much more complex over a worldwide network, where the trade is in digital materials that can easily be duplicated or modified. On the Internet, the parties to a transaction need not even declare from what country they are operating.

Liability

Responsibility for the content of library materials is a social and legal issue of particular importance to digital libraries. Society expects the creators of works to be responsible for their content, and it expects the people who make decisions about content to behave responsibly too. However, digital libraries will not thrive if legal liability for content is placed upon parties whose only function is to store and transmit information.

Because of the high esteem in which libraries are held, they have a privileged legal position in most democratic countries. It is almost impossible to hold a library liable for libelous statements or subversive opinions expressed in the books it holds. In a similar way, telecommunications law protects common carriers, so a telephone company does not have to monitor the conversations that take place on its lines; in fact, the telephone companies are prohibited from deliberately listening to such conversations.

Traditionally, the responsibility for the content has fallen on the creators and publishers, who are aware of the content, rather than on the libraries. This allows libraries to collect materials from all cultures and all periods without having to scrutinize every item for possible invasions of privacy, libel, copyright violations, and so on. Most people would accept that this is a good policy that should be extended to digital libraries. Whereas organizations have a responsibility to account for information that they create and distribute, it is not reasonable to expect libraries or Internet service companies to monitor everything that they transmit.

The liability of service providers is one of the central topics of the Digital Millennium Copyright Act of 1998, described in panel 6.2. This act removes the liability for copyright violations from online service providers, including libraries and educational establishments. As is usual with emerging law, developing this act was not a simple process, and the process did not end with the legislation. Digital libraries welcome this part of the Digital Millennium Copyright Act, but how the courts interpret it will be interesting to see.

Copyright

Some of the most heated legal arguments about online information concern the interaction between economic issues and copyright law. Such arguments seem to emerge every time a new technology is developed. In the early days of printing there was no copyright. Shakespeare's plays were freely pirated. In the nineteenth century, the United States had copyright protection for American authors but none for foreigners; the books of European authors were not protected and were shamelessly copied despite the pleas of Dickens, Trollope, and other authors.

In the United States, copyright applies to almost all literary works, including textual materials, photographs, computer programs, musical scores, and video and audio tapes. A major exception is materials created by government employees. Initially, the creator of a work or the employer of the creator owns the copyright. In general, intellectual property can be bought and sold like any other property. Other countries have different approaches; in some countries, notably France and Canada, the creator has personal rights (known as *moral rights*) that cannot be transferred.

Panel 6.2
The Digital Millennium Copyright Act

In 1998 the U.S. Congress passed the Digital Millennium Copyright Act, which made significant changes in copyright law. Apart from a section dealing with the design of boat hulls, almost all of the act concerns digital works on networks. On the surface, the act appears a reasonable balance between commercial interests that wish to sell digital works and the openness of information that is central to libraries and education.

Under the act, providers of online services in the United States, including libraries and educational establishments, are largely protected from legal claims of copyright infringement that take place without their knowledge. To qualify for this exception, specific rules must be followed: the organization must provide users with information about copyright, have a policy for termination of repeat offenders, comply with requirements to "take down" infringing materials, support industry-standard technical measures, and advise the Copyright Office of an agent to receive statutory notices under the act. The act explicitly permits many of the activities that are fundamental to the operation of digital libraries. It allows service providers to offer users facilities to store materials such as web sites, to follow hyperlinks, and to use search engines. It recognizes that service providers make copies of materials for technical reasons, (e.g., for caching and to transmit or route material to other sites). These activities are permitted by the act, and service providers are not liable for violations by their users if they follow the rules and correct problems when notified.

For universities and other institutes of higher education, the act makes an important exception to the rule that organizations are responsible for the actions of their employees. It recognizes that administrators do not oversee the actions of faculty members and graduate students and are not necessarily liable for their acts.

The act prohibits the circumvention of technical methods used by copyright owners to restrict access to works. It also prohibits the manufacture or distribution of methods to defeat such technology. However, the act recognizes several exceptions, all of which are complex and need careful interpretation: software developers can reverse engineer protection systems to permit interoperability, researchers can study encryption and system security, law enforcement agencies can be authorized to circumvent security technology, and libraries can examine materials to decide whether to acquire them. Finally, users are permitted to identify and disable techniques that collect private information about users and usage.

The act provides rules on tampering with copyright management information about a work, such as title, author, performer, and copyright owner. This information must not be intentionally altered or removed.

Panel 6.3
Events in the History of Copyright

Outside the U.S. Copyright Office is a series of display panels that summarize some major legal decisions about copyright law that have been decided by federal courts, including the Supreme Court. They illustrate how, over the years, legal precedents have shaped and clarified the law and allowed it to evolve into areas (such as photography, broadcasting, and computing) that were not thought of when the Constitution was written and the laws enacted. Some of the decisions are summarized below.

Wheaton vs. Peters (1834)   This landmark case, established the principle that copyright is not a kind of natural right but rather is the creation of the copyright statute and subject to the conditions it imposes.

Baker vs. Selden (1880)   This case established that copyright law protects what an author writes and the way ideas are expressed, but the law does not protect the ideas themselves.

Burrow-Giles Lithographic Co. vs. Sarony (1884)   This decision expanded the scope of copyright to cover media other than text, in this case a photograph of Oscar Wilde.

Bleistein vs. Donaldson Lithographic Co. (1903)   This case concerned three circus posters. The court decided that they were copyrightable, whether or not they had artistic value or were aesthetically pleasing.

Fred Fisher, Inc. vs. Dillingham (1924)   This dispute concerned the similarity in two musical passages. The court ruled that unconscious copying could result in an infringement of copyright.

Nichols vs. Universal Pictures Corp. (1931)   The court ruled that it was not an infringement of copyright for a film to copy abstract ideas of plot and characters from a successful Broadway play.

Sheldon vs. Metro-Goldwyn Pictures Corp. (1936)   The court ruled that "no plagiarist can excuse the wrong by showing how much of his work he did not pirate."

G. Ricordi & Co. vs. Paramount Pictures, Inc. (1951)   This was a case about how renewal rights and rights in derivative works should be interpreted, in this instance the novel *Madame Butterfly* by John Luther Long, Belasco's play based on the novel, and Puccini's opera based on the play. The court ruled that copyright protection in derivative works applies only to the new material added.

Warner Bros. Pictures, Inc. vs. Columbia Broadcasting System, Inc. (1955)   This case decided that the character Sam Spade in *The Maltese Falcon* was a vehicle for the story, not a copyrightable element of the work.

Mazer vs. Stein (1954)   The court decided that copyright does not protect utilitarian or useful objects, in this case a sculptural lamp. It is possible to register the separable pictorial, graphic, or sculptural features of a utilitarian piece.

King vs. Mr. Maestro, Inc. (1963) This was a case about the speech "I have a dream" by Martin Luther King, Jr. Although he had delivered the speech to a huge crowd with simultaneous broadcast by radio and television, the court decided that this public performance did not constitute publication and the speech could be registered for copyright as an unpublished work.

Letter Edged in Black Press, Inc., vs. Public Building Commission of Chicago (1970) This case, about the public display of a Picasso sculpture, has been superseded by later legislation.

Williams Electronics, Inc. vs. Artic International, Inc. (1982) This case involved copying a video game. The court ruled that video game components were copyrightable and that computer read-only memory can be considered a copy.

Norris Industries, Inc. vs. International Telephone and Telegraph Corp. (1983) The court ruled that, even if the Copyright Office rejects a work because it is not copyrightable, the owner is still entitled to file suit and to ask for a court ruling.

Even these major decisions cannot be considered irrevocable. Many were never tested by the Supreme Court and could be reversed. Recently, a federal court made a ruling that explicitly disagreed with the *King vs. Mr. Maestro* decision.

Historically, a copyright has had a finite life, expiring a certain number of years after the creator's death. The U.S. Congress has extended that period a number of times, most recently when Hollywood feared that the copyright on older films was about to expire—a sad example of the public good being secondary to the financial interests of a few corporations.

The owner of the copyright in a work has an exclusive right to make copies, to prepare derivative works, and to distribute the copies by selling them or in other ways. This helps to ensure authors that their works do not get corrupted, either accidentally or maliciously. It also allows publishers to develop products without fear that their markets will be destroyed by copies from other sources.

Although a copyright holder has considerable control over how material may be used, copyright law is not absolute. Two important concepts in U.S. law are *first sale* and *fair use*.

First sale applies to a physical object, such as a book. The copyright owner can control the sale of a new book, and can set the price; however, once a customer buys a copy of the book, that customer has full ownership of the copy and may sell it or dispose of it in any way without having to get permission.

Fair use is a legal right that allows certain uses of copyright information without permission of the copyright owner. Under fair use, a reviewers or a scholar has the right to quote short passages, and an article or a portion of a book may be photocopied for private study. The boundaries of fair use are deliberately vague, but there are four basic factors: the purpose and character of the use (including whether such use is of a commercial nature or is for nonprofit educational purposes), the nature of the copyrighted work, the amount and substantiality of the portion used relative to the work as a whole, and the effect of the use on the work's potential market or value. Because these factors are imprecise, judges have discretion in how they are interpreted. In general, fair use allows reproduction of parts of a work but not the whole, single copies rather than many, and private rather than commercial use. The exact distinctions can be clarified only by legal precedents. Court cases are so expensive that many important copyright issues (even with regard to traditional print materials) have never been tested in court or have been addressed only in the lower courts.

The doctrine of first sale and the right of fair use do not transfer easily to digital libraries. While the first-sale doctrine can be applied to physical media that store electronic materials, such as CD-ROMs, there is no parallel for information that is delivered over networks. The guidelines for fair use are equally hard to translate from physical media to the online world. This uncertainty was one of the things that led to a series of attempts to rewrite copyright law, both in the United States and internationally. Though most people accept that copyright law should provide a balance between the public's right of access to information and economic incentives to creators and publishers of information, there was no consensus what that balance should be. Furthermore, there were extremists on both sides. Vested interests, motivated by fear and greed, attempted to push through one-sided legislation. For several years, bills were introduced in Congress to change or clarify the copyright law relating to online information, usually in such a way as to favor some group of interested parties. Some commercial organizations lobbied for draconian rights to control information and for criminal sanctions on all activities not explicitly authorized. In response, public-interest groups argued that there was no evidence that fair use hurts any profits, and that unnecessary restrictions on information flow are inherently harmful. Until 1998 there a stalemate, which was probably good. Existing legislation was adequate to permit the first phase of electronic publishing and digital libraries. The fundamental difficulty was to understand the underlying issues. Legal clarification was needed eventually, but it was better to observe the patterns that emerged than to rush into premature legislation. The 1998 legislation described in panel 6.2 is probably good enough to allow digital libraries to thrive.

Privacy

At least in the United States, libraries feel strongly that users have a right to privacy. No one should know that a certain user is consulting books on sensitive issues, such as unpleasant diseases. Libraries have gone to court rather than divulge to the police whether a patron was reading books about communism. Many states have laws that prohibit libraries from gathering data that violates the privacy of their users. The Internet community has a similar tradition. Although corporations have the legal right to inspect the activities of their employees, most people in technical jobs expect their electronic mail and their computer files to be treated as private under most normal circumstances.

But much of the technology of digital libraries is also used for electronic commerce. Advertisers and merchants strive to gather information about their customers (often without the customers' knowledge), and they sell such information to one another. Technology that is used for purposes such as recording when a user of a web site has been authenticated can also be used to track a user's behavior without his or her knowledge.

As is discussed in panel 6.4, digital libraries must gather data on use. Good data is needed to tune computer systems, to anticipate problems, and to plan for growth. With care, use statistics can be gathered without identifying any specific individuals. But not everyone takes care. When troubleshooting a computer network, a system administrator may need to look at any file on a server computer or to inspect every message passing over the network. Occasionally they stumble across highly personal information or criminal activities. What is the correct behavior in these circumstance? What should the law say?

Panel 6.4
Digital Libraries and Privacy

Anyone who runs a service needs to have data about how it is used. To manage a computer system, such as a digital library, requires data about performance and reliability, about utilization of capacity, and about trends and peaks. Libraries and publishers need statistical data about how the collections are used and which services are popular. Designers of user interfaces depend on knowledge of how people interact with the library. Security requires careful tracking of use patterns and analysis of anomalies.

This information is not easy to gather. Web sites gather data about how often each file is accessed. One widespread practice is for sites to boast about how many hits they have received. Since every graphic image is usually a separate file, a single user who reads one page may generate many hits. This statistic is important for configuring the computer system, but not for anything else. The manager of an online journal would like to know how many people read the journal, with data about the use of individual articles. The number of times that the contents page is accessed is probably useful information; so is the frequency with which the first page of each article is accessed. These are indirect measures that cannot distinguish between one person who reads a story several times and several different people who each read it once. They measure how often the computer system is accessed, but they have no way of estimating how many readers are accessing copies of the materials through caches or mirror sites. If the users are identified, it becomes much easier to gather track usage and gather precise statistics; but then privacy becomes a problem.

At Carnegie Mellon we handled this problem as follows: Every time a user accessed an item, a temporary record was created that included a scrambled version of the user's computer ID. The temporary records were kept in a special part of the file system, which was never copied onto backup tapes. Once a week, the records were analyzed, creating a report that could not be used to identify individual users. It contained information such as the number of different people who had searched each collection and the number of total searches. The temporary records and all traces of the users' IDs were then discarded.

Software Patents

Although the legal system has its faults, in general it has dealt well with the rapid growth of computing and the Internet. The worst exception concerns software patents. Few areas of the law are so far removed from the reality to which they are applied. In too many cases, the U.S. Patent Office approves patents that the entire computer industry knows to be foolish. Until recently, the Patent Office did not even employ trained computer scientists to evaluate patent applications. The examiners still award patents that are overly broad, that cover concepts that have been widely known for years, or that apply to simple applications of standard practice.

One reason for this mess is that the concept of invention on which patent law is based—Archimedes leaping from his bath, crying "Eureka!"—is not suited to computer science. New ideas in software are created incrementally. The community of computer science is quite homogeneous. People are trained at the same universities, and they use the same computers and the same software. There is open exchange of ideas through many channels. As a result, parallel groups work on the same problems and adapt the same standard techniques in the same incremental ways.

The success of the Internet and the rapid expansion of digital libraries have been fueled by the open exchange of ideas. Patent law, with its emphasis on secrecy, litigation, and confrontation, can only harm such processes.

7

Access Management* and Security

This chapter looks at two related topics: methods for controlling who has access to materials in digital libraries, and techniques of security in networked computing.

One obvious reason for controlling access is economic. When publishers expect revenue from their products, they permit access only to users who have paid. It might be thought that access management would be unnecessary except when revenue is involved; however, there are other reasons to control access to materials in a digital library. Some materials may have been donated with conditions attached (perhaps conditions tied to external events, such as the lifetimes of certain individuals). Organizations may have in their private collections information that they wish to keep confidential, such as commercial secrets, police records, and classified government information. The boundaries of art, obscenity, and invasion of privacy are never easy to draw. Even when access to collections is open, controls are needed over the processes of adding, changing, and deleting content and metadata. A well-managed digital library will keep a record of all changes, so that the collections can be restored if mistakes are made or computer files are corrupted.

Uncertainty is a fact of life in access management. People with a computing background sometimes assume that every object can be labeled with metadata that lists all the rights, permissions, and other factors relevant to

---

* This book uses the term *access management* to describe the control of access to digital libraries, but other words are also used. Some people refer to "terms and conditions." In publishing, where the emphasis is usually on generating revenue, the strange expression "rights management" is common. Each of these terms has a different emphasis, but they are essentially synonymous.

access management. People with a library background, especially those who manage historic collections or archives, know that assembling such information is always time consuming and often impossible. Projects such as the Library of Congress's American Memory project convert millions of items from historic collections. In the case of these older materials, it seems natural to assume that copyright has expired and there need be no access restrictions—but this is far from true. The expiration of copyright on published material is linked to the death of the creator. That date is often hard to determine, and libraries often do not know whether a particular item has been published.

As was noted in chapter 6, many of the laws that govern digital libraries, such as copyright, have fuzzy boundaries. Access-management policies that are based on these laws are subject to this fuzziness. As the boundaries become clarified through new laws, treaties, or legal precedents, policies have to be modified accordingly.

Elements of Access Management

Figure 7.1 shows a framework that is useful for thinking about access management. At the left of this figure, information managers create policies for access. Policies relate users (top of figure) to digital material (bottom). Authorization (center) specifies the access (right). Each of these sections requires elaboration. Policies that information managers establish must take into account relevant laws and agreements made with others (such as licenses from copyright holders) Users must be authenticated, and their role in accessing materials must be established. Digital materials in collections must be identified and their authenticity established. Access is expressed in terms of permitted operations.

When a user requests access to digital material, the request passes through an access-management process. After the user's identity has been established through a process of *authentication, authorization* procedures grant or refuse that user permission to carry out specified operations.

The responsibility for access lies with whoever manages the digital material. The manager may be a library, a publisher, a webmaster, or the creator of the information. Parts of the responsibility may be delegated. If a library controls the materials and makes them available to users, the library sets the policies and implements them—usually guided by external restraints, such

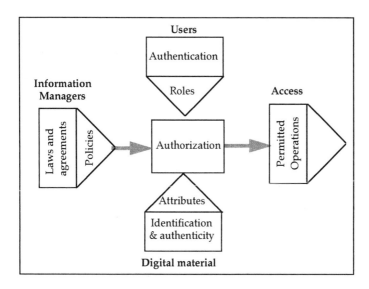

Figure 7.1

as legal restrictions, licenses from publishers, or agreements with donors. If a publisher mounts materials and licenses access, then the publisher is the manager; however, in this case the publisher may delegate key activities, such as authorization of users, to others.

Users
Authentication

A wide variety of techniques are used to authenticate users. Some have the virtue of simplicity but the shortcoming of being easy to circumvent; others, more secure, have the drawback of complexity. The techniques of authentication can be divided into four main categories:

What does the user know? One standard and widely used method of authentication is to provide each user with a login name and a password. This is widely used but is vulnerable to abuse. Passwords are easily stolen, and people often select passwords that are easy to remember and hence easy to guess.

What does the user possess? Two kinds of cards that are used for authentication are the magnetically encoded cards used by automated teller machines and digital "smart cards" that execute an authentication program. Smart cards are one of the best systems of authentication; they are highly secure and quite convenient to use.

Where is the user? A common form of authentication is the network address of a computer. Anyone who has access to a computer with an approved IP address is authenticated. Data on many personal computers is unprotected except by physical access; anyone who has access to the computer can read the data.

What are the physical characteristics of the user? Authentication by the user's physical attributes, such as voice recognition, is used in a few esoteric applications but has been little used in digital libraries.

Roles

Policies for access management rarely specify users by name. They are usually tied to categories of users or to the *role* of an individual user. A user can have many roles. At different times, the same person may use a digital library for teaching, for private reading, or in a part-time business. A digital library may have different policies for the same individual in each of these roles. The following roles may be important:

Membership of a group   The user may be, for example, a member of the (European) Institute of Physics, or a student at the U.S. Naval Academy.

Location   The user may be using a computer in the Carnegie Library in Pittsburgh, or may be located in New Zealand.

Subscription   The user may have a current subscription to *Journal of the Association for Computing Machinery*, or may belong to a university that has a site license to all JSTOR collections.

Automatic indexing program   The user may be using a web crawler or some other computer program.

Payment   The user may have a credit account with Lexis, or may be paying $10 to access the material.

Most users of digital libraries are human beings using personal computers. However, a user can be a computer running, without a human operator present, a program that is indexing web pages, or a mirroring program that replicates an entire collection. Some sites explicitly ban access by automatic programs or give them higher privileges.

Digital Material
Identification and authentication of materials

For access management, digital materials must be clearly identified. Identification associates some name or identifier with each item of material. This is a major topic in both digital libraries and electronic publishing.

Authentication of digital materials assures both users and managers of collections that the materials have not been altered. In some contexts this is crucial. For example, some colleagues and I once worked with a U.S. government agency to assemble a collection of documents relevant to foreign affairs, such as trade agreements and treaties. With such documents the exact wording is essential: if, for example, a document claims to be the actual text of the North American Free Trade Agreement, the reader must be confident that it is accurate. Texts with wrong wording, whether created maliciously or by error, have caused international incidents.

In most digital libraries, the accuracy of the materials is not verified explicitly. Where the level of trust is high and the cost of mistakes is low, no formal authentication of documents is needed. Deliberate alterations are rare, and mistakes are usually obvious. In some fields, however, such as medicine, errors are serious. Digital libraries in these areas should seriously consider using formal methods of authenticating materials.

To ensure the accuracy of an object, a *digital signature* can be associated with it. (Techniques for doing this will be described at the end of this chapter.) A digital signature ensures that a file or other set of bits has not changed since the signature was calculated. Panel 7.1 describes the use of digital signatures in the U.S. Copyright Office.

A group of methods that are related to authentication of materials are described by the term *watermarking*. They are defensive techniques used by publishers to deter and track unauthorized copying. The basic idea is to embed a code into the material in a subtle manner that is unobtrusive to the user but can be retrieved to establish ownership, much as when a broadcaster adds a corporate logo to a television picture to identify the source of the picture if is copied. Digital watermarks can be completely imperceptible to users yet almost impossible to remove without trace.

Attributes of digital material

Access-management policies often treat different materials in varying ways, depending on their attributes. Attributes can be encoded as administrative metadata and stored with the object, or they can be derived from some other source. Some attributes can also be computed; thus, the size of an object can be measured. Here are some typical examples:

Division into subcollections   Collections often divide material into items for public access and items with restricted access. Publishers may separate

Panel 7.1
Electronic Registration and Deposit for Copyright

The U.S. Copyright Office is a separate department of the Library of Congress. Under federal law, the library is entitled to receive two copies of every work published in the United States for its collections. While deposit of published works is mandatory, the copyright law since 1978 has not required registration of copyrighted works, though registration is encouraged since it confers significant benefits.

The method of copyright registration is straightforward. The owner of the copyright sends two copies of the work to the Copyright Office with an application form and a fee. The copyright claim and the work are examined. Upon approval, a registration certificate is produced. Published works are transferred to the Library of Congress, which decides whether to retain them for its collections or to use them in its exchange programs with other libraries.

In 1993, the Copyright Office and the Corporation for National Research Initiatives began work on a system, known as CORDS (Copyright Office Electronic Registration, Recordation and Deposit System), for registering and depositing electronic works. CORDS mirrors the traditional procedures. The submission consists of a web form and a digital copy of the work, delivered securely over the Internet. The fee is processed separately. Digital signatures are used to identify claims that are submitted for copyright registration. Using a private key, the submitter submits a signed claim along with the work, the digital signature, the public key, and associated certificates. The digital signature verifies to the Copyright Office that the submission was received correctly and confirms the submitter's identity. If at any future date there is a copyright dispute over the work, the digital signature can be used to authenticate the claim and the registered work.

the full texts of articles from indexes, abstracts, and promotional materials. Web sites, in addition to their public areas, may have private areas for use only by members of an organization.

Licensing and other external commitments   A digital library may contain materials licensed from a publisher or acquired subject to terms and conditions that govern access, such as materials that the Library of Congress receives through copyright deposit.

Physical and temporal properties   Digital libraries may have policies that depend on time since date of publication, or on physical properties such as size. Some newspapers provide open access to selected articles soon after they are published but require licenses for access to the same articles later.

Media types   A digital library may have access policies that depend on format or media type. For example, digitized sound, textual material, computer programs, and images may be treated differently.

Attributes must be assigned at varying "granularity." If all the materials in a collection have the same property, then it is convenient to assign the attribute to the collection as a whole. At the other extreme, there are times when parts of objects may have specific properties. Often the rights associated with images differ from those associated with the text in which they are embedded and have to be distinguished. Someone may donate a collection of letters to a library for public access but may request that access to certain private items be restricted. Digital libraries must be able to associate attributes with entire collections, with subcollections, with individual library objects, or with elements of individual objects.

Operations

Access-management policies often specify or restrict the operations and the various actions that a user is authorized to carry out on library materials. Two categories of operation are the following:

Computing actions   Some operations are defined in computing terms, such as writing data to a computer, executing a program, transmitting data across a network, displaying on a computer screen, printing, or copying from one computer to another.

Extent of use   A user may be authorized to extract individual items from a database, but not to copy the entire database.

The operations mentioned above can be controlled by technical means. However, many policies that an information manager might state are essentially impossible to enforce technically. They include the following:

Business or purpose   Authorization of a user might refer to the reason for carrying out an operation. Examples include commercial, educational, and government use.

Intellectual operations   Operations may specify the intellectual use that is to be made of an item. The rules that govern the creation of a new work that is derived from the content of another are most important here. The criteria may need to consider both the intent and the extent of use.

Subsequent Use

Systems for access management have to consider both direct operations and subsequent use of material. *Direct operations* are actions initiated by a repository, or another computer system that acts as a agent for the managers of the collection. *Subsequent use* covers all the operations that can occur once material leaves the control of the digital library, including all the ways that a copy can be made (from replicating computer files to photocopying paper documents). Intellectually, subsequent use can include extracting short sections, the creation of derivative works, and outright plagiarism.

When an item or part of a item has been transmitted to a personal computer, it is technically difficult to prevent a user from copying what is received, storing it, and distributing it to others. This is comparable to photocopying a document. If the information is for sale, the potential for such subsequent use to reduce revenue is clear. Publishers naturally are concerned that readers may distribute unauthorized copies of materials. At an extreme, if a publisher sells one copy of an item that is subsequently widely distributed over the Internet, the publisher may end up selling only that one copy. Often, in partial response to this fear, digital libraries allow readers access to individual records but do not provide any way to copy complete collections. Though this does not prevent a small loss of revenue, it is a barrier against anyone's undermining the economic interests of the publisher by wholesale copying.

Policies

An informal definition of a policy is that it is a rule, made by information managers that states who is authorized to do what to which material. The following policies are typical in digital libraries:

• A publication has a policy of open access. Anyone may read the material, but only members of the editorial staff may change it.

• A publisher of online journals has a policy that only subscribers have access to all materials. Others may read the contents pages and abstracts, but only those who pay a fee per use may have access to the full contents.

• A government organization classifies materials (e.g., "top secret") and has strict policies about who has access to the materials, under what conditions, and what they may do with them.

Policies are rarely as simple as in these examples. For example, *D-Lib Magazine* has a policy of open access, but the authors of the individual articles own copyright to their articles. The access policy is that all are encouraged to read the articles and to print copies for private use, but some subsequent uses (e.g., creating a derivative work, or selling copies for profit) require permission from the copyright owner.

Because access-management policies can be complex, a formal method is needed to express them for exchange of information among computer systems. Perhaps the most comprehensive work in this area is that carried out by Mark Stefik of the Xerox Corporation. The Digital Property Rights Language, which Stefik developed, is a language for expressing rights, conditions, and fees for the use of digital works. The purpose of the language is to specify attributes of material and policies for access, including subsequent use. The manager of a collection can specify terms and conditions for copying, transferring, rendering, printing, and similar operations. The language allows fees to be specified for any operation, and it envisages links to electronic payment mechanisms. The notation used by the language is based on Lisp, a language used for natural-language processing. Some have suggested that a more convenient notation for digital libraries would use XML. However, the real test is not notation but how effective the language will prove to be in large-scale applications.

Enforcing Access-Management Policies

Access management is not simply a question of developing appropriate policies. Information managers want the policies to be followed, which requires some form of enforcement.

Some policies can be enforced technically, but not all. There are straightforward technical methods to enforce a policy of who is permitted to change material in a collection or to search a repository. There are no technical means of enforcing a policy against plagiarism or against invasion of privacy, or to guarantee that all use is educational. Such policies, though reasonable, are extremely difficult to enforce by technical means; they must be enforced by social and legal methods.

There are tradeoffs between strictness of enforcement and convenience to users. Technical method of enforcing policies can be annoying. Few people object to typing in a password when they begin a session, but no one wants to be asked repeatedly for passwords or other forms of identification. Information managers sometimes decide to relax their enforcement of policies in the interest of satisfying users. Satisfied customers contribute to the growth of the market even if some revenue is lost as a result of unauthorized users. The publishers who are least aggressive about enforcement keep their customers happy and often generate more total revenue than any other publishers. As is discussed in panel 7.2, this is the strategy now used for most personal computer software. Data from publishers such as HighWire Press is beginning to suggest the same result with electronic journal publishing.

If technical methods are relaxed, social and legal pressures can be effective. Among the social objective are to educate users about the policies that apply to the collections and to coax or persuade people to follow them. Those objectives require policies that are easy to understand and to follow. Users must be informed of the policies and educated as to what constitutes reasonable behavior. One useful tool is to display an *access statement* when the material is accessed. An access statement is text that states some policy,

Panel 7.2
Access-Management Policies for Software

Early experience with software for personal computers provides an example of what happens when attempts to enforce policies are unpleasant for the users.

Software is usually licensed for a single computer. The license fee covers use on one computer only, but software is easy to copy. Manufacturers lose revenue from unlicensed copying, particularly if there is widespread distribution.

In the early days of personal computers, software manufacturers attempted to control unlicensed copying by technical means. One approach was to supply their products on disks that could not be copied easily. This was called "copy protection." Every time a program was launched, the user had to insert the original disk. This had a powerful effect on the market, but not what the manufacturers had hoped. It was inconvenient for legitimate customers to use the software they had purchased. Hard disk installations were awkward and backup difficult. Users objected. Those software suppliers who were most assertive about protection lost sales to competitors who supplied software without copy protection.

Microsoft was one of the companies that realized that technical enforcement was not the only option. It has become extremely rich by selling products that are not technically protected against copying. It has worked hard to stimulate adherence to its policies by non-technical methods. Marketing incentives, such as customer support and low-cost upgrades, encouraged customers to pay for licenses. Social pressure was used to educate people, legal methods to frighten the worst offenders.

Unlicensed copying still costs the software manufacturers money; however, companies that concentrate on satisfying their responsible customers are able to thrive.

such as "For copyright reasons, this material should not be used for commercial purposes." Other non-technical methods of enforcement are more assertive. For example, if members of an organization repeatedly violate a licensing agreement or abuse policies that they should respect, a publisher can revoke a license. In extreme cases, a single well-publicized legal action may persuade many others to behave responsibly.

Access Management at a Repository

Most digital libraries implement policies at the repository level or at the collection level. Although there are variations in the details, the methods all follow the outline in figure 7.1. Digital libraries are distributed computer systems in which information is passed from one computer to another. If access is managed only at the repository, it is effectively controlled locally; once material leaves the repository, few technical controls are possible.

The issue of subsequent use has already been introduced; once a user's computer receives information, it is hard for the original manager of the digital library to retain effective control without obstructing a legitimate user. With networks, there is a further complication: Numerous copies of the material made in networked computers, including caches, mirrors, and other servers, are beyond the control of the local repository.

To date, most digital libraries have been satisfied to provide access management at the repository while relying on social and legal pressures to control subsequent use. Usually such pressures are adequate, but some publishers are concerned that the lack of control could damage their revenues. Therefore, there is interest in technical methods that control copying and subsequent use, even after the material has left the repository. The methods fall into two categories: *trusted systems* and *secure containers*.

Trusted Systems

A repository is an example of a trusted system. The managers of a digital library have confidence that the hardware, the software, and the administrative procedures provide an adequate level of security for storage and provision of access to valuable information. There may be other systems, linked to the repository, that are equally trusted. Within such a network of trusted systems, digital libraries can use methods of enforcement that are simple extensions of those used for single repositories. Attributes and policies can be passed among systems, with confidence that they will be processed effectively.

Implementing networks of trusted systems is not easy. The individual systems' components must support a high level of security, and so must the processes by which information is passed among the various computers. For these reasons, trusted systems are typically used only in restricted situations or on special-purpose computers. If all the computers are operated by the same team, or by teams working under strict rules, many of the administrative problems diminish. An example of a large trusted system is the network of computers that support automatic teller machines for banks.

No assumptions can be made about users' personal computers and how they are managed. In fact, it is reasonable not to trust them. For this reason, early applications of trusted systems in digital libraries are likely to be restricted to special-purpose hardware, such as smart cards or secure printers, or to dedicated servers running tightly controlled software.

Secure Containers

Since networks are not secure, and since trusted systems are difficult to implement, several groups are developing secure containers for transmitting information across the Internet. Digital material is delivered to the user in a package that contains data and metadata about access policies. Some or all of the information in the package is encrypted. Access to the information requires a digital key, which might be received from an electronic payment system or from some other method of authentication. An advantage of this approach is that it provides some control over subsequent use. The package can be copied and distributed to third parties, but the contents cannot be accessed without the key. Panel 7.3 describes one such system.

Secure containers face a barrier to acceptance. They are of no value to a user unless the user can acquire the cryptographic keys that are needed to unlock them and make use of the content. This requires widespread deployment of security service and methods of electronic payment. Until recently, the spread of such services has been rather slow, so publishers have had little market for information delivered via secure containers.

Panel 7.3
Cryptolopes

IBM's Cryptolope system uses secure containers to let users buy and sell content securely over the Internet. The figure in this panel gives an idea of the structure of information in a Cryptolope.

Information is transmitted in a cryptographic envelope called a *container*. Information suppliers seal their information in the container. It can be opened by recipients only after they have satisfied any access-management requirements, such as paying for use of the information. The content is never separated from the access-management and payment information in the envelope. Thus, the envelope can later be passed on to others, who also must pay if they want to open it. (Each user must obtain the code to open the envelope.)

In addition to the encrypted content, Cryptolope containers may include an abstract in clear text to provide users with a description of the product. The information in this abstract may include a summary, the source, the author, the time of the last update, the size, the price, and the terms of sale. Once the user has decided to open the contents of a Cryptolope container, a digital key is issued that unlocks them. To view a free item, the user clicks on the abstract and the information appears on the desktop. To view priced content, the user agrees to the terms of the Cryptolope container as stated in the abstract.

The contents of a Cryptolope container can be dynamic, since the system has the potential to wrap JavaScripts, Java programs, and other live content into secure containers. In the interest of standardization, IBM has licensed Xerox's Digital Property Rights Language for specifying the rules governing the use and the pricing of content.

Bill of Materials	
Clear Text	
Encrypted fingerprinting and watermarking instructions	
Encrypted document part	Key record
Encrypted document part	Key record
Encrypted document part	Key record
Terms and Conditions	
Integrity protection and signatures	

Security of Digital Libraries

The remainder of this chapter looks at some of the basic methods of security that are used in networked computer systems. These are general-purpose methods with applications far beyond digital libraries; however, digital libraries have special needs because of the highly decentralized networks of suppliers and users of information.

Security begins with the system administrators, the people who install and manage the computers and the networks that connect them. Their honesty must be above suspicion, since they have privileges that provide access to the internals of the system. Good systems administrators will organize networks and file systems so that users have access to appropriate information. They will manage passwords, install firewalls to isolate sections of the networks, and run diagnostic programs to anticipate problems. They will back up information so that the system can be rebuilt after an incident such as an equipment breakdown, a fire, or a security violation.

The Internet is not secure. People can tap into it and observe the packets of information traveling over it. This is often done for legitimate purposes, such as troubleshooting, but it can also be done for less honest reasons. The general security question is how to build secure applications across this insecure network.

Since the Internet is not secure, security in digital libraries begins with the individual computers that constitute the library and the data on them, with special attention paid to the interfaces between computers and local networks. For many personal computers, the only method of security is physically restricting who uses the computer. Other computers have some form of software protection, usually a simple login name and password. When computers are shared by many users, controls are needed to determine who may read or write to each file.

The next step in protection is to control the interface between local networks and the broader Internet and to provide some barrier to intruders from outside. The most complete barrier is isolation—that is, having no external network connections. A more useful approach is to connect the internal network to the Internet through a special-purpose computer called a *firewall*. The purpose of a firewall is to screen every packet that attempts to pass through and to refuse those that might violate security. Firewalls can refuse attempts from outside to connect to computers within the organization, or they can reject packets that are not formatted according to a list of approved protocols. Well-managed firewalls can be quite effective in blocking intruders.

Universities have been at the heart of networked computing for many years. Despite the diversity of their users, they have succeeded in establishing adequate security for campus networks with thousands of computers. Incidents of abusive, anti-social, or malicious behavior occur on every campus, yet major disruptions are rare.

With careful administration, computers connected to a network can be made reasonably secure. However, there are many ways by which a malicious person can attempt to violate security. At universities, most problems are attributable to insiders, such as disgruntled employees or students who steal a user's login name and password. More sophisticated methods of intrusion take advantage of the complexity of computer software. Every operating system has built-in security, but design errors or programming bugs may have created gaps. Some of the most useful programs for digital libraries, such as web servers and electronic mail, are among the most difficult to secure. For these reasons, everyone who builds a digital library must recognize that security can never be guaranteed. With diligence troubles can be kept rare, but there is always a chance of a flaw. Managers of digital libraries should have a balanced attitude toward security. Though absolute security is impossible, moderate security can be built into networked computer systems without excessive cost (though it requires thought and attention).

Encryption

Encryption is the name given to a group of techniques that are used to store and transmit private information, encoding it in a way that the information appears completely random until the procedure is reversed. Even if the encrypted information is read by someone who is unauthorized, no damage is done. In digital libraries, encryption is used to transmit confidential information over the Internet, and some information is so confidential that it is encrypted wherever it is stored. Passwords are an obvious example of information that should always be encrypted, whether it is stored on computers or transmitted over networks. In many digital libraries, passwords are the only information that needs to be encrypted.

The basic concept of encryption is shown in figure 7.2. The data that is to be kept secret, X, is input to an encryption process which performs a mathematical transformation and creates an encrypted set of data, Y. The encrypted set of data will have the same number of bits as the original data. It appears to be a random collection of bits, but the process can be reversed by means of a reverse process that regenerates the original data, X. These two processes, encryption and decryption, can be implemented as computer programs, in software, or with special-purpose hardware.

The commonly used methods of encryption are controlled by a pair of numbers known as *keys*. One key is used for encryption, the other for decryption. The methods of encryption vary in the choice of processes and in the way the keys are selected. The mathematical forms of the processes are not secret; the security lies in the keys. A key is a string of bits, typically from 40 to 120 bits but sometimes more. Long keys are intrinsically much more secure than short keys, since any attempt to violate security by guessing keys becomes twice as difficult with every bit added to the key length.

Historically, the use of encryption has been restricted by computer power. The methods all require considerable computation to scramble and

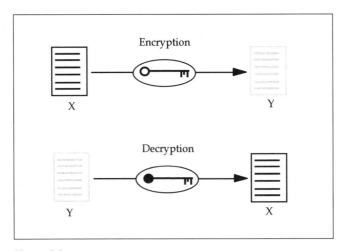

Figure 7.2

unscramble data. Early implementations of DES, the method described in panel 7.4, required special hardware to be added to every computer. With today's fast computers, this is much less serious, but the time to encrypt and decrypt large amounts of data is still noticeable. The methods are excellent for encrypting short messages (such as passwords) or occasional highly confidential messages, less suitable for large amounts of data if response times are important.

Private-Key Encryption

Private-key encryption is a family of methods in which the key used to encrypt the data and the key used to decrypt the data are the same and must be kept secret. Private-key encryption is also known as single-key or secret-key encryption. Panel 7.4 describes DES, one of the most commonly used methods.

Private-key encryption is only as secure as the procedures that are used to keep the key secret. If one computer wants to send encrypted data to a remote computer, it must find a completely secure way to get the key to the remote computer. Thus, private-key encryption is most widely used in applications in which trusted services are exchanging information.

Panel 7.4
The Data Encryption Standard

The Data Encryption Standard, a method of private-key encryption originally developed by IBM, has been a U.S. standard since 1977. The calculations used by DES are fairly slow when implemented in software, but the method is fast enough for many applications. A present-day personal computer can encrypt about a million bytes per second.

The Data Encryption Standard uses 56-bit keys. It divides a set of data into 64-bit blocks and encrypts each of them separately. From the 56-bit key, 16 smaller keys are generated. The heart of the algorithm is 16 successive transformations of the 64-bit block, using these smaller keys in succession. Decryption uses the same 16 smaller keys to carry out the reverse transactions in the opposite order. This sounds like a simple algorithm, but there are subtleties. Most important, the bit patterns generated by encryption appear to be entirely random, with no clues about the data or the key.

Fanatics argue that the 56-bit keys can be broken simply by trying every conceivable key, but this is a huge task. For digital library applications, the Data Encryption Standard is perfectly adequate.

Dual-Key Encryption

When private-key encryption is used over a network, the sending computer and the destination computer must both know the key. This poses the conundrum of how to get started if one computer cannot pass a key secretly to another. *Dual-key encryption* permits all information to be transmitted over a network. For this reason, it has the alternate name *public-key encryption*. Even if every message is intercepted, the encrypted information is still kept secret.

The Rivest-Shamir-Adleman (RSA) method is the best-known method of dual-key encryption. It requires a pair of keys. The first key is made public; the second is kept secret. An individual A wishing to send encrypted data to another, individual, B, encrypts the data using B's public key. On receiving the data, B decrypts it using the private key, which only B knows.

This dual-key system of encryption has many advantages and one major disadvantage. The disadvantage is the need to make sure that a key is genuinely the public key of a specific individual. The usual approach to doing this is to have all keys generated and authenticated by a trusted *certification authority*. The certification authority then generates *certificates*—signed messages specifying an individual and a public key. This works well, so long as security at the certificate authority is never violated.

Digital Signatures

As has already been mentioned, a digital signature can be used to check that a computer file has not been altered. Digital signatures are based on the concept of a *hash function*—a mathematical function that can be applied to the bytes of a computer file to generate a fixed-length number.

One commonly used hash function, called MD5, carries out a special transformation on the bits of a file and ends up with an apparently random 128 bits. MD5 can be applied to files of any length. If two files differ by even one bit, their MD5 hashes will be completely different. Conversely, if two files have the same hash, the probability that they are not identical is infinitesimal. Thus, a simple way to establish whether a file has been altered is to calculate the MD5 hash when the file is created; then, later to check that no changes have taken place, recalculate the hash and compare it against the original. If the two are the same, the files are almost certainly the same.

The MD5 function has many strengths, including being fast to compute for large files; however, as with any security device, there is always a possibility that some bright person may discover how to reverse engineer the hash function and create a file that has a specific hash value. As this book was being written, there were hints that MD5 may be vulnerable in this way. In any case, other hash functions are available.

A hash value gives no information as to who calculated it. A digital signature goes one step further toward guaranteeing the authenticity of a library object: When the hash value of an object is calculated, it is encrypted using the private key of the object's owner. This, together with the public key and the certificate authority, creates a digital signature. Before checking the hash value, the user decrypts the digital signature using the public key. If the hash results match, then the object has not been altered and that the digital signature was generated using the corresponding private key.

Digital signatures have a shortcoming, however: Although users of a digital library want to be confident that objects have not been altered, they are not concerned with bits; their interest lies in the content. For example, the U.S. Copyright Office pays great attention to intellectual content, such as words of text, but does not care if a computer system attached some control information to a file or if the font used for the text was changed; yet the test of a digital signature fails completely when even one bit is changed. As yet, no one has suggested an effective way to ensure authenticity of content rather than of bits.

Deployment of Public-Key Encryption

Since the basic mathematics of public-key encryption is now almost twenty years old, one might expect such encryption to have been in wide use for many years. Sadly, this is not the case.

There are significant technical issues, many concerning the management of the keys, how they are generated, how private keys are stored, and what precautions can be taken if the agency creating the keys suffers a breach of security. However, the main reasons for the delay have to do with policy.

First, there is the problem of software patents (already discussed in chapter 6). Public-key encryption is one of the few areas of computing in which most computer scientists would agree there have been real inventions. The methods of encryption are not obvious, and their inventors deserve the rewards that go with invention. Unfortunately, the patent holders and their agents have followed narrow licensing policies, which have slowed the pace of deployment.

A more serious obstacle has been interference from U.S. government agencies. The Central Intelligence Agency claims that encryption technology is a military secret and that exporting it would jeopardize the security of the United States. Police forces—notably the Federal Bureau of Investigation—claim that public safety depends on their ability to intercept and read any message on the Internet when authorized by an appropriate warrant. The export argument is hard to defend when the methods are widely published overseas and when reputable companies in Europe and Japan are marketing encryption products. The public-safety argument is more complicated, but it is undercut by the simple fact that the American public does not trust either the technical competence or the administrative procedures of the CIA and the nation's police forces. People want to be able to transmit confidential information without being monitored.

It is appropriate that this chapter ends with a case in which a technical solution is being held up by policy difficulties. This echoes a theme that recurs throughout the field of digital libraries and is especially important in access management. People, technology, and administrative procedures are intimately linked. Successful digital libraries combine aspects of all three and do not rely solely on technology.

8

User Interfaces and Usability

A person who uses a library is conventionally called a *patron* or a *reader*. In computing, the usual term is *user* or *end user*. Whatever word is chosen, digital libraries are of little value unless they are easy to use effectively.

The relationship between people and computers is a subject of intensive research drawing on fields as diverse as cognitive science, graphic design, rhetoric, and mathematical modeling of computer systems. Some of the research aims to develop a theoretical understanding of how people interact with computers so that models of human information processing can be used to design appropriate computer systems. Other research helps the user comprehend the principles behind a computer system, thereby stimulating productive use of the services and the information that the system provides. This chapter is less ambitious. It concentrates on the methods that are in wide use today, offering some illustrations of experimental systems that show promise.

Change is one of the themes of digital libraries, and change is one of the problems in designing user interfaces. Traditional libraries are not easy to use effectively; however, they change slowly, and over the years their users develop expertise. Digital libraries evolve so quickly that every month brings new services, new collections, new interfaces, and new headaches. Users do not enjoy having to relearn basic skills, but change appears to be a necessary evil.

Partly because of the rapidity with which digital libraries change, their users' levels of expertise vary greatly. Much of the development of digital libraries has come out of universities, where there are many experts. Colleagues and librarians are at hand to help users; system administrators configure computers, install software, and track changes in the marketplace.

But with the spread of the Internet, digital libraries are being used by people who do not have access to such expertise and do not want to spend their own time learning techniques that may be of only transitory value. This creates tension: Advanced features are valuable to specialists, and they enable skilled users to work faster and be more effective, but digital libraries must be usable by individuals with minimal training.

Usability and the Design of User Interfaces

In discussing the usability of a computer system, it is easy to focus on the design of the interface between the user and the computer. But usability is a property of the entire system. All the components of a digital library must work together smoothly to make the library effective and convenient for patrons, for librarians, and for systems administrators.

Figure 8.1 shows a way to think about usability and the design of user interfaces. Any computer system's user interface is built on a *conceptual model* that describes the manner in which the system is used. Here are some typical conceptual models that are used to design digital libraries. (In practice, most digital libraries combine concepts from several such models.)

- In the classical library model, the user searches a catalog or index, selects objects from the results, then retrieves the objects from a repository.
- In the basic web model, the user follows hyperlinks between files.
- The Z39.50 protocol supports a conceptual model of searching a collection and then storing sets of results for subsequent manipulation and retrieval.

The right side of figure 8.1 illustrates the layers of design needed to implement any conceptual model. *Interface design* encompasses what

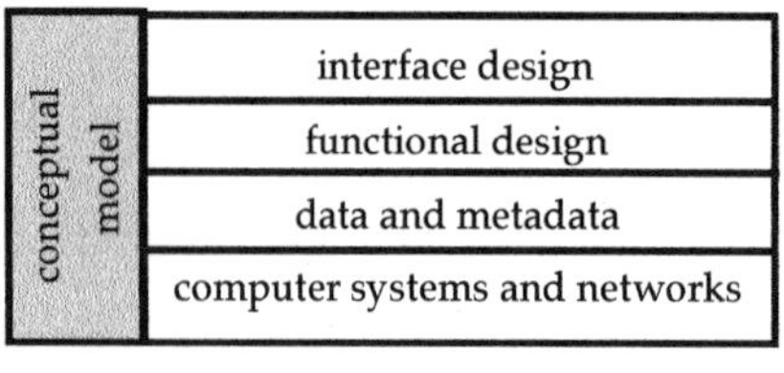

Figure 8.1

appears on the screen and how the user manipulates it; among its aspects are fonts, colors, logos, keyboard controls, menus, and buttons. *Functional design* specifies the functions that are offered to the user. Typical functions include selecting parts of a digital object, searching a list or sorting results, obtaining help, and manipulating objects that have been rendered on the screen. These functions are made possible by the *data and metadata* that are provided by the digital library, and by the underlying *computer systems and networks*. Panel 8.1 details how these aspects of usability apply to an important application.

Almost all present-day personal computers have a user interface of the style made popular on Apple's Macintosh computers, which was derived from earlier research at Xerox PARC. It uses the metaphor of files and folders on a desktop. Its characteristics include overlapping windows, menus, and a pointing device such as a mouse. Despite numerous attempts at improvement, this style of interface continues to dominate the computer market. An early Macintosh user transported through fifteen years and presented with a computer running Microsoft's latest system would find the interface familiar. Some new conventions have been introduced, and hardware has been improved greatly, but the same basic metaphor is still used.

The conceptual model is the desktop metaphor; files are thought of as documents that can be moved to the desktop, placed in folders, or stored on disks. Every windows-based user interface has this same conceptual model, although the interface designs vary (for example, Apple uses a mouse with one button, Microsoft uses two buttons, and Unix systems usually have three). The functions that support this model include open and closing files and folders, selecting them, moving them from one place to another, and so on. These functions differ little from one manufacturer to another, but the systems differ in the metadata that they use to support the functions. The desktop metaphor requires that applications be associated with data files. Microsoft and Unix systems use file-naming conventions; for example, the names of files that are to be used with a PDF viewer end in .pdf. Apple stores such metadata in a separate data structure, hidden from the user. Differences in the underlying computer systems permit some user interfaces to carry out several tasks simultaneously.

Panel 8.1
Page Turning

Page turning illustrates the aspects of user-interface design shown in figure 8.1. Conversion projects such as JSTOR and American Memory have collections of digital objects, each consisting of page images scanned from a book or some other printed material. The *conceptual model* is that the user interacts with an object in much the same manner as with a book. Often the pages will be read in sequence, but the reader may also go back a page or jump to a different page. Some pages, such as a table of contents or an index, may be identified as special. Since many personal computers have screens that are smaller than printed pages and have lower resolution, the conceptual model includes zooming and panning across a single page.

The *interface design* defines the actual appearance on the screen, such as the choice of frames, icons, colors, and visual clues. It also includes decisions about how the individual functions are offered to the user. The interface design determines the appearance of icons, the wording on the buttons, and their position on the screen. The design also specifies whether panning and zooming are continuous or in discrete steps. When we built a page turner at Carnegie Mellon University, the interface design maximized the area of the screen that was available for displaying page images. Most manipulations were controlled from the keyboard; the arrow keys were used for panning around an individual page, with the tab key used for going to the next page. An alternative design would have these functions controlled by buttons on the screen, but with less space on the screen for the page images.

The *functional design* must provide services that are equivalent to turning the pages of a book, including going to the first, the next, the previous, or the last page. There will be functions that relate to the content of a specific page, such as going to the page that has a specific page number printed on it and going to the table of contents. To support panning and zooming within a page, other functions of the user interface move the area displayed up or and down one screen, and zoom in or out.

The functions offered by a user interface depend on the digital objects in the collections and especially on the *structural metadata*. Typically, page images are stored as compressed files that can be retrieved in any sequence. To allow pages to be turned in sequence, structural metadata must identify the first page image and list the sequence of the other images. Going to the page with a specific page number printed on it requires structural metadata that relates the page numbers to the sequence of page images, since it is rare that the first page of a set is the page numbered 1. Zooming and panning require metadata that states the dimensions of each page.

A user interface is only as good as the performance of the underlying *computer system*. Delays in transmitting a page image across a network can be annoying to the user. One possible way to reduce this annoyance is to anticipate the user's demands by sending pages from the repository to the user's computer before the user requests them, so that at least the next page in a sequence is ready in memory. This is known as *pre-fetching*. In the case of the Carnegie Mellon page turner, priority was given to achieving quick response—about a second to read and display a page image, even one transmitted over the busy campus network. This led to a "pipelined" implementation in which the first part of a page was being rendered on the user's computer even before the final section was read into the repository computer from disk storage.

Browsers

The introduction of browsers (notably Mosaic, introduced in 1993) stimulated the design of better user interfaces for networked applications. Although browsers were designed for the web, they are so flexible that they are used as interfaces to almost every type of application on the Internet, including digital libraries. Before the emergence of general-purpose browsers, developers had to provide a separate user interface for each type of computer and each computing environment. These interfaces had to be modified whenever the operating systems changed—a monumental task that few attempted and almost none did well. By relying on web browsers for the actual interaction with the user, the designer of a digital library can now focus on how to organize the flow of information to the user, leaving complexities of hardware and operating systems to the browser.

Basic Functions

The basic function of a browser is to retrieve a remote file from a web server and render it on the user's computer.

• To locate the file on the web server, the browser needs a Uniform Resource Locator. The URL can be typed in by the user, or it can be a link within an HTML page, or it can be stored as a bookmark.

• From the URL, the browser extracts the protocol. If it is HTTP, the browser then extracts from the URL the domain name of the computer on which the file is stored. The browser sends a single HTTP message, waits for the response, and closes the connection.

• If all goes well, the response consists of a file and a MIME type. To render the file on the user's computer, the browser examines the MIME type and invokes the appropriate routines. These routines may be built into the browser or may be an external program invoked by the browser.

A simple web browser would offer little more than support for the HTTP protocol and routines to render pages in the HTML format. Since both HTTP and HTML are straightforward, a web browser need not be a complex program.

Extending Browsers beyond the Web

Browsers were developed for the web, and every browser supports the web's basic protocols and a few standard formats. However, browsers can be extended to provide other services while retaining the browser interface. Much of the success of browsers, of the web, and indeed of the whole Internet is due to this extensibility.

Mosaic and its successors have had the same three types of extensibility: one for data types, one for protocols, and one for the execution of programs.

Data types

With each data type, browsers associate routines to render files of that type. A few types have been built into all recent browsers, including plain text, HTML pages, and images in GIF format, but users can add additional types through mechanisms such as helper applications and plug-ins. A *helper application* is a separate program that is invoked by selected types of data. The source file is passed to the helper as data. For example, browsers do not have built-in support for files in the PostScript format, but many users have a PostScript viewer on their computer which is used as a helper application. When a browser receives a file of type PostScript, it starts this viewing program and passes to it the file to be displayed. A *plug-in* is similar to a helper application, except that it is not a separate program. It is used to render source files of non-standard formats, within an HTML file, in a single display.

Protocols

HTTP is the central protocol of the web, but browsers also support other protocols. Some, such as Gopher and WAIS, were important historically because they allowed browsers to access older information services. Others, such as NetNews, electronic mail, and FTP, remain important. A weakness of most browsers is that the list of protocols supported is fixed and does not allow for expansion. Thus, there is no natural way to add Z39.50 or other protocols to browsers.

Execution of programs

An HTTP message sent from a browser can do more than retrieve a static file of information from a server. It can run a program on a server and return the results to the browser. The earliest method of achieving this was the common gateway interface (CGI), which provides a simple way for a browser to execute a program on a remote computer. The CGI programs are often called *CGI scripts*. CGI is the mechanism that most web search programs use to send queries from a browser to the search system. Publishers store their collections in databases and use CGI scripts to provide user access. An informal interpretation of the URL

http://www.dlib.org/cgi-bin/seek?author='Arms'

is "On the computer with domain name www.dlib.org, execute the program in the file cgi-bin/seek, pass it the parameter string author='Arms', and return the output." The program might search a database for records having the word Arms in the author field.

The earliest uses of CGI were to connect browsers to older databases and other information. By a strange twist, now that the web has become a mature system, the roles have been reversed. People who develop advanced digital libraries often use CGI as a method to link the old system (the web) to their newer systems.

Mobile Code

Browsers rapidly became big business, with new features added continually. Some of these features are clearly good for the users; others are marketing features. The improvements include performance enhancements, elaboration to HTML, built-in support for other formats (an early addition was JPEG images), and better ways to add new formats. Two changes that are more than incremental improvements are the steady addition of security features and the introduction of *mobile code* (which permits servers to send computer programs to the client, to be executed by the browser on the user's computer).

Mobile code gives the designer of a web site the ability to create web pages that incorporate computer programs. Panel 8.2 describes one approach, which uses *applets* (small programs) written in the Java programming language. An applet can be copied from a web site to a client program and executed on the client. Because Java is a full programming

Panel 8.2
Java

Java is a general-purpose programming language that was explicitly designed for creating distributed systems, especially user interfaces, in a networked environment.

The conventional approach to making user-interface software that runs on several types of computers (e.g., web browsers and email systems) has been to write different versions. Even when versions are written in a standard language, such as C, the differences among the Windows, Unix, and Macintosh operating systems force the creator to write several versions and to modify them continually as the operating systems change. A user who wants to run a new user interface must first find and install a version of the user interface for his or her specific type of computer. At best, this is awkward and time consuming; at worst, the new program will disrupt the operation of some existing program or will introduce viruses.

Computer programs are written in a high-level language known as the *source code*. After a program has been written, it is usually compiled into the machine language of the specific computer. A Java compiler is different, however. Rather than create machine code for a specific computer system, it transforms the Java source into an intermediate code, known as *Java bytecode*, that is targeted for a software environment called a Java Virtual Machine. To run the bytecode on a specific computer requires a second step, in which each statement in the bytecode is interpreted as machine-code instructions for that computer as it is executed. Modern browsers support the Java Virtual Machine and incorporate Java interpreters.

A Java applet is a short computer program that is compiled into a file of Java bytecode and can be delivered across the network to a browser, usually by means of an HTTP command. The browser recognizes the file as an applet and invokes the Java interpreter to execute it.

Since Java is a full-feature programming language, almost any computing procedure can be incorporated in a web application. The Java system also provides programmers with a set of tools that can be incorporated into programs. These include basic programming constructs, such as strings, numbers, input and output, and data structures; the conventions used to build applets; networking services, such as URLs, TCP sockets, and IP addresses; help for writing programs that can be tailored for scripts and languages other than English; security, including electronic signatures, public/private key management, access control, and certificates; software components, known as JavaBeans, which can plug into other software architectures; and connections to databases. Since the basic functions are permanent parts of the web browser, they do not have to be delivered across the Internet with every applet; in addition, they can be written in the machine code of the individual computer, so that they can be executed faster than the interpreted bytecode.

Java has much to offer to the digital library community, but it is not perfect. Some of its defects are conventional technical ones: It is large, complex, and difficult to learn. Interpreted languages always execute slowly, and Java is no exception. Design decisions that prevent Java applets from bringing viruses across the network and infecting the user's computer also constrain legitimate programs. However, Java's biggest drawback is non-technical: Its developer, Sun Microsystems, set out to develop a standard language. Unfortunately, other companies, notably Microsoft, have created incompatible variants.

language, it can be used for complex operations such as sending an authentication form from a web site to a browser so that the user can then type in an ID and a password, which a Java applet encrypts and sends securely back to the server.

Java is not the only means of providing mobile code. An alternative is for an HTML page to include a script of instructions, usually written in the JavaScript language. JavaScript is simpler to write than Java and executes quickly. A typical use of JavaScript is to check data that a user provides as input as soon as it has been typed, without the delays of transmitting everything back to the server for validation. (Java and JavaScript are completely different languages. The similarity of the names is purely a marketing device. Java has received most of the publicity; however, JavaScript has some advantages, and both are widely used.)

Recent Advances in Design of User Interfaces

Designing user interfaces for digital libraries is part art and part science. Ultimately the success of an interface depends on the designers' instincts and their understanding of users. New concepts are steadily being introduced to the design repertoire. This section looks at some of the new ideas and topics of research. Chapter 12 describes recent research into structural metadata. This is a topic of great importance to user interfaces, since the manner in which digital objects are modeled and the structural metadata associated with them provide the raw material on which user interfaces act.

Conceptual Models

Several research groups have been looking for conceptual models that will help users navigate through the vast collections now available online. There are few landmarks on the Internet, few maps, few signposts. Hyperlinks, which are the heart of the web, lead to unexpected places, and a user can easily get lost. Users of digital libraries often have little formal training and work alone. This argues for interfaces based on conceptual models that will guide users along well-established paths, although with a little ingenuity some people are remarkably adept at finding information on the Internet. Observations suggest that experienced people meet a high percentage of their library needs with networked information, but less experienced users often get lost and have difficult evaluating the information that they find. Panel 8.3 describes two research projects that have explored novel conceptual models for digital libraries.

Interface Design

Interface design is partly an art, but a number of general principles have emerged from recent research. Consistency in appearance, in controls, and in function is important to users. Users need feedback; they need to understand what the computer system is doing and why they see certain results. They should be able to interrupt or reverse actions. Error handling should be simple and easy to comprehend. Skilled users should be offered shortcuts, while beginners should have simple, well-defined options. Above all, the user should feel in control.

Control—particularly over graphic design and the appearance of materials—creates a continuing tension between the designers of digital libraries and the users. Many designers want the user to see materials exactly as they were designed. They want to control graphical quality, typography, window size, location of information within a window, and everything else that is important to good design. Unfortunately for designers, browsers are generic tools. The designer does not know which browser the user has, what type of computer, how fast the network, or whether the display is large or small. Users may wish to reconfigure their computer. They may prefer a large font, or a small window. They may turn off the displaying of images to reduce network delays. Therefore, a good design must be effective in a range of computing environments. The best designers have a knack of

Panel 8.3
New Conceptual Models: DLITE and Pad++

Several interesting experiments have searched for user-interface metaphors other than the desktop. Since these were research projects, the interfaces will probably never be used in a production system; however, they are important for developing concepts that can be used in other interfaces and for illustrating a design process that is based on systematic analysis of users' needs and expectations.

DLITE is an experimental user interface developed by Steve Cousins at Stanford University as a part of the Digital Libraries Initiative. Created as a user interface for the Stanford InfoBus, DLITE uses concepts from object-oriented programming. Each component is implemented as a CORBA object. (The InfoBus and CORBA are described in chapter 13.)

The conceptual model of DLITE is based on an analysis of the tasks that a user of digital libraries carries out. The following requirements were identified:

• Digital libraries consist of heterogeneous collections that must be accessible from anywhere on the Internet.
• Results created by one service may become the input to another.
• The interface must be extensible, so that new resources can be integrated easily with existing ones.
• Resources may be retained over long periods of time.
• Users must be able to collaborate.

The DLITE model describes digital libraries in terms of components, the four major types being documents, queries, collections, and services. These components are represented by icons that can be manipulated directly by a user viewing windows on the screen. For example, dragging a query onto a search service causes the search to be carried out, thus creating a collection of results. DLITE allows users to create task-specific interfaces by assembling interface elements on the screen.

The functional design of DLITE was motivated by two considerations: rapid response and the ability to add new services with minimal effort. For these reasons, the functional design is divided into user-interface clients and a user-interface server. The clients carry out the manipulations of the components. Several can run at the same time. The server provides an interface to the external services and can operate even when the clients are shut down.

Extensibility is provided by the server. When a new service is added, a new interface must be programmed in the server; the clients, however, need not be modified. Support for a variety of computers and operating systems is provided by having separate client programs for each.

Pad++, a user-interface concept conceived by Ken Perlin at New York University, has been developed by researchers at several universities and research centers. Its fundamental concept is the viewing of a large collection of information at many different scales. Pad++ takes the metaphor of the desktop far beyond the confines of a computer display, as though a collection of documents were spread out on an enormous wall. User interactions are based on the familiar ideas of panning and zooming. A user can zoom out and see the whole collection with little detail, zoom in part way to see sections of the collection, or zoom in to see every detail. This spatial approach makes extensive use of research in human perception. Since people have good spatial memory, Pad++ emphasizes shape and position as clues to help users explore information and to recall later what they found.

When Pad++ zooms out, details do not grow ever smaller; if it did, the program would be forced to render huge numbers of infinitesimal details. Features have thresholds. Below a certain scale, they are merged into other features or are not displayed at all. In a process known as *semantic zooming*, objects change appearance when they change size. This approach is familiar from mapmaking, in which a map of a large area represents cities but not individual buildings.

Pad++ is not intended as a universal interface for all applications. For some purposes, such as exploring large hierarchical collections in digital libraries, it may serve as a complete user interface; for other purposes, it may be a visualization component, alongside other user-interface concepts, within a conventional windowing system.

Pad++ is an interesting example of user-interface research on the relationship between system performance and usability. Several versions of the Pad++ concept have been developed, some free-standing and some as parts of web browsers. Each contains internal performance monitoring. The rendering operations are timed so that the frame refresh rate remains constant during pans and zooms. When the interface starts to be slow, medium-size features are rendered approximately; the details are added when the system is idle.

building interfaces that are convenient to use and attractive on a variety of computers, but some designers encounter difficulty in making the transition from traditional media (where they control everything) to digital libraries and the web. A common mistake is overelaboration, so that an interface is almost unusable without a fast network and a high-performance computer.

One unnecessary complication is that Netscape and Microsoft, the two leading vendors of browsers, deliver products that they have chosen to make different from one another. If a designer wishes to use some specialized features, the user must be warned that the application cannot be used on all browsers. A user interface that works beautifully on one browser may be a disaster on the other. The manufacturers' competitive instincts have been given priority over the convenience of the user.

Functional Design

Digital libraries are distributed systems, with many computers working together as a team. Research into functional design provides designers with choices about what functions belong on which of the various computers and about the relationships between them. Between a repository (where collections are stored) and the end user (typically using a web browser) lie an assortment of computer programs which are sometimes called *middleware*. Middleware programs act as intermediaries between the user and the repository. They interpret instructions from users and deliver them to repositories. They receive information from repositories, organize it, and deliver it to the user's computer. Often the middleware provides supporting services, such as authentication or error checking, but its most important task is to match the services that a user requires with those provided by a repository.

Figures 8.2 and 8.3 show two common configurations. In each case, a user at a personal computer is using a standard web browser as a front-end interface to digital library services: a repository and a search system.

In figure 8.2, the middleware is implemented as independent computer programs (usually CGI scripts) that run on server computers somewhere on the network. The browser sends messages to the interface in a standard protocol (probably HTTP). The scripts can run on the remote service, or they can communicate with the service by means of any convenient protocol. The link between the interface scripts and the search system might use the Z39.50 protocol. The technical variations are important to the system's flexibility and performance, but functionally they are equivalent. This configuration has the disadvantage that each of the user's actions must be transmitted across the network to be processed; the user then waits for a response.

Figure 8.3 shows a more advanced configuration in which mobile code is executed on the user's computer by the browser. The code may be Java applets. Until used, the code is stored on the remote server; it is loaded into the user's computer automatically when required. This configuration has

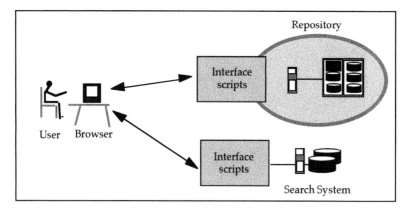

Figure 8.2
User interface with interface scripts.

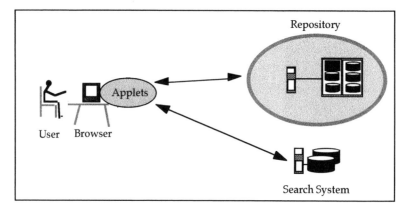

Figure 8.3
User interface with mobile code (applets).

many advantages. Since the user-interface code runs on the user's computer, it can be very responsive. The protocol between the user interface and the services can be any standard protocol or can be tailored specially for the application.

A *presentation profile* is an interesting concept that has recently emerged. Managers of a digital library associate guidelines with stored information. The guidelines suggest how the objects might be presented to the user. For example, the profile might recommend two ways to render an object, one offering small file size and one offering full detail. The user interface is encouraged to follow the profile in rendering the data but has the option of following different approaches.

Computer Systems and Networks

The performance of computer systems and networks has a considerable impact on usability. The creator of a digital library can make few assumptions about the equipment that a user possesses, beyond the basic knowledge that every user has a personal computer attached to the Internet. However, this simple statement covers a multitude of situations. Some personal computers are more powerful than others. The quality of displays vary greatly. Some people have their own private computer, which they can configure as they wish; others may share a computer, or use more than one computer. Any digital library must assume that users will have a variety of computers, with a variety of operating systems and environments. The environments include the various versions of Microsoft's Windows, Macintosh, and a plethora of types of Unix. Differences among operating systems can be minimized by using a web browser for the user interface, but performance differences are not so easily mediated.

The usability of a computer system depends on how quickly it responds to instructions. The designer of a digital library has little or no knowledge of the quality of network connections between the user and the library. Connections vary from spectacularly fast to frustratingly slow, and even the best connections occasional experience long pauses. A user interface that is a delight to use over a 10 million bits per second local network may be unusable over an erratic dial-up link that rarely reaches its advertised speed of 28,000 bits per second. Thus, digital libraries have to balance effective use of advanced services (which require fast equipment and up-to-date software) with decent service to users who are less well provided for.

Improving the Responsiveness of Browsers
Web browsers incorporate several tricks to improve the responsiveness seen by the user. One is *internal caching*. Information that has been used once is likely to be used again (for example, when the user clicks the "back" button on a web browser), and some graphics (such as logos and buttons) may

be repeated often. Web browsers retain recently used files by storing them temporarily on the disk of a user's personal computer. These files may be HTML pages, images, or files of mobile code (perhaps in JavaScript). When a user requests a file, the browser first checks to see if it can read the file from the local cache rather than having to retrieve it from a distant server.

Another family of methods that improve the responsiveness of browsers carry out many operations in parallel. Browsers display the first part of a long file before the whole file has arrived; images are displayed in outline, and the details are filled in later as more data arrives. Several separate streams of data can be requested in parallel. In aggregate, these techniques do much to mitigate the slow and erratic performance that often plagues the Internet.

Mirroring and Caching

Replication of data is a technique widely used to enhance the performance of systems on the Internet.

If a digital library collection is to be used by people around the world, duplicate copies of the entire collection may be placed at several sites—perhaps two in Europe, two in the United States, one in Australia, and one in Japan. This is called *mirroring*. Generally, users select the nearest mirror site, which is likely to provide the best performance for those users. Mirroring also allows a user to turn to another site if one site breaks down or if a section of the network is giving trouble.

The replication of specific information (rather than an entire library) is referred to as *caching*. A cache is any store that retains recently used information, to avoid delays the next time it is used. Caches are found within the computer hardware used to help computer processors run quickly. They are found in the controllers that read data from computer disks. In the domain-name system, they are used to improve the speed and reliability of the conversion of domain names to Internet addresses.

Digital libraries have caches in many places. For example, an organization may maintain local caches of documents that have been read recently. A digital library that stores large collections on slow but cheap mass storage devices will maintain a cache on faster storage devices.

All methods of replicating data suffer from the danger that the versions may differ and that some users may therefore be receiving obsolete material. Elaborate procedures are needed to discard replicated information after a stated time, or to check the source to see if changes have taken place.

Caches are vulnerable to security breaches. A computer system is only as secure as its weakest link, and a cache can easily be the weakest link.

Reliability and User Interfaces

Few computer systems are completely reliable, and digital libraries depend on many subsystems scattered across the Internet. In view of the number of independent components, it is remarkable that any world-wide system ever works.

Well-designed computer systems provide the user with feedback about progress in carrying out tasks. One simple form of feedback is an animation that keeps moving while the user interface is waiting for a response; this at least tells the user that something is happening. More advanced feedback is provided by an indication of the fraction of the task that has been completed and an estimate of the time to completion. In all cases, the user should be allowed to cancel a time-consuming operation.

The term *graceful degradation* describes methods that identify when a task is taking a long time and attempt to provide partial satisfaction to the user. One simple technique is to allow users of web browsers to turn off images in web pages and to see only the text. Several methods of delivering images allow a crude image to be displayed as soon as part of the data has been delivered; full resolution is added later.

User Interfaces for Multimedia Information

The materials in digital libraries are steadily becoming more varied in kind. User interfaces designed for collections of textual material may be inadequate when faced with collections of music, maps, computer software, images, statistical data, and even video games. Nonetheless, some general principles apply:

Summarization   When the user has many items to choose from, it is convenient to represent each by some small summary information that conveys its essence. A book is usually summarized by the author's name and the title (e.g., Arms, *Digital Libraries*). For a picture, a thumbnail-size image is usually sufficient. More esoteric information, such as a computer program or a film, is difficult for a digital library to summarize.

Sorting and categorization   Libraries organize information by classification or by ordering, but many types of information (e.g., musical tunes) lack easily understood ways of organization. Fields guides to birds are easy to use because they divide birds into well-known categories, such as ducks, hawks, and finches; guides to wildflowers are more awkward because flowers lack equivalent divisions.

Presentation   Many types of information require specialized equipment for the best presentation to the user. High-quality digitized video, for example, requires specialized displays, powerful computers, high-speed network connections, and appropriate software. A digital library should make full use of such capabilities, if they are available; to present such information to users who have lesser equipment, alternative means of presentation must be provided.

There is no single way to design digital libraries for different types of information. User interfaces have to be tailored for the different classes of material and probably also for different categories of users. Panel 8.4 describes one good example of a user interface: the Informedia digital library of digitized segments of video.

User Interfaces and the Effectiveness of Digital Libraries

During the past few years, the quality of user-interface design has improved dramatically. It is now assumed that new users can begin productive work without any training. Most important, there are now numerous examples of fine interfaces on the Internet that others can use for inspiration and as models. Standards of graphical design get better every year. (The materials for *D-Lib Magazine* were redesigned three times in as many years. Each design was considered elegant in its day but needed a face lift a year later.)

Good support for users is more than a cosmetic flourish. Elegant design, appropriate functionality, and responsive systems make a measurable difference in the effectiveness of digital libraries. When a system is hard to use, the users may fail to find important results, may misinterpret what they do find, or may give up in disgust. A digital library is only as good as its interface.

Panel 8.4
Informedia

Informedia, a program at Carnegie Mellon University led by Howard Wactlar, is carrying out research on digital libraries of video materials—specifically, broadcast news and documentary programs. The programs are automatically broken into short segments, such as the individual items in a news broadcast. The emphasis is on developing automatic methods for extracting information from the video objects, so as to minimize human intervention. More than 1000 hours of digitized video material (obtained from the Cable News Network, the British Open University, the Pittsburgh public television station WQED, and other sources) are being used.

One of the questions associated with video or audio material is how to provide users with an quick overview of an item. The reader of a book can look at the contents page or flick through the pages to see the chapter headings, but there is no way to flick through a video. *Video skimming*, a technique developed by the Informedia project, uses automatic methods to extract important words and images. In combination, the selected words and images provide a video abstract that conveys the essence of the full video segment. Informedia's research on video skimming has gone far beyond what was expected at the start of the project.

The Informedia user interface employs the conceptual model of searching an index of the collection, obtaining a set of hits, then browsing through the items found. Queries may be entered by typing or by means of a speech-recognition program. After a search, the interface presents ranked results. Each video clip is represented by an image. When the cursor is moved over the image, a text summary is provided. The image is selected automatically as representative of the video segment as it relates to the current query; the summary is created through natural-language processing. The user may then click on an image to view the segment. The interface consists of a video viewer with controls (such as "play" and "stop") similar to those of a home video player. The interface is sufficiently intuitive to be used by individuals who have not been trained on the system. It maximizes feedback to the user at each step. Much of the testing has been done with Pittsburgh high school students.

9

Text

Textual materials have a special place in all libraries, including digital libraries. Though sometimes a picture may indeed be worth a thousand words, more often the best way to convey complex ideas is through words. The richness of concepts, the detail, and the precision of ideas that can be expressed in text are remarkable.

Textual documents in digital libraries may come from many sources. Some may have been created for online use. Some may have been converted from print or other media. Some may be digitized soundtracks from films or television programs. Textual records have a special function as metadata that describes other materials.

This chapter looks at how textual documents are represented for storage in computers, and how they are rendered for printing and display to users. Metadata records and methods for searching textual documents are covered in later chapters.

Markup, Page Description, and Style Sheets

Methods for storing textual materials must represent two different aspects of a document: its structure and its appearance.

The *structure* describes the division of a text into elements, such as characters, words, paragraphs, and headings. It identifies parts of the documents that are emphasized, materials placed in tables or footnotes, and everything that relates one part to another. The structure of text stored in computers is often represented by a *markup* specification. In recent years, SGML (Standard Generalized Markup Language) has become widely accepted as a generalized system for structural markup.

The *appearance* is how the document looks when displayed on a screen or printed on paper. The appearance is closely related to the choice of format: the font and its size, the margins and the line spacing, how headings are represented, the location of figures, and the display of mathematics or other specialized notation. In a printed book, decisions about the appearance extend to the choice of paper and the type of binding. *Page-description languages* are used to store and render documents in a way that precisely describe their appearance. This chapter looks at three rather different approaches to page description: TeX, PostScript, and PDF.

Structure and appearance are related by the design of the document. In conventional publishing, a designer creates a set of design specifications that describe how each structural element is to appear, with comprehensive rules for every situation that can arise. The specifications enable a compositor to create a well-formatted document from a manuscript marked up by an editor and/or a designer.

Figure 9.1 illustrates a procedure that several journal publishers use to produce electronic journals. Articles received from authors are marked up with SGML tags, which describe the structure and content of the article. A so-called *style sheet* specifies how each structural element should appear. The SGML markup and the style sheet are input to rendering software, which creates the formatted document.

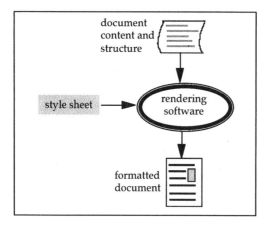

Figure 9.1
The relationship between structure and appearance.

In the early days of digital libraries, a common question was whether digital libraries would replace printed books. The initial discussion concentrated on questions of readability. Under what circumstances would people read from a screen rather than printed paper? With experience, people have realized that computers and books are not directly equivalent. Each has strengths that the other cannot approach. Computing allows powerful searching, which no manual system can provide. The "human factors" of a printed book are superb: it is portable, it can be annotated, it can be read anywhere, it can be spread out on a desktop or carried in one hand; no special equipment is needed to read it.

Since digital texts and printed materials serve different purposes, some publishers create print and online versions of the same materials. Figure 9.2 shows how a markup language can be used to manage texts that will be both printed and displayed on computer screens. With separate style sheets, a single document, represented by structural markup, can be rendered in different ways for different purposes. It can be displayed on a screen or printed. The layout and the graphic design may differ, but they are derived from the same source and they present the same content.

Strictly controlling the appearance of documents via SGML markup and style sheets is difficult. The ways in which textual materials are organized, displayed, and interpreted have many subtleties. Markup languages can

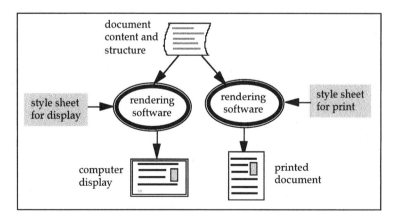

Figure 9.2
Alternative renderings of a single document.

represent almost all structures; however, the variety of structural elements in a document may be great, and the details of appearance that authors and designers can choose may be equally varied. For example, many articles in journals published by the Association for Computing Machinery contain mathematical notation. Authors often supply their articles in the TeX format, which provides precise control over the layout of mathematics. During the production process, it is converted to SGML markup. When rendered using a style sheet, the output may appear slightly different from the author's original.

Converting Text

Today most documents are created digitally, by means of computers, but libraries are full of valuable documents that exist only on paper.

Panel 9.1
The Oxford English Dictionary

The second edition of the *Oxford English Dictionary*, published in 1989, is a fine example of the use of a markup language to describe structure and content so that the same material can be used as the basis for a variety of products.

The first edition of the *OED* was created by James Morris and his colleagues over four decades. Nineteenth-century photographs of Morris at work in his grandly named Scriptorium in Oxford show a primitive shack filled with slips of paper. The dictionary was a landmark in lexicography, but it existed only as static printed pages. Keeping it up to date by hand proved impossible.

The first stage in producing the new edition was to type the entire text of the original edition into a database, identifying all the typographic distinctions. The typography of the original dictionary is loaded with semantic information. Capitals, boldface, italics, parentheses, smaller type, and other formatting conventions convey subtleties that are recorded nowhere else. A sophisticated computer program was written to extract this buried semantic information and to mark the textual elements with SGML tags. The effort involved a team of lexicographers in Oxford, a team of computational linguists at Waterloo University in Ontario, and corporate support from IBM.

The new *OED* is maintained as a computer database, in which the SGML markup is as important as the words. Lexicographers update it continually. A wide variety of publications can be created with minimal effort, including CD-ROMs, other digital versions, and printed books.

Consequently, there is a demand to convert print documents to computer formats. A conversion project involving important documents may both capture the appearance and identify the structure of the originals.

The basic conversion technique is scanning. A document is scanned by sampling its image on a grid of points. Each point is represented by a brightness code. In the simplest form, only black and white are distinguished. With a resolution of 300 dots per inch (horizontally and vertically), good images can be made of most printed pages. If the resolution is increased to 600 dots per inch, or if eight levels of gray are coded, the clarity becomes excellent, and halftone illustrations can be represented. High-quality artwork requires at least 24 bits per dot to represent color combinations. This creates very large files. The files are compressed for convenience in storage and processing, but even simple black-on-white text files need at least 50,000 bytes to store a single page.

A scanned page reproduces the appearance of the printed page but represents text simply as an image. In many applications, this is a poor substitute for marked-up text or even simple ASCII characters. In particular, it is not possible to search a page image for specific words. Serious scholars sometimes need to work from originals and often needs to know exactly how the originals look. On other occasions, an electronic version that identifies the structure is superior; for example, a marked-up electronic text is more convenient than an image of the original for creating a concordance, or for textual analysis, since the text can be tagged to indicate its linguistic structure or its historical antecedents. Therefore, the next stage of conversion is to provide an electronic text from the page image.

Optical character recognition is the technique of converting scanned images of characters to their equivalent characters. The basic technique is for a computer program to separate out the individual characters and then to compare each character to mathematical templates. Despite decades of research, optical character recognition remains an inexact process. The error rate varies with the legibility of the original. If the original document is clear and legible, the error rate is less than 1 percent. With low-quality materials, the error rate can be much higher. For many purposes, an error rate of even a fraction of a percent is too high; it corresponds to many incorrect characters on every page.

Various processes have been devised to get around these errors. One technique is to use several different character-recognition programs on the same materials in the hope that characters that cause difficulty for one program may be resolved by the others. Another approach is to use a dictionary to check the results. However, all high-quality conversion requires human proofreading. In some systems, a computer program displays the converted text on a screen and highlights doubtful words, providing suggestions that an editor may accept or correct. One organization that has developed efficient processes of this type is UMI, which converts huge numbers of theses every year. Since most of the theses it receives consist of new, clean copy, UMI achieves low error rates by using optical character recognition combined with manual resolution of doubtful words.

When the individual words have been recognized, the next stage of conversion is to identify the structure of a document and to tag headings and other structural elements. Despite steady progress by researchers, this too requires human proofreading and editing.

An alternative method of conversion, widely used in practice, is to retype the document from scratch and add markup tags manually. This approach is often cheaper than a combination of automatic and human processing. Since the work is labor intensive, it is usually carried out in countries where labor costs are low. One of the largest conversion projects is the Library of Congress's American Memory program. The documents to be converted are selected from the library's historic collections and are often less clear than recently printed documents. The conversion is carried out by contractors who guarantee a specified level of accuracy but are at liberty to carry out the conversion by any convenient method. All the early contractors decided that the most economical method was retyping.

Encoding Characters

ASCII
The most basic elements of text are characters, such as A and 5. It is important to distinguish between the concept of a character as a structural element and the various representations of that character stored within a computer or displayed for reading. A character is an abstract concept, independent of the encoding used to store it in a computer or the format used to display it.

Computers store characters as sequences of bits, each distinct character being encoded as a different sequence. Early computers had codes for the 26 letters of English (sometimes in upper case only), the ten digits, and a few punctuation marks and special symbols. The internal storage representation within most computers is still derived from this limited character set. Most modern computers use the American Standard Code for Information Interchange (ASCII).

Originally, ASCII represented each character by seven bits. This seven-bit encoding is known as *standard ASCII*. For example, the character A is encoded as the seven-bit sequence 1000001. Considered as a binary number, this sequence is the number 65. Hence, it is conventional to state that, in the standard ASCII code, the number 65 represents the character A. There are 128 different patterns that can be made with seven bits. Standard ASCII associates a specific character with each number between 0 and 127. Of these, the characters 0 through 31 represent control characters (e.g., "carriage return"). Table 9.1 shows the ASCII codes 32–127, known as the *printable ASCII* character set. (The space character is considered a printable character.)

The printable ASCII character set is truly a standard. The same codes are used in a very wide range of computers and applications. Therefore, the 96 printable ASCII characters are used in applications where interoperability has high priority. They are the only characters allowed in HTML and in many electronic mail systems. Almost every computer keyboard, display, and software program interprets these codes in the same way. There is also an extended version of ASCII that uses eight bits. It provides additional character encodings for the numbers 128–255, but it is not as widely accepted as seven-bit ASCII.

Unicode

Textual materials use a much wider range of characters than the printable ASCII set, which has its basis in the English language. Some European languages have additional letters or use diacritics. Even Old English requires extra characters. Greek and Russian have different alphabets. Rather than letters, Chinese, Japanese, and Korean use Han characters, which represents complete words or syllables with a single character. Indeed, the ASCII characters are not always adequate for current English. Certain disciplines

Table 9.1
Printable characters in seven-bit ASCII.

32	[space]	52	4	72	H	92	\	112	p
33	!	53	5	73	I	93	]	113	q
34	"	54	6	74	J	94	^	114	r
35	#	55	7	75	K	95	_	115	s
36	$	56	8	76	L	96	`	116	t
37	%	57	9	77	M	97	a	117	u
38	&	58	:	78	N	98	b	118	v
39	'	59	;	79	O	99	c	119	w
40	(	60	<	80	P	100	d	120	x
41	)	61	=	81	Q	101	e	121	y
42	*	62	>	82	R	102	f	122	z
43	+	63	?	83	S	103	g	123	{
44	,	64	@	84	T	104	h	124		
45	-	65	A	85	U	105	i	125	}
46	.	66	B	86	V	106	j	126	~
47	/	67	C	87	W	107	k	127	□
48	0	68	D	88	X	108	l		
49	1	69	E	89	Y	109	m		
50	2	70	F	90	Z	110	n		
51	3	71	G	91	[	111	o		

(e.g., mathematics, music, and chemistry) use highly refined notation that require large numbers of characters, and comprehension often depends critically on the use of accepted conventions of notation.

The computer industry sells its products worldwide and recognizes the need to support the characters used by their customers around the world. This is an area in which the much-maligned Microsoft Corporation has been a leader. Since it is impossible to represent all languages using the 256 possibilities represented by an eight-bit byte, there have been several attempts to represent a greater range of character sets using a larger number of bits. Recently, one of these approaches has emerged as a standard that most computer manufacturers and software houses are supporting. It is called *Unicode*.

In strict Unicode, each character is represented by 16 bits. This allows for up to 65,536 distinct characters. Through the painstaking efforts of a number of dedicated specialists, the scripts used in a wide range of languages can now be represented in Unicode.

Panel 9.2
Scripts Represented in Unicode

Version 2.0 of the Unicode standard contains 16-bit codes for 38,885 distinct characters. The encoding is organized by scripts rather than by languages. Where several languages use a closely related set of characters, the set of symbols that covers the group of languages is identified as a single script. The Latin script, for example, contains all the characters used by English, French, Spanish, German, and related languages. Unicode 2.0 also supports Arabic, Armenian, Bengali, Bopomofo, Cyrillic, Devanagari, Georgian, Greek, Gujarati, Gurmkhi, Han, Hangul, Hebrew, Hiragana, Kannada, Katakana, Lao, Malayalam, Oriya, Phonetic, Tamil, Telugu, Thai, and Tibetan scripts. In addition to the above primary scripts, there are a number of other collections of symbols, including numbers, general diacritics, general punctuation, general symbols, mathematical symbols, technical symbols, dingbats, arrows, blocks, box drawing forms, geometric shapes, and presentation forms. Several more modern languages (e.g., Ethiopic and Sinhala) will eventually be supported, and numerous archaic scripts (e.g., Aramaic, Etruscan, runes) will probably be supported in the future.

One especially important aspect of Unicode is its support for the Han characters used in Chinese, Japanese, and Korean. Unicode is compatible with Unihan, the result of an earlier project to reconcile the encoding systems previously used for those languages.

The acceptance of Unicode is not simply a result of the efforts of linguistic scholars. The developers have thought carefully about the relationship between Unicode and existing software. If every computer program had to be changed, Unicode would never be adopted. Therefore, there is a special representation of the Unicode characters, known as UTF-8, that allows gradual transformation of ASCII-based applications to the full range of Unicode scripts.

UTF-8 is an encoding that uses from one to six bytes to represent each Unicode character. The most commonly used characters are represented by a single byte, the next most common by two bytes, the least common by six bytes. The crucial aspect of the design is that each printable ASCII character is represented by a single byte, which is identical to the corresponding ASCII character. Thus, the same sequence of bytes can be interpreted as either Unicode characters (in UTF-8 representation) or as printable ASCII. For example, a page of HTML text created using printable ASCII characters requires no modification to be used with a program that expects its data to be in UTF-8 encoding.

Transliteration

Unicode is not the only method that has been used to represent a wide range of characters in computers. Another approach is *transliteration*, a systematic way of converting characters in one alphabet into another set of characters. For example, the German 'ö' is sometimes transliterated 'oe'. A phonetic system of transliteration known as pinyin is often used to represent Chinese (especially Mandarin) in the English alphabet. Transliteration may have been acceptable in the days when typewriters were manual devices with a physically constrained character set. With computers, however, transliteration should not be needed, and it should soon become ancient history.

Libraries were using a wide range of alphabets long before the computing industry paid attention to scripts. In fact, libraries were well advanced in this area in the days when most computers supported only upper-case letters. As a result, MARC catalogs and other library systems contain huge volumes of material that are encoded in pinyin and in other systems besides Unicode; they face a daunting task of conversion or coexistence.

SGML

Markup languages have been used since the early days of computing to describe the structure of text and the format in which text is to be displayed. Today, the most commonly used markup languages are those in the SGML family.

SGML is not a single markup language; it is a system used to define markup specifications. An individual specification defined within the SGML framework is called a *document type definition* (DTD). Many publishers and other agencies have developed their own private DTDs. Two DTDs that are of particular importance to scholarly libraries are the Text Encoding Initiative and the Encoded Archival Description, described in panel 9.3.

A DTD is built up from the general concepts of *entities* and *elements*. It defines what entities and elements are allowable in a particular class of documents, and it declares the *base character set encoding* used for the document.

Panel 9.3
DTDs for Scholarship

The Text Encoding Initiative was an early and very thorough effort to represent existing texts in digital form, with an emphasis on addressing the needs of humanities scholars. Texts from the past exhibit every technique ever used to represent text on paper, velum, papyrus, and even stone: print, handwriting, typewriting, and more. The documents include annotations, deletions, and damaged portions that cannot be read. Any character set ever used may be present.

SGML proved effective in describing these materials, but designing a suitable DTD was a challenge. It would have been easy to have created a DTD so complex as to be unwieldy. The solution was to use components to build a family of DTDs. The *core* tag set defines elements likely to be needed for all documents and therefore is included in all DTDs. Each DTD also has a *base* set of tags, which is selected from among those created for prose, verse, drama, dictionaries, and data files. Usually only one base set is appropriate for a given document. Finally, a variety of additional tag sets are available for specialized purposes. (The authors call this the Chicago Pizza model: every pizza has cheese and tomato sauce, one base, and optional extra toppings.)

The term *finding aid* covers a wide range of lists, inventories, indexes, and other textual documents created by archives, libraries, and museums to describe their holdings. Some finding aids provide fuller information than is normally contained within cataloging records; others are less specific and do not necessarily include detailed records for every item in a collection. Some are short; others run to hundreds of pages.

The Encoded Archival Description is a DTD used to encode electronic versions of archival aids. The first version of the EAD was developed by a team at the University of California at Berkeley. The effort drew on experience from the Text Encoding Initiative; the result reflects the conventions and practices established by archivists and the heavily structured nature of finding aids. Much of the information is derived from hierarchical relationships; however, there are many other interrelationships that one must recognize explicitly when encoding a finding aid for use in a digital library.

The EAD has been embraced by many archivists, who have worked collaboratively to refine it, to test it against existing finding aids, and to provide extensive documentation. It has become a highly specialized tool, tailored to a specialized community's needs to exchange and share information.

Entities are specified by identifiers that begin with an ampersand and end with a semicolon, such as the following.

α

&logo;

In a typical DTD, the allowable entities include most of the ASCII characters and some other characters (known as *character entities*); however, any symbol or group of symbols can be defined as a entity. The name of the entity is simply a name. In standard character sets, α is the entity used to encode the first letter of the Greek alphabet; however, a DTD could use this code for some entirely different purpose. The DTDs used by scientific publishers define as many as 4000 separate entities to represent all the special symbols and the variants used in scientific disciplines.

Entities provide a stream of symbols that can be grouped together into elements. A DTD can define any string as the name of an element. The element is bracketed by two tags in angle brackets, with a slash used to denote the end tag. Thus, the Text Encoding Initiative uses the tags <del> and </del> to bracket text that has been crossed out in a manuscript. For example, to mark the words "men and women" as crossed out, one would tag them as follows.

<del>men and women</del>

Examples of elements include the various types of headings, footnotes, expressions, and references. Elements can be nested in hierarchical relationships. Each DTD has a grammar that specifies the allowable relationships as a set of rules that can be processed by a computer program.

Simplified Versions

SGML is firmly established as a flexible approach for recording and storing high-quality texts. Its flexibility permits creators of textual materials to generate DTDs that are tailored to their particular needs. Panels 9.1 and 9.3 describe some examples. Publishers of scientific journals have developed their own DTDs, which they use to mark up journal articles as they are created and to store them on computers. Digital library projects, such as JSTOR and American Memory, use DTDs that are derived from the work of the Text Encoding Initiative.

The disadvantage of SGML's flexibility is the complexity of the software needed to process it. Though a program to parse and render a simple DTD is not hard to write, it is a forbidding task to create a general-purpose package that can parse any DTD, combine information from any style sheet and render the document either on a computer screen or printer. The market for such software is quite small. Only one company has persevered and created a general package for rendering SGML. Even this package is not perfect; it does not implement all of SGML, it runs only on some types of computers, and it uses its own private form of style sheets. Hence, full SGML is not suitable for use in digital libraries that emphasize interoperability with other systems.

HTML

The web has stimulated the development of simplified versions of SGML. HTML, the markup language used by the web, can be considered an unorthodox DTD. In many ways, however, it diverges from the philosophy of SGML, because it mixes structural information with format. At first HTML may have been intended for structural markup, relying on browsers to determine how to format the text for display, but its subsequent development has added a large number of features that give the designer of web pages control over how their material appears when rendered for screen display or printing. Panel 9.4 illustrates how far HTML has diverged from purely structural markup.

HTML continues to grow. Depending on one's viewpoint, the additions can be described as making HTML more powerful or as adding complexity and inconvenience. No one would dispute the great value of some additions, such as being able to embed images through the <img> tag (which was introduced in Mosaic). The value of other additions is a matter of opinion. Simple formatting commands such as <center> (introduced by Netscape) can do little harm, but other features have added a great deal of complexity. Perhaps the most notable of these are tables and frames. No longer can an author learn HTML in a morning, and no longer can a programmer write a program to render HTML in a week.

The tension between structural markup in HTML and formatting to control appearance has become serious. Many creators of web pages, wanting to control what the user sees, use every opportunity that HTML

Panel 9.4
Features of HTML

Most HTML tags occur in pairs. For example, <h1>Text</h1> indicates that the enclosed text is a first-level head. A few tags are self-contained and do not bracket any text; an example of this is <hr>, which indicates a horizontal rule. Elements are often nested; for example, a list may contain many paragraphs, and a table may contain other tables.

The examples below are typical of the features provided by HTML and illustrate how HTML combines structural markup with formatting and support for online applications. (There are many more features, and several of those shown below have wide selections of options.)

Tags used to describe the *structural elements* of a document include the following:

<body> (body of document)

<p> (paragraph)

<h1>, <h2>, . . . , <h6> (headings—six standard levels)

<em> (emphasis)

<ul>, <ol>,< dl> (unordered list, ordered list, definition list)

<table> (table).

Tags that define the appearance of the document when it is rendered for display on a computer or printed include the following:

 (line break)

<i> (italic)

<font> (details about the font to be used)

<center> (centered text)

<pre> (pre-formatted text).

Tags designed for online applications include the following:

<a> (anchor—used with hyperlinks)

<img> (location of an image)

<form> (online form).

provides to control appearance. One unfortunate trend is for designers to use structural elements to manipulate the design; many web pages are laid out as a single huge table, so that the designer can control the margins seen by the user. Skilled designers construct elegant web pages using such tricks. Less skilled designers impose on the users pages that are awkward to use. The worst abuses occur when a designer imposes a page layout that will not fit in the window size that the user chooses or that overrides the user's preferences, perhaps preventing a user with poor eyesight from using large type.

Almost all of the features that have been added to HTML have come from the developers of browsers, who have added features to enhance their products or to keep pace with their competitors. Some are indeed improvements, but others are not necessary. The World Wide Web Consortium and the Internet Engineering Task Force provide valuable coordination and attempt to provide standards, but the fundamental control of HTML is exercised by the two principal browser manufacturers, Netscape and Microsoft.

XML

XML is a variant of SGML that attempts to bridge the gap between the simplicity of HTML and the power of SGML. Simplicity is the key to the success of HTML, but simplicity is also its weakness. Every time a new feature is added to HTML it becomes less elegant, harder to use, and less of a standard shared by all browsers. SGML, in contrast, is so flexible that almost any text description is possible, but the flexibility comes at the cost of complexity. Even after many years, only a few specialists are really comfortable with SGML, and general-purpose software is still scarce.

XML is a subset of SGML designed explicitly for use with the web. The design is based on two important criteria: that it be simple to write computer programs to manipulate XML and that people and systems be able to migrate to XML from HTML with a minimum of pain.

The underlying character set for XML is 16-bit Unicode, and in particular the UTF-8 stream encoding. This encoding permits documents to be written in standard ASCII, but it supports a wide range of languages and character sets. For convenience, some character entities are pre-defined, such as < and > for the less-than and greater-than symbols. XML does not specify particular methods for representing mathematics, but a separate effort known as MathML is addressing that need.

Standard HTML is acceptable as XML with minimal modifications. One modification is that end tags are always needed. For example, in HTML, the tags <p> and </p> delimit the beginning and the end of a paragraph, but the </p> is optional when another paragraph follows. In XML the end tag is always needed. The other major modification concerns HTML tags that do not delimit any content. For example, the tag <br> indicates a line break. Standard HTML does not use a </br> tag. With XML, a line break is tagged either with the pair
</br> or with the special shortened tag <br/>.

Since XML is a subset of SGML, every document is based on a DTD, but the DTD does not have to be specified explicitly. If the file contains previously undefined pairs of tags, which delimit some section of a document, the parser automatically adds them to the DTD.

The developers of XML have worked hard to gain wide acceptance for their work. Their strategy follows the philosophy of the Internet mainstream. The design has been an open process hosted by the World Wide Web Consortium. From the start, members of the design team wrote demonstration software and distributed it freely to interested parties. Leading corporations, notably Microsoft and Netscape, have lent their support. This deliberate building of consensus and support seems to have been successful, and XML looks likely to become widely adopted.

Style Sheets

Markup languages describe the structure of a document. SGML and XML use tags to describe the semantics of a document and its component parts, but not the appearance of a document. Thus, SGML tags might be used to identify a section of text as a chapter heading, but they would not indicate that a chapter heading starts on a new page and is printed in a specific font and with specific alignment.

A common need is to take a document that has SGML or XML markup and render it according to a set of specific design specifications. For example, a publisher who creates journal articles according to a DTD may wish to render them in two different ways: printed output for conventional publication, and a screen format for delivery over the Internet and display on a computer screen. The first will be rendered in a format that is input to a typesetting machine. The second will be rendered in one of the formats that are supported by web browsers, usually HTML or PDF.

The process requires that the structural tags in the markup be translated into formats that can be displayed either in print or on a screen. A style sheet is used for this. For example, a DTD may define an element as a second-level heading, denoted by <h2> and </h2> tags. The style sheet may state that this should be displayed in 13-point Times Roman font, bold, left aligned. It will also specify other important characteristics, such as the appropriate line spacing and how to treat a heading that falls near the bottom of the page. A style sheet provides detailed instructions for how to render every conceivable valid document that has been marked up according to a specific DTD.

In creating style sheets, the power of SGML is a disadvantage. Readers are accustomed to beautifully designed books. Much of this beauty comes from the skill of the craftsmen who carry out the composition and page layout. Much of their work is art. The human eye is very sensitive; the details of how statistical tables are formatted or of the layout and pagination of an art book have never been reduced to mechanical rules. Style sheets can easily be very complex yet still fail to be satisfactory for the rendering of complex documents.

Since SGML is a general framework, people have been working on a general method of specifying style sheets for any DTD, called Document Style Semantics and Specification Language (DSSSL). This is a forbidding task. To date, DSSSL rendering programs have been written for some simple DTDs, but the general task appears too ambitious. It is much easier to create a satisfactory style sheet for a single DTD that is used in a well-understood context. Many books and journals are printed from SGML markup, with special-purpose style sheets, and the results can be excellent.

With HTML, there has been no formal concept of style sheets. The markup combines structural elements (such as various types of lists) with formatting tags (such as those that specify bold or italic). The tags provide general guidance about appearance, which individual browsers interpret and adapt to the computer display in use. The appearance that the user sees comes from a combination of the markup provided by the designer of a web page, the formatting conventions built into a browser, and options chosen by the user. Authors of HTML documents wishing for greater control can embed various forms of scripts, applets, and plug-ins.

Panel 9.5 describes CSS (Cascading Style Sheets) and XSL (Extensible Style Language), which are methods of providing style sheets for (respectively) HTML and XML. The developers of XML, realizing that the greatest challenge to be faced by XML before it becomes widely accepted is how to control the appearance of documents, have been supportive of both CSS and XSL. It is still too early to know what will succeed, but the combination is promising. These methods have the important concept of laying down precise rules for actions to be taken when the styles specified by the designer and the user disagree.

Page-Description Languages

Since creators and readers both attribute much importance to the appearance of documents, it is desirable to have methods that specify the appearance of a document directly, without structural markup. The methods used to accomplish this differ greatly in their details, but the underlying objective is the same: to render textual materials with the same graphic quality and precision seen in the best documents printed by traditional methods. This is not easy. Few things in life are as pleasant to use as a well-printed book. Over the years, typography, page layout, paper manufacturing, and binding have been refined to a high level of usability. Early text-formatting methods were designed for printed output, but display on computer screens has become equally important. This section looks at three page-description languages: TeX, PostScript, and PDF. These three languages have different objectives and address them differently, but they are all practical approaches that perform well in production systems.

TeX

TeX, the earliest of the three languages, was developed by Donald Knuth around 1980. It is aimed at high-quality printing, with a special emphasis on mathematics. In addition to the numerous special characters, mathematical notation relies on complex expressions that are not naturally represented as a single sequence of characters. TeX provides rules for encoding mathematics as a sequence of ASCII characters for input, storage, and manipulation by computer, with tags to indicate the format for display.

Panel 9.5
Cascading Style Sheets and Extensible Style Language

Markup languages describe the structural elements of a document. Style sheets specify how the elements appear when rendered on a computer display or printed on paper. Cascading Style Sheets (CSS) were developed for use with HTML markup. The Extensible Style Language (XSL) is an extension of CSS for XML markup. Much as XML is a simplified version of full SGML that provides a simple conversion from HTML, XSL is derived from Document Style Semantics and Specification Language (DSSSL), and any CSS style sheet can be converted to XSL by a purely mechanical process. The original hope was that XSL would be a subset of DSSSL, but there are divergences. Currently XSL is only a specification, but there is every hope that, as XML is widely adopted, XSL will become equally important.

In CSS, a rule defines styles to be applied to selected elements of a document. For example, the simple rule

h1 {color: blue}

states that for elements tagged h1 (the HTML tag for top-level headings) the property color should have the value blue. More formally, each rule consists of a *selector*, which selects certain elements of the document, and a *declaration* (enclosed in braces, and having two parts, separated by a colon: a *property* and a *value*), which states the style to be applied to the elements.

A CSS style sheet is a list of rules. Various conventions are provided to simplify the writing of rules. For example,

h1, h2 {font-family: sans-serif; color: blue}

specifies that headings h1 and h2 are to be displayed in blue in a sans-serif font.

The markup for an HTML document defines a structure that can be represented as a hierarchy. Thus, headings, paragraphs, and lists are elements of the HTML body; list items are elements within lists; and lists can be nested within other lists. The rules in CSS style sheets also inherit styles from other rules. If no rule explicitly selects an element, it inherits the rules for the elements higher in the hierarchy. For example, consider the following pair of rules.

body {font-family: serif}

h1, h2 {font-family: sans-serif}

Headings h1 and h2 are elements of the HTML body but have an explicit rule: they will be displayed in a sans-serif font. Because in this example there is no explicit rule for paragraphs or lists, they inherit the styles that apply to body, which is higher up the hierarchy; thus, they will be displayed in a serif font.

A style sheet must be associated with an HTML page. The designer has several options, including embedding the style at the head of a page and providing a link to an external file that contains the style sheet. Every browser has its own implicit style sheet, which may be modified by the user. A user may have a private style sheet.

Since several style sheets may apply to the same page, conflicts can occur if rules conflict. Mechanisms based on simple principles have been developed to handle these situations. The most fundamental principle is that when rules conflict, one is selected and the others are ignored. Rules that explicitly select elements have priority over inherited rules. The most controversial convention is that when the designer's rule conflicts directly with the user's, the designer's rule has precedence. A user who wishes to override this rule can flag a rule "!important." Though this is awkward, it does permit special style sheets to be developed—e.g., for users with poor eyesight who wish to specify large type.

Most users make use of one of two TeX packages: plainTeX and LaTeX. Each of these packages defines a set of formatting tags that cover most situations that are normally encountered in typesetting. Closely allied with TeX is a system for designing fonts called Metafont. Knuth has taken great pains to produce versions of his standard font for a wide range of computer systems.

TeX remains unsurpassed for the preparation of mathematical papers. It is widely used by authors in mathematics, physics, and related fields.

PostScript

PostScript was the first product of Adobe Systems, which spun off from Xerox in 1984. PostScript is a programming language used to create graphical output for printing. Few people ever write programs in PostScript, but many computers have printer routines that will take text or graphics and create an equivalent PostScript program. The program can then be sent to a printer controller that executes the PostScript program and creates control sequences to drive the printer.

Explicit support for fonts is one of PostScript's strengths. Much of the early success of the Apple Macintosh computer came from the combination of bit-mapped designs on the screen with PostScript printers that provided a quality of output previously available only on very expensive computers. With both laser printing and screen display, characters are built up from small dots. Simple laser printers use 300 dots per inch, and typesetting machines may have a resolution of 1200 dots per inch or more, but most computer screens are about 75 dots per inch. The fonts that appear attractive on a computer screen are not quite the same as the ones used for printing, and the displays of text on a screen must be fitted to the coarse resolution. Usually, the operating system functions that display text on a screen are different from the PostScript commands used for printing. Unless great care is taken, this can lead to different page breaks and other unacceptable variations.

Although PostScript is primarily a graphical output language, and although its initial impact was in the area of representing computer output to laser printers, PostScript programs are also used in other applications. One of PostScript's uses is to store and exchange representations of any text or graphical output. PostScript is not ideal for this purpose, however, since the language has many variations and since the programs make assumptions about the capabilities of the computer on which they will be executed.

Portable Document Format

Adobe built on its experience with PostScript to create Portable Document Format (PDF), a better format for storing page images in a portable format that is independent of any particular computer. PDF, the most popular page-description language in use today, consists of a powerful format and a set of tools for creating, storing, and displaying documents in it.

PDF is widely used in commercial document-management systems, but some digital libraries have been reluctant to use it. One reason is technical. PDF is best suited for representing documents that were generated from computer originals. PDF can also store bit-mapped images, and Adobe provides optical-character-recognition software for the creation of PDF files, but many of PDF's advantages are lost when it is used to store image files. The file sizes can be unpleasantly large, and much of the flexibility that digital libraries require is lost.

In addition, some digital libraries and archives reject PDF because the format is proprietary. There is a fear that the decision to use PDF in a digital library is more vulnerable to future events than using a format blessed by one of the standards bodies. This reasoning appears misguided. PDF had its first success in corporate America, which welcomes well-supported commercial products. The academic and scholarly community should recognize that a format maintained by a corporation may be more stable in

Panel 9.6
Portable Document Format

Adobe's Portable Document Format (PDF) is an important format. It is also interesting as an example of how a corporation can create a standard, make it available to the world, and yet still generate good business. PDF is a document-representation format that is independent of applications and computer systems. A PDF document consists of pages, made up of text, graphics, and images, and supporting data. However, PDF pages can go beyond the static print view of a page, since PDF supports hyperlinks, searching, and other features that are only possible electronically.

PDF is an evolution of the PostScript programming language (also created by Adobe). One way to generate a PDF file is to divert a stream of data that would usually go to a printer. Alternatively, the file can be converted from PostScript or from another format, then stored, transmitted over a network, displayed on a screen, or printed.

PDF has many technical strengths. When viewed on a computer screen, most PDF documents are very legible, yet they the retain the design characteristics of print. Except when they include bit-mapped images, the files are of moderate size. If the computer that is displaying a PDF document does not have the fonts that were used to generate it, font descriptors enable the PDF viewer to generate an artificial font, which is usually close to the original. Although it has difficulty distinguishing among certain types of files and working with unusual fonts, PDF has become a important format for online documents.

PDF provides many features that users want, including the creation of hyperlinks (either within the document or to external URLs). The PDF viewer provides a tool for searching for words within text, though searching across documents is a problem. Annotation is supported. Printer support is excellent. There is even a method by which the creator of a document can prevent users from printing or otherwise using the document in ways that the creator has not approved.

After a hesitant introduction, Adobe has marketed PDF shrewdly, in part by making excellent PDF viewers for almost all types of computers freely available over the Internet. Adobe makes money from people who buy products that are used to create PDF files, not from the users of those files; thus, it illustrates how a corporation can create a standard, make it available to the world, and yet still generate good business. Adobe owns the copyright in the PDF specification; however, to promote the use of PDF as an interchange format, it gives broad permission for creating PDF files, for writing applications that produce PDF output, and for writing software that reads and processes PDF files. Competitors could create products that would undercut those that Adobe sells, but Adobe accepts that risk.

the long run than official standards that are not backed by good products and a wide user base. The definition of PDF is widely published, and the broad use of this format in commercial applications guarantees that programs will be available for it even if Adobe should go out of business or cease to support it.

Structure versus Appearance of Documents

This chapter began with a discussion of two requirements for storing documents in digital libraries: representations of structure and of appearance. They should not be seen as alternatives or competitors, but as twin needs, both of which deserve attention. In some applications a single representation serves both purposes, but many digital libraries are storing two versions of each document. Textual materials are at the heart of digital libraries and electronic publishing. Authors and readers are very demanding, but methods suitable for meeting their demands exist.

10

Information Retrieval and Descriptive Metadata

Helping users find information is among the core services provided by digital libraries. This chapter, the first of two on this general subject, begins with a discussion of *descriptive metadata*—the catalogs, indexes, and other summary information used to describe objects in a digital library. This is followed by a discussion of the methods by which bodies of text are searched for specific information. Chapter 11 extends the concepts discussed here to discuss distributed searching—that is, searching for information that is spread across separate collections or scattered over many computer systems.

These two chapters concentrate on methods used to search for specific information. Direct searching is just one of the strategies that people use to discover information, however. Browsing—unstructured exploration of a body of information—is a popular and effective method for discovering the unexpected. Most traditional libraries arrange their collections by subject so as to facilitate browsing. Dewey Decimal classification and Library of Congress classification provide both subject information and a hierarchical structure that can be used to organize collections. The most widely used web information service, Yahoo, is fundamentally a classification of web resources augmented by searching. Digital libraries, with their hyperlinks, lend themselves to strategies that combine searching and browsing.

The range of the needs of users of digital libraries illustrates why information discovery is such a complex topic and why no single approach satisfies all users or suits all materials. The objective of a *comprehensive search* is to find everything on a specified topic. Serious scholarly, scientific, or legal study typically begins with a comprehensive search to discover prior work in the field. In a *known-item search*, the user is looking for a specific item, such as the opening chapter of *Moby Dick*. Often the reference is not perfect and a search must be done to find the item; however, there is indeed a specific item, and the user will recognize it when it is found. Then there are *searches for facts*. Facts (e.g., the name of the capital of Barbados, or the atomic weight of mercury) are specific items of information that may be found in many sources of information. A search for a fact is complete when the fact is found. The source of the fact must be reliable, but there may be many possible sources. *Overview information on a topic* is yet another common need. A request such as "How does one organize a wedding?" or "What is public-key encryption?" may lead to many suitable sources of information, but usually the user wants a small selection. Once one useful item has been found, a user may wish to know about *related items*. In research, for example, a common question is "Is there any later research that builds on the work reported in this article?"

Descriptive Metadata

Many methods of information discovery do not search the actual objects in the collections; rather, they work from descriptive metadata about the objects. The metadata for an object may be a catalog entry, an indexing record, or an abstract. Descriptive metadata usually is stored separately from the objects that it describes, but sometimes it is embedded in the objects.

Descriptive metadata is usually expressed as text; however, it can be used to describe information that is in formats other than text, such as images, sound recordings, maps, and computer programs. A single catalog can combine records for all genres, media, and formats. This enables users of digital libraries to discover materials in all media by searching textual records.

Descriptive metadata is usually created by professionals. Library catalogs and scientific indexes represent huge investments of work by skilled people, sustained over decades or even centuries. This economic fact is crucial to understanding current trends. On one hand, it is important to build on the investments and the expertise behind them. On the other, there is a great incentive to find cheaper and faster ways to create metadata, either by automatic indexing or through the use of computer tools that enhance human expertise.

Catalogs

Catalog records are short records that provide summary information about a library object. The word *catalog* is applied to records that have a consistent structure, organized according to systematic rules. An *abstract* is a short summary of a longer document. Other types of indexing records are less formal than a catalog record but have more structure than a simple abstract.

Library catalogs serve many functions, not only information retrieval. Some catalogs provide comprehensive bibliographic information that cannot be derived directly from the objects. This includes information about authors or the provenance of museum artifacts. For managing collections, catalogs contain administrative information, such as where items are stored (whether online or on library shelves). Catalogs are usually much smaller than the collections they represent; in conventional libraries, materials that are stored on miles of shelving are described by records that can be contained in a group of card drawers at one location or in an online database. Indexes to digital libraries can be mirrored for higher performance and greater reliability.

Information in catalog records is divided into *fields* and *subfields*, with tags to identify them. For example, there might be a field for an author's name with a subfield for the author's surname. The Anglo-American Cataloging Rules and the MARC format are used for many types of material, including monographs, serials, and archives. Because of the labor required to create a detailed catalog record, materials are cataloged once (often by a national library, such as the Library of Congress) and the records are then distributed to other libraries through utilities such as the OCLC.

The role of MARC and the related cataloging rules in digital libraries is a subject of debate. How far can traditional methods of cataloging migrate to support new formats, media types, and methods of publishing? MARC cataloging retains its importance for conventional materials. Librarians have extended it to some of the newer types of object found in digital libraries, but it has not been adopted by organizations other than traditional libraries.

Abstracting and Indexing Services

The sciences and other technical fields rely on abstracting and indexing services more than they rely on catalogs. Each scientific discipline has a service to help users find information in journal articles—e.g., Medline for medicine and biology, Chemical Abstracts for chemistry, and Inspec for physics, computing, and related fields. Each service indexes the articles in a large set of journals. The record for an article includes basic bibliographic information (authors, title, date, etc.) and subject information, organized for information retrieval. The details differ, but the services have many similarities. Since abstracting and indexing services emerged at a time when computers were slower and more expensive than they are today, the information is structured to support simple textual searches; however, the records have proved useful in more flexible systems.

Scientific users often want information on a specific subject. Because of the subtleties of language, subject searching is unreliable unless there is indexing information that describes the subject of each object. The subject

Panel 10.1
Medical Subject Headings

The National Library of Medicine has provided information-retrieval services for medicine and related fields since the 1960s. Since in medicine (a complex field with a huge terminology) it is often the case that the same concept may be described by scientific terms or by any of multiple vernacular terms, the NLM has developed a controlled-vocabulary, known as MeSH, that provides a thesaurus of subject headings for each of the 400,000 articles it indexes every year and for every book acquired by the library. These subject headings can be used for information retrieval. In addition to MeSH (which has about 18,000 primary headings), there is a separate thesaurus of about 80,000 chemical terms. The terms in MeSH are organized in a hierarchy. At the top are general terms, such as *anatomy*, *organisms*, and *diseases*. Going down the hierarchy, anatomy (for example) is divided into sixteen topics, beginning with *body regions* and *musculoskeletal system*. *Body regions* is further divided into sections, such as *abdomen*, *axilla*, and *back*. Some of the sections are then subdivided. Thousands of cross-references are provided.

The success of MeSH depends on the professionals who maintain the thesaurus and on those who assign subject terms to documents. Successful use of MeSH also depends on users or reference librarians who understand medicine and are able to formulate queries using the terms and the structures that MeSH employs.

Panel 10.2
The Art and Architecture Thesaurus

The Art and Architecture Thesaurus was developed by the J. Paul Getty Trust as a controlled vocabulary for describing and retrieving information on fine art, architecture, decorative art, and material culture. It has almost 120,000 terms for objects, textual materials, images, architecture and culture from all periods and all cultures, with an emphasis on Western civilization. The thesaurus can be used by archives, museums, and libraries to describe items in their collections. It also be used to search for materials.

Serious work on this thesaurus began in the early 1980s, when the Internet was in its infancy; however, the data was created in a flexible format that allowed the creation of many versions, including an open-access version on the web, a printed book, and various computer formats. The Getty Trust explicitly organized the thesaurus so that it could be used by computer programs for information retrieval and for natural-language processing.

The Art and Architecture Thesaurus is arranged in seven categories, each containing a hierarchies of terms. The categories are *associated concepts, physical attributes, styles and periods, agents, activities, materials,* and *objects.* A single concept is represented by a cluster of terms, one of which is established as the *descriptor* (i.e., the preferred term). The thesaurus provides not only the terminology for objects but also the vocabulary used to describe them (e.g., style, period, shape, color, construction, use) and scholarly concepts such as theories and criticism.

The costs of developing and maintaining a large, specialized thesaurus are huge. Even in a mature field, such as art and architecture, terminology is changing continually, and the technical staff has to support new technology. Even though the Getty Trust is extremely rich, developing the thesaurus took many years.

information can be an abstract, keywords, subject terms, or other information. Some services ask authors to provide keywords or an abstract, but this leads to gross inconsistencies. It is far better to have professional indexers assign subject information to each item.

An effective but expensive approach is to use a *controlled vocabulary.* That is, where several terms could be used to describe a concept, one is used exclusively. The indexer is given a list of approved subject terms and rules for applying them. No other terms are permitted. This is the approach used for the Library of Congress subject headings and the National Library of Medicine's MeSH headings.

The controlled-vocabulary approach requires trained indexers. It also requires skilled users, because the terms used in a search query must be consistent with the terms assigned by the indexer. Medicine in the United States is especially fortunate in having a cadre of reference librarians. In digital libraries, the trend is to provide users with tools that permit them to find information directly, without the help of a reference librarian. A thesaurus, such as MeSH or the Art and Architecture Thesaurus, can be used to relate the terminology that a user provides to the controlled terms used in indexing.

The Dublin Core
Since 1995, an international group led by Stuart Weibel of OCLC has been working to devise a set of simple metadata elements that can be applied to a wide variety of digital library materials. The set of elements developed by this group is known as the Dublin Core, after Dublin, Ohio, the home of OCLC, where the first meeting was held. Several hundred people have participated in Dublin Core workshops and have discussed the design by electronic mail. Their spirit of cooperation is a model of how individuals with diverse interests can work together. The fifteen elements they have selected are summarized in panel 10.3.

Simplicity is both the strength and the weakness of the Dublin Core. Whereas traditional cataloging rules are long and complicated, requiring professional training to apply effectively, the Dublin Core can be described simply. However, simplicity conflicts with precision. The team has struggled with this tension. The initial aim was to create a single set of metadata elements for untrained people who publish electronic materials to use in describing their work. Some people continue to hold this minimalist view; they would like to see a simple set of rules that anyone can apply. Others prefer the benefits that come from more tightly controlled cataloging rules and would accept the additional labor and cost. They point out that extra structure in the elements results in extra precision in the metadata records. For example, if entries in a subject field are drawn from the Dewey Decimal Classification, it is helpful to record that fact in the metadata. To further enhance the effectiveness of the metadata for information retrieval, several of the elements are expected to have recommended lists of values. Thus, there might be a specified set of types, and indexers would be advised to select from the list.

Panel 10.3
The Dublin Core

The following fifteen elements constitute the metadata set of the Dublin Core. All elements are optional, and all can be repeated. (These descriptions were condensed from the official Dublin Core definitions with the permission of the design team.)

Title   The name given to the resource by the creator or publisher.

Creator   The person or organization primarily responsible for the intellectual content of the resource (authors in the case of written documents; artists, photographers, or illustrators in the case of visual resources).

Subject   The topic of the resource. Typically, subject will be expressed as a keyword or a phrase that describes the subject or the content of the resource. The use of controlled vocabularies and formal classification schemes is encouraged.

Description   A textual description of the content of the resource, including abstracts in the case of document-like objects and content descriptions in the case of visual resources.

Publisher   The entity responsible for making the resource available in its present form—e.g., a publishing house, a university department, or a corporate entity.

Contributor   A person or organization not specified in a creator element that has made significant intellectual contributions to the resource but whose contribution is secondary to any person or organization specified in a creator element—e.g., an editor, a transcriber, an illustrator.

Date   A date associated with the creation or availability of the resource.

Type   The category of the resource—e.g., home page, novel, poem, working paper, preprint, technical report, essay, dictionary.

Format   The data format of the resource (used to identify software and possibly hardware that might be needed to display or operate the resource).

Identifier   A string or number used to uniquely identify the resource. Examples for networked resources include URLs and URNs.

Source   Information about a second resource from which the present resource is derived.

Language   The language of the intellectual content of the resource.

Relation   An identifier of a second resource and its relationship to the present resource. This element permits links between related resources and resource descriptions to be indicated. Two examples are an edition of a work and a chapter of a book.

Coverage   Spatial locations and temporal durations characteristic of the resource.

Rights   A rights-management statement, an identifier linked to such a statement, or an identifier linked to a service providing information about rights management for the resource.

A proposed strategy is to have two options: "minimalist" and "structuralist." The minimalist option will meet the original criterion of being usable by people who have no formal training. The structured option will be more complex, requiring fuller guidelines and a trained staff.

Automatic Indexing

Cataloging and indexing are expensive when carried out by skilled professionals. A rule of thumb is that each record costs about $50 to create and distribute. In certain fields, such as medicine and chemistry, the demand for information is great enough to justify the expense of comprehensive indexing, but these disciplines are the exceptions. Usually the cataloging of a monograph is restricted to an overall record, without detailed cataloging of individual topics. Most items in museums, archives, and library special collections are not cataloged or indexed individually.

In digital libraries, many items are worth collecting but the costs of cataloging them individually cannot be justified. The collections may be very large, and continual changes in objects may inhibit long-term investments in cataloging. Each object may go through several versions in quick succession. A single object may be composed of many other objects, all changing independently. New categories of objects are being devised continually, while others are being discarded. Often the user's perception of an object is the result of executing a computer program and is different with each interaction. These factors increase the complexity and the cost of cataloging digital library materials.

For all these reasons, professional cataloging and indexing are likely to be less central to digital libraries than they are to traditional libraries. The alternative is to use computer programs to create index records automatically. Records created by automatic indexing are normally of poor quality, but they are inexpensive. A powerful search system will go a long way toward compensating for the low quality of individual records. The web search programs, which build their indexes automatically, prove this point. The records are not very good, but the success of the search services shows that the indexes are useful. At least they are better than the alternative, which is to have nothing.

Much of the development that led to automatic indexing came out of research in text skimming. A typical problem in that field is how to organize electronic mail. A user has a large volume of electronic mail messages and wants to file them by subject. A computer program is expected to read through them and assign them to subject areas. This is difficult for humans to carry out consistently, and it is very difficult for a computer program, but steady progress has been made. The programs look for clues within the document—structural elements (such as the subject field of an electronic mail message), linguistic clues, or simply key words.

Automatic indexing also depends on clues to be found in a document. The first of the examples in panel 10.4 is a success, because the underlying web document provides useful clues. The AltaVista indexing program was able to identify the title and author. For example, the page includes the following tagged element.

<title>Digital library concepts</title>

Panel 10.4
Automatic Indexing

The two records reproduced below (lightly edited versions of records that were created by AltaVista in 1997) are typical of indexing records created automatically by web search programs.

Digital Library Concepts
Key Concepts in the Architecture of the Digital Library. William Y. Arms Corporation for National Research Initiatives Reston, Virginia . . . http://www.dlib.org/dlib/July95/07arms.html - size 16K - 7-Oct-96 - English

Repository References
Notice: HyperNews at union.ncsa.uiuc.edu will be moving to a new machine and domain very soon. Expect interruptions. Repository References. This is a page. http://union.ncsa.uiuc.edu/HyperNews/get/www/repo/references.html - size 5K - 12-May-95 - English

The first example shows automatic indexing at its best. It gives the author, the title, the date, and the location of an article in an electronic journal. For many purposes, it is an adequate substitute for a record created by a professional indexer.

The second example illustrates some of the shortcomings of automatic indexing. No one who understood the content would bother to index this web page. The information about location and date is probably all right; however, the title is strange, and the body of the record is simply the first few words of the page.

The author inserted these tags to guide web browsers in displaying the article. They are equally useful in providing guidance to automatic indexing programs.

One of the potential uses of markup languages such as SGML and XML is that the structural tags can be used by automatic indexing programs to build records for information retrieval. Within the text of a document, the string 'Marie Celeste' might be the name of a person, a book, a song, a ship, a publisher, or a play, or it might not even be a name. With structural markup, the string can be identified and labeled for what it is. Thus, information provided by the markup can be used to distinguish specific categories of information, such as author, title, or date.

Automatic indexing is fast and cheap. The exact costs are commercial secrets, but they are a tiny fraction of one cent per record. For the cost of a single record created by a professional cataloger or indexer, computer programs can generate 100,000 or more records. It is economically feasible to index huge numbers of items on the Internet, and even to index them again at frequent intervals.

Creators of catalogs and indexes can balance costs against perceived benefits. The most expensive forms of descriptive metadata are the traditional methods used for library catalogs and by indexing and abstracting services. The structuralist Dublin Core will be moderately expensive, keeping most of the benefits while saving some costs. The minimalist Dublin Core will be cheaper, but not free. Automatic indexing has the poorest quality at a tiny cost.

Attaching Metadata to Content

Descriptive metadata must be associated with the material it describes. In the past, descriptive metadata has usually been stored separately, as an external catalog or index. This has many advantages, but it requires links between the metadata and the object referenced. Some digital libraries are moving in the other direction, storing the metadata and the data together (either by embedding the metadata in the object or by having two tightly linked objects). This approach is convenient in distributed systems and for long-term archiving, since it guarantees that computer programs have access to the data and to the metadata at the same time.

Mechanisms for associating metadata with web pages have been a subject of considerable debate. For an HTML page, a simple approach is to embed the metadata in the page using the special HTML tag <meta>, which comes from an HTML description of the Dublin Core element set. Table 10.1 illustrates the use of <meta> tags. (The choice of <meta> tags is a system-design decision. The Dublin Core itself does not specify how the metadata is associated with the material.)

Since meta tags cannot be used with file types other than HTML and rapidly become cumbersome, a number of organizations working through the World Wide Web Consortium have developed a more general structure known as the Resource Description Framework (RDF). RDF is described in panel 10.5.

Techniques of Information Retrieval

Information retrieval is a field in which computer scientists and information professionals have worked together for many years. It is still an active area of research, and it is one of the few areas of digital libraries to have a systematic methodology for measuring the performance of various methods.

Basic Concepts and Terminology

The various methods of information retrieval use some simple concepts to search large bodies of information. A *query* is a string of text describing the information that the user is seeking. Each word of the query is called a

Table 10.1
Metadata represented with HTML <meta> tags.

<meta name="DC.subject" content="dublin core metadata element set">

<meta name="DC.subject" content="networked object description">

<meta name="DC.publisher" content="OCLC Online Computer Library Center, Inc.">

<meta name="DC.creator" content="Weibel, Stuart L., weibel@oclc.org.">

<meta name="DC.creator" content="Miller, Eric J., emiller@oclc.org.">

<meta name="DC.title" content="Dublin Core Element Set Reference Page">

<meta name="DC.date" content="1996-05-28">

<meta name="DC.form" scheme="IMT" content="text/html">

<meta name="DC.language" scheme="ISO639" content="en">

<meta name="DC.identifier" scheme="URL"
content="http://purl.oclc.org/metadata/dublin_core">

Panel 10.5
The Resource Description Framework

The Resource Description Framework (RDF) is a method for the exchange of metadata that was developed by the World Wide Web Consortium, drawing on concepts from several other efforts (including the PICS format for rating labels identifying characteristics such as violence and pornography in web pages.) The Dublin Core team is working closely with the RDF designers.

A metadata scheme, such as Dublin Core, can be considered as having three aspects: *semantics*, *syntax*, and *structure*. The semantics describes how to interpret concepts such as *date* and *creator*. The syntax specifies how the metadata is expressed. The structure defines the relationships among metadata elements (e.g., day, month, and year as components of a date). RDF provides a simple, general structural model for expressing syntax. It does not stipulate the semantics used by a metadata scheme. XML is used to describe a metadata scheme and for exchange of information among computer systems and among schemes.

The structural model consists of *resources*, *property types*, and *values*. Consider the simple statement that Shakespeare is the author of the play *Hamlet*. In the Dublin Core metadata scheme, this can be represented as follows:

Resource		Property type		Value
Hamlet	→	creator	→	Shakespeare
	→	type	→	play

A different metadata scheme might use 'author' in place of creator, and might use 'type' with an entirely different meaning. Therefore, the RDF markup would make explicit that this metadata is expressed in the Dublin core scheme, as follows.

<DC:creator>Shakespeare</DC:creator>
<DC:type>play</DC:type>

To complete this example, *Hamlet* must be identified more precisely. If it were referenced by the imaginary URL http://hamlet.org/, the full RDF record, with XML markup, would be as follows.

<RDF:RDF>
   <RDF:description RDF:about = "http://hamlet.org/">
      <DC:creator>Shakespeare</DC:creator>
      <DC:type>play</DC:type>
   </RDF:description>
</RDF:RDF>

The markup in this record makes explicit that 'description' and 'about' are defined in the RDF scheme, while 'creator' and 'type' are defined in the

Dublin Core (DC). One more step is needed to complete this record: the schemes RDF and DC must be defined as XML namespaces.

The RDF structural model permits resources to have property types that refer to other resources. For example, a database might include a record about Shakespeare containing metadata about him, such as when and where he lived and the various ways he spelled his name. The DC:Creator property type could reference this record as follows.

<DC:creator RDF:about = "http://people.net/WS/">

In this manner, arbitrarily complex metadata descriptions can be built up from simple components. Using the RDF framework for syntax and structure and using XML representation, computer systems can associate metadata with digital objects and can exchange metadata from different schemes.

search term. A query can be a single search term, a string of terms, a phrase in natural language, or a stylized expression using special symbols.

Some methods of information retrieval compare the query with every word in the entire text, without distinguishing the function of the various words; this is called *full-text searching*. Other methods identify bibliographic or structural fields (such as author or heading) and allow searching on specified field (e.g., "author = Gibbon"); this is called *fielded searching*. Full-text and fielded searching are both powerful, and modern methods of information retrieval often use them in combination.

Whereas fielded searching requires some method of identifying the fields, full-text searching does not require such support. With the power of modern computers, full-text searching can be effective even on unprocessed text; however, heterogeneous texts of varying length, style, and content are difficult to search effectively, and the results can be inconsistent. Although the legal information systems Westlaw and Lexis are based on full-text searching, when descriptive metadata is available most services prefer either fielded searching or free text searching of abstracts and other metadata.

Some words, such as common pronouns, conjunctions, and auxiliary verbs, occur so frequently that they are of little value for retrieval. Most systems have a list of common words that are ignored in queries. This is called a *stop list*. The selection of stop words is difficult. The choice clearly depends on the language of the text; it may also be related to the subject matter. For this reason, instead of having a predetermined stop list, some systems use statistical methods to identify the most commonly used words and reject them. Even then, no system is perfect. There is always the danger that a perfectly sensible query—for example, "To be or not to be?"—may be rejected because every word is in the stop list.

The basic computational method that is used to compare search terms against a collection of textual documents is to use an *inverted file* as described in panel 10.6.

Boolean searching

A *Boolean query* consists of two or more search terms related by a logical operator, such as *and, or,* or *not.* Consider the query "abacus *and* actor" applied to the inverted file in panel 10.6. The query includes two search terms separated by a Boolean operator. The first stage in carrying out this query is to read the inverted lists for 'abacus' (documents 3 and 19) and for 'actor' (documents 2, 19, and 29). The next stage is to compare the two lists for documents that are in both lists. Both words are in document 19, which is the only document that satisfies the query. When the inverted lists are short, Boolean searches with a few search terms are almost as fast as simple queries, but the computational requirements increase dramatically with large collections of information and complex queries.

Inverted files can be used to extend the basic concepts of Boolean searching. Since the location of words within documents are recorded in the inverted lists, they can be used for searches that specify the relative position of two words, such 'West' followed by 'Virginia.' They can also be used with *truncation*—i.e., searching for words that begin with certain letters. In many search systems, the query "comp?" will lead to a search for all words that begin with the letters c, o, m, and p. This will find the related words 'compute', 'computing', 'computer', 'computers', and 'computation'. Unfortunately, this approach will not distinguish unrelated words that begin with the same letters, such as 'company.'

Ranking closeness of match

Boolean searching is a powerful tool, but it finds only exact matches. A search for 'library' will miss 'libraries'. 'John Smith' and 'J. Smith' are not treated as the same name. Yet everyone recognizes that these are similar. A range of techniques address such difficulties.

Panel 10.6
Inverted Files

An *inverted file* is a list of the words in a set of documents and their locations within those documents. Here is a small part of an inverted file:

Word	Document	Location
abacus	3	94
	19	7
	19	212
actor	2	66
	19	200
	29	45
aspen	5	43
atoll	11	3
	34	40

This shows that 'abacus' is word 94 in document 3 and words 7 and 212 in document 19; that 'actor' is word 66 in document 2, word 200 in document 19, and word 45 in document 29; and so on.

An inverted file can be used to search a set of documents for every occurrence of a single search term. In the example above, a search for 'actor' would look in the inverted file and find that the word appears in documents 2, 19, and 29. A simple reference to an inverted file is typically a fast operation for a computer.

The list of locations for a given word is called an *inverted list*. Most inverted lists give the locations of the word in the document. This is important for displaying the result of searches, particularly with long documents. The appropriate section of the document can be displayed, with the search terms highlighted.

Since inverted files contain every word in a set of documents (except stop words), they are large. The inverted file for typical digital library materials may approach half the size of all the documents in the collection, even after compression. Thus, at the cost of storage space, an inverted file provides a fast way to find every occurrence of a single word in a collection of documents. Most methods of information retrieval use inverted files.

A modern approach is not to attempt to match documents exactly against a query, but to define some measure of similarity between a query and each document. Suppose that the total number of different words in a set of documents is n. A given document can be represented by a vector in n-dimensional space. If the document contains a given word, the vector has the value 1 in the corresponding dimension; otherwise, it has the value 0. A query can also be represented by a vector in the same space. The closeness with which a document matches a query is measured by how close these two vectors are to each other. This might be measured by the angle between these two vectors in n-dimensional space. Once these measures have been calculated for every document, the results can be ranked from the best match to the worst. Several ranking technique are based on the same general concept. A variety of probabilistic methods make use of the statistical distribution of the words in the collection. These methods derive from the observation that the exact words chosen by an author to describe a topic or by a user to express a query were chosen from a set of possibilities, but that other words might be equally appropriate.

Natural-Language Processing and Computational Linguistics

The words in a document are not simply random strings of characters; they are words in a language (such as English), and they are arranged in phrases, sentences, and paragraphs. Natural-language processing is the branch of computer science that uses computers to interpret and manipulate words as part of a language. The spelling checkers that are used with word processors are a well-known application; they use methods of natural-language processing to suggest alternative spellings for words they do not recognize.

One of the achievements of computational linguistics (the branch of linguistics that deals with grammar and linguistics) has been to develop computer programs that can parse almost any sentence with good accuracy. A parser analyzes the structure of a sentence, categorizes the words by part of speech (verb, noun, adjective, etc.), groups the words into phrases and clauses, and identifies the structural elements (subject, verb, object, etc.). For this purpose, linguists have been required to refine their understanding of grammar, recognizing far more subtleties than were contained in traditional grammars. Considerable research in information retrieval has been carried out using noun phrases. In many contexts, the content of a sentence can be found by extracting the nouns and noun phrases and searching on them. Work of this kind has not been restricted to English; it has been applied to many languages.

Parsing requires an understanding of the morphology of words so that variants derived from the same stem—such as plurals (library, libraries) and verb forms (look, looks, looked)—can be recognized. For information retrieval, it is often effective to reduce morphological variants to a common stem and to use the stem as a search term. This is called *stemming*. Stemming is more effective than truncation, since it separates words with entirely different meanings (such as 'computer' and 'company') while recognizing that 'computer' and 'computing' are morphological variants from the same stem. In English, a language in which the stem is almost always at the beginning of a word, stemming can be carried out by truncating words and perhaps making adjustments to the final few letters. In some other languages, including German, it is also necessary to trim at the beginnings of words.

Computational linguists have developed a range of dictionaries and other tools, including lexicons and thesauruses, for natural-language processing. A *lexicon* contains information about words, their morphological variants, and their grammatical usage. A *thesaurus* relates words by meaning. Some of these tools are general in purpose; others (such as the Art and Architecture Thesaurus and the MeSH headings for medicine) are tied to specific disciplines.

Lexicons and thesauruses can greatly augment information retrieval by recognizing words as more than random strings of characters. For example, they can recognize synonyms ('car' and 'automobile'), relate a general term and a particular instance ('science' and 'chemistry'), or relate a technical term and a vernacular equivalent ('cranium' and 'brain').

A lexicon or a thesaurus is a major undertaking and is never complete. Languages change continually, and terminology changes especially rapidly in fields of active research.

User Interfaces and Information-Retrieval Systems

Information-retrieval systems depend for their effectiveness on the user's making good use of the tools provided. When the user is a trained medical librarian or a lawyer whose legal education included training in search systems, these objectives are usually met. Untrained users typically do much less well at formulating queries and understanding the results.

The vector-space and probabilistic methods of information retrieval are most effective with long queries. An interesting experiment is to use a very long query, perhaps an abstract from a document. This is equivalent to asking the system to find documents that match the abstract. Many modern search systems are remarkably effective when given such an opportunity, but methods based on vector space or linguistic techniques require a worthwhile query to display their full power.

In practice, statistics show, most queries consist of a single word. One reasons for the shortness of many queries is that many users' first searches were done with Boolean systems, which yield only exact matches and therefore seldom find any matches to long queries. Another characteristic of the early systems that encouraged short queries was that computers' performance deteriorated terribly in the face of a long or complex query. Many individuals have retained habits they learned when using such systems.

However, the tendency of users to supply short queries is more entrenched than can be explained by historical factors or by the tiny input boxes that are sometimes provided. The pattern is repeated almost everywhere. There appears to be an inhibition in regard to long queries. Another unfortunate characteristic of users—widely observed—is that few people read even the simplest instructions. Digital libraries are failing to train their users in effective searching, and users do not take advantage of the potential of the systems that are now available.

Evaluation

Information retrieval has a long tradition of performance evaluation. Two long-standing criteria are *precision* (the percentage of relevant hits—i.e., the extent to which the set of hits retrieved by a query satisfies the requirement that generated the query) and *recall* (the percentage of the relevant items found—i.e., the extent to which the query found all the items that satisfy the requirement). Each of these criteria refers to the results of a single search on a given body of information. Suppose that, in a collection of 10,000 documents, 50 documents are on a specific topic. An ideal search would find these 50 documents and reject all others. If an actual search identifies 25 documents, of which 20 prove to be relevant and 5 prove to be about other topics, the precision is $20/25 = 0.8$ and the recall is $20/50 = 0.4$.

Precision is much easier to measure than recall. To calculate precision, a knowledgeable person looks at each document that is identified and decides whether it is relevant. In the example, only the 25 documents that are found need be examined. In the case of recall, however, there is no way to know all the items in a collection that satisfy a specific query other than to go systematically through the entire collection, looking at every object to decide whether it fits the criteria—often an imposing task.

The criteria of precision and recall have been very important in the development of information retrieval, but they were devised in days when computers were much slower and more expensive than they are today. Information retrieval then consisted of a single search of a large set of data, and success or failure was a one-time event. Today, searching is usually interactive. A user will formulate a query, carry out an initial search, examine the results, and repeat the process with a modified query. In the jargon of the field, this is called "searching with a human in the loop." The effective precision and recall of such a session should be judged by the overall results, not by the results of a single search.

Performance criteria such as precision and recall measure technical properties of aspects of computer systems. They do not measure how a user interacts with a system, or what constitutes an adequate result of a search. Many newer search programs have a strategy of ranking all possible hits. This creates a high level of recall at the expense of many irrelevant hits. Criteria are needed that measure the effectiveness of the ranking in giving high ranks to the most relevant items.

Users look for information for many different reasons, and they use many different strategies to seek for information. Sometimes they are looking for specific facts; sometimes they are exploring a topic. Only rarely are they faced with the standard problem of information retrieval: to find every item relevant to a well-defined topic, with the minimal number of extraneous items. With interactive computing, users do not carry out a single search. They iterate through a series of steps, combining searching, browsing, interpretation, and filtering of results. The effectiveness of information discovery depends on the users' objectives and on how well the digital library meets them.

Panel 10.7
Tipster and TREC

Tipster was a long-running project sponsored by DARPA to improve the quality of text processing. The focus was on several problems, all of which are important in digital libraries: document detection (which combines information retrieval on stored documents and identification of relevant documents from a stream of new text), information extraction (location of specified information within a text), and summarization (to condense the size of a document or a collection).

Over the years, Tipster shifted its emphasis from standard information retrieval to the development of components that can tackle specific tasks and an architecture for sharing these components. The architecture is an ambitious effort that uses concepts from object-oriented programming to define standard classes for the basic components of textual materials, notably documents, collections, attributes, and annotations.

At the annual Text Retrieval Conferences (known as "TREC conferences"), researchers demonstrate their methods on standard bodies of text. The TREC conferences, an outstanding example of quantitative research on digital libraries, are held under the auspices of the National Institute of Standards and Technology, with the help of many other organizations. The organizers of the conferences have created a corpus of several million textual documents—more than 5 gigabytes of data. Researchers evaluate their work by attempting a standard set of tasks. One task is to search the corpus for topics provided by a group of 20 surrogate users. Another test evaluates systems that match a stream of incoming documents against standard queries. Among the participants in the TREC conferences are representatives of large commercial companies, small information-retrieval vendors, and university research groups.

The TREC conferences provide an opportunity to compare the performance of various techniques involving such methods as automatic thesauruses, sophisticated term weighting, natural-language techniques, relevance feedback, and advanced machine learning. In recent years, other aspects of information retrieval, including methods intended for use with Chinese texts, spoken documents, and cross-language retrieval, have been evaluated. Another track has experimented with methods of evaluating interactive retrieval.

11

Distributed Information Discovery

How to discover information that is spread across many computer systems is an aspect of the broad challenge of interoperability. The world's digital libraries are managed by many organizations, with different management styles and different attitudes toward collections and technology. Few libraries have more than a small percentage of the materials that users might want. Hence, users need to draw from collections and services provided by many different sources. How does a user discover and gain access to information when there are so many potential sources?

Distributed computing is the overall term for the technical aspects of coordinating separate computers so that they can provide coherent service. Distributed computing requires that the various computers share some technical standards. With distributed searching, for example, a user might want to search many independent collections with a single query, compare the results, choose the most promising ones, and retrieve selected materials from the collections. Beyond the underlying networking standards, this requires a method of identifying the collections, conventions for formulating the query, techniques for submitting the query, means of returning results, and methods for obtaining the items that are discovered. The standards may be formal ones blessed by official standards bodies, local ones developed by a small group of collaborators, or agreements to use specific commercial products.

An ideal approach would be to develop a comprehensive set of standards that all digital libraries would adopt. However, this notion fails to recognize the costs of adopting standards, especially in times of rapid change. Digital libraries are in a state of flux. Every library is striving to improve its collections, services, and systems, and no two libraries are the same. Altering part of a system to support a new standard is time consuming. By the time the alteration is completed, there may be a new version of the standard, or the community may be pursuing some other direction. Comprehensive standardization is a mirage.

In regard to interoperability, digital libraries are faced with the challenge of developing distributed computing systems in a world of independently operated and technically dissimilar computers. This requires formats, protocols, and security systems so that messages can be exchanged. It also requires semantic agreements on the interpretation of the messages. But the central challenge is to find approaches that independent digital libraries have incentives to incorporate.

Adoption of shared methods provides digital libraries with extra functionality, but it also has costs. Some costs are directly financial: purchasing equipment and software, hiring and training staff. More often, however, the major costs are organizational. Rarely can one aspect of a digital library be changed in isolation. Introducing a new standard requires interrelated changes in existing systems, changes in the flow of work, changes in relationships with suppliers, and perhaps other changes.

Figure 11.1 illustrates a conceptual model that is useful in thinking about interoperability. In this instance, the model is used to compare three methods of distributed searching. The horizontal axis of the figure indicates the functionality provided by various methods; the vertical axis indicates the costs of adopting them. The ideal method would be at the bottom right of

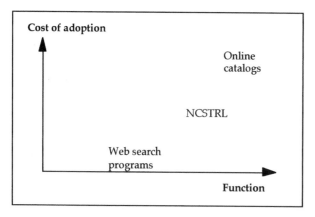

Figure 11.1
Comparison of three strategies for distributed searching.

the graph, where high functionality is achieved at low cost. Web search programs have moderate functionality; they are widely used because they have low costs of adoption. Online catalogs based on MARC cataloging and the Z39.50 protocol have much more functionality, but because the standards are complex they are less widely adopted. The NCSTRL system (described in panel 11.4) falls somewhere in between.

The methods that might be used for interoperability fall into three broad classes:

• Most of the methods that are in widespread use for interoperability today have moderate functionality and low cost of acceptance. The main web standards—HTML, HTTP, and URLs—have these characteristics. Their simplicity has led to wide adoption, but it limits their functionality.

• Some high-end services provide great functionality but are costly to adopt. Z39.50 and SGML are examples. Such methods are popular in restricted communities where their functionality is valued, but their cost of adoption keeps them from reaching broader communities.

• Many current developments in digital libraries are attempts to find the middle ground: substantial functionality with moderate cost of adoption. Examples include the Dublin Core, XML, and Unicode. In each instance, the designers have paid attention to providing a moderate-cost route for adoption. The Dublin Core allows every field to be optional. Unicode provides UTF-8, which accepts existing ASCII data. XML's cost of adoption is reduced by its close relationships with HTML and SGML.

Figure 11.1 has no scale, and the dimensions are only conceptual, but it illustrates the fundamental principle that the cost of adopting new technology is a factor in every aspect of interoperability. Technology can never be considered in isolation, without consideration of organizational impact. When the creators of a digital library hope to have it interoperate with other libraries, they are often faced with choosing between the methods that are best for their particular community and more generally accepted standards that offer lesser functionality. New versions of software illustrate this tension. Often a new version will provide the digital library with more functionality, but fewer users will have access to it. For example, the creator of a web site can use the most basic HTML tags, a few well-established formats, and the services provided by every version of HTTP to produce a simple site that can be accessed by every browser in the world. Alternatively, the creator can choose the latest version of web technology, with Java applets,

HTML frames, built-in security, style sheets, and audio and video inserts. These features will provide superior service to users who have high-speed networks and the latest browsers, but others may find them unusable.

Web Search Programs

The most widely used systems for distributed searching are web search programs, such as Infoseek, Lycos, AltaVista, and Excite. These are automated systems that index materials on the Internet. In the scheme of figure 11.1, they provide moderate functionality with low barriers to use: web sites need take no special action to be indexed by them, and the only cost to the user is the tedium of looking at the advertisements. The combination of respectable functionality with almost no barriers to use makes web search programs extremely popular.

Most of these programs have the same basic architecture, though there are many differences in the details. The notable exception is Yahoo, which has its roots in a classification system. The other systems have two major parts: a *web crawler* (which builds an index of material on the Internet) and a *retrieval engine* (which allows users on the Internet to search the index).

Web Crawlers

A web crawler is an indexing program that follows hyperlinks continuously and assembles a list of the pages it finds. It builds an ever-increasing index of web pages by repeating a few basic steps. Internally, it maintains a list of the URLs known to the system, whether or not the corresponding pages have yet been indexed. From this list, it selects the URL of an HTML page that has not been indexed. It retrieves this page and brings it back to a central computer system for analysis. An automatic indexing program examines the page and creates an index record for it, which is then added to the overall index. Hyperlinks from the page to other pages are extracted, and those that are new are added to the list of URLs for future exploration.

Behind this simple framework lie many variations and some deep technical problems.

One question is which URL to visit next. At any given moment, a web crawler has millions of unexplored URLs, but it has little information that is of use in selecting the next URL. Criteria for choice might include how current a URL is, how many other URLs link to it, and whether it represents a home page or a page deep within a hierarchy.

The biggest problem, however, concerns indexing. Web crawlers rely on automatic indexing (discussed in chapter 10) to create records that can be presented to users. They are faced with automatic indexing at its most basic: millions of pages created by thousands of people with different concepts of how information should be structured. Typical web pages provide only meager clues for automatic indexing. Some creators and publishers are even deliberately misleading; they fill their pages with terms that are likely to be requested by users, hoping that their pages will be highly ranked against common search queries. Without better-structured pages or systematic metadata the quality of the indexing records will never be high, but they are adequate for simple retrieval.

Searching an Index of Web Pages

Web search programs allow users to search their indexes by means of information-retrieval methods of the kind described in chapter 10. The indexes are organized for efficient searching by large numbers of simultaneous users. Since the index records are of low quality and the users are likely to be untrained, the search programs follow the strategy of identifying all records that vaguely match the query and supplying them to the user in some ranked order.

Most users of web search programs would agree that they are remarkable programs but that they have several significant difficulties. The ranking algorithms have little information on which to base their decisions. As a result, the programs may give high ranks to pages of marginal value. Important materials may be far down the list, trivial items at the top. The index programs have difficulty recognizing items that are duplicates, though they attempt to group similar items; since similar items tend to rank together, the programs often return long lists of nearly identical items. One interesting approach to ranking is that of the Google search system, which counts links. Google is particularly effective in finding introductory or overview material on a topic.

The crawlers are continually exploring the web, and eventually almost everything will be found. But important materials may not be indexed until months after they are mounted on the web. Conversely, the programs do

Panel 11.1
Page Ranks and Google

Citation analysis is a commonly used tool in the sciences. Articles that cite one another are probably on related topics, and heavily cited articles are likely to be more important than articles that are never cited. Lawrence Page, Sergey Brin, and their colleagues at Stanford University have applied this concept to the web, using the patterns of hyperlinks among web pages as a basis for ranking pages, and have developed an experimental web search program known as Google.

As an example, imagine using various web search programs to search for "Stanford University." There are more than 200,000 web pages at Stanford. Most search programs have difficulty separating pages that are of only local or ephemeral interest from those that are of broader interest. All web search programs find enormous numbers of web pages that match the query "Stanford University," but in most cases the order in which sites are ranked fails to identify the sites that most people would consider to be the most important.

When "Stanford University" was submitted to Google, the top ten results were the following:

Stanford University Homepage (www.stanford.edu/)
Stanford University Medical Center (www-med.stanford.edu/)
Stanford University Libraries & Information Resources
(www-sul.stanford.edu/)
Stanford Law School (www-leland.stanford.edu/group/law/)
Stanford Graduate School of Business (www-gsb.stanford.edu/)
Stanford University School of Earth Sciences (pangea.stanford.edu/)
SUL: Copyright & Fair Use (fairuse.stanford.edu/)
Computer Graphics at Stanford University (www-graphics.stanford.edu/)
SUMMIT (Stanford University) Home Page (summit.stanford.edu/)
Stanford Medical Informatics (camis.stanford.edu/)

Most people would agree that this is a good list.

The basic method used by Google is simple: pages to which many other pages provide links are ranked higher than pages with fewer links, and links from high-ranking pages are given greater weight than links from other pages. Since web pages around the world link to the home page of the Stanford Law School, that page has a high rank. In turn, that home page links to about a dozen other pages, such as the university's home page, which gain rank from being referenced by a high-ranking page.

Calculating page ranks requires elegant computation. To understand the basic concept, imagine a huge matrix listing every page on the web and identifying every page that links to it. At first, every page is ranked equally. New rankings are then calculated on the basis of the number of links to each page, weighted according to the rank of the linking pages and proportional to the number of links from each. These ranks are then used for another iteration, and the process continued until the calculation converges.

The actual computation is a refinement of this approach. In 1998, Google had a set of about 25 million pages, selected by a process derived from the ranks of pages that link to them. The program has weighting factors to account for pages with no links and for groups of pages with link only to one another. It rejects pages that are generated dynamically by CGI scripts. That the system was able to gather, index, and rank these pages in five days, using only standard workstation computers, testifies to the power of today's computers.

Using links to generate page ranks helps solve two problems that bedevil web search programs: Since they cannot index every page on the web simultaneously, which should they index first? How should they rank the pages found from simple queries to give priority to the most useful ones?

not do a very good job of going back to see if materials have been withdrawn, so many of the index entries refer to items that no longer exist or have moved.

Another threat to the effectiveness of web indexing is that a web crawler cannot index material that it cannot access directly. If a web page is protected by some form of authentication, or if a web page is an interface to a database or a digital library collection, the indexing program will know nothing about the resources behind the interface. Because more and more web pages are interfaces controlled by Java programs or other scripts, indexing programs miss a lot of high-quality information.

These weaknesses are significant, but they should not be overemphasized. The proof lies in the practice. Experienced users of the web, using a combination of tools and often several web search services, can usually find the information they want. The programs are far from perfect, but they are remarkably good—and use of them is free.

Most of the search services had roots in research groups but rapidly became commercial companies. The fact that there is no charge for the basic service has had a profound effect on the Internet and on the companies. Their search for revenue has led to aggressive solicitation of advertising. They have rapidly moved into related markets through such tactics as licensing their software to other organizations wanting to build indexes to their own web sites.

A less desirable aspect of this business model is that it limits the incentive to have a comprehensive index. At first, the indexing programs aimed to index the entire web. However, as the web has grown, and as managing search programs has become a commercial venture, comprehensiveness has become secondary to improvements in interfaces and ancillary services. To build a really high-quality index of the Internet, and to keep it up to date, requires a considerable investment. Most of the companies are content to do a reasonable job, but if they had more incentives their indexes would be better.

Federated Digital Libraries

Resolving the tension between functionality and cost of adoption depends on the context. It is sometimes appropriate to select simple technology and strive for broad but shallow interoperability. At other times, it is wise to select technology with great functionality and high associated costs; only highly motivated digital libraries will adopt such expensive methods, but they will realize higher functionality.

The term *federated digital library* describes a group of organizations, working together formally or informally, that agree to support a set of common services and standards, thus providing interoperability among their members. The partners in a federation may have very different systems, so long as they support an agreed-upon set of services. They will need to agree both on technical standards and on policies (including financial agreements, intellectual-property guidelines, security, and privacy).

Research at the University of Illinois at Urbana-Champaign provides a revealing example of the difficulties of interoperability. In the period 1994–1998, as a part of the Digital Libraries Initiative, a team based at the Grainger Engineering Library set out to build a federated library of journal articles from several leading science publishers. Since each publisher planned to make its journals available with SGML markup, this appeared to be an opportunity to build a federation. The university would provide central services, such as searching; the collections would be maintained by the publishers. However, incompatibility in the ways that the various publishers used SGML caused problems. Each publisher has its

Panel 11.2
The University of Illinois Federated Library of Scientific Literature

The Grainger Engineering Library at the University of Illinois is the center of a prototype library that is a federation of collections of scientific journal articles. The work began as part of the Digital Libraries Initiative under the leadership of Bruce Schatz and William Mischo. By 1998, the test-bed collection had 50,000 journal articles from the Institute of Electrical and Electronic Engineers (IEEE), the IEEE Computer Society, the American Physical Society, the American Society of Civil Engineers, and the American Institute of Aeronautics and Astronautics. Each of those organizations provides journal articles with SGML markup at the same time as its printed journals are published.

This prototype has put into practice concepts of information retrieval from marked-up text that have been discussed often but used little. The first phase (which proved extremely tough) was to reconcile the DTDs used by the various publishers, each of which uses its own DTD to represent the structural elements of its documents. Some of the differences are syntactic—for example, an author tag is sometimes <author>, sometimes <aut>, and sometimes <au>. Other variations reflect significant semantic differences. For indexing and retrieval, the project has written software that maps each DTD's tags onto a canonical set. The interfaces to the digital library use these tags, so users can search for text in a given context—e.g., in figure legends. In the scheme of figure 11.1, the use of this set of tags lies to the top right. Converting the markup for all the collections to this set imposes a high cost whenever a new collection is added to the federation, but it provides powerful functionality.

Because of technical difficulties, the first implementation loaded all the documents into a single repository at the University of Illinois. Future plans call for the federation to use repositories maintained by individual publishers. There is also interest in expanding the collections to embrace bibliographic databases, catalogs, and other indexes.

Even the first implementation proved to be fertile ground for studying users and their wishes. Giving users more powerful methods of searching was welcomed, but it also stimulated requests. Users pointed out that figures and mathematical expressions often are more revealing of an article's content than abstracts and conclusions. And these experiments have demonstrated, once again, that users have great difficulty finding the right words to include in search queries when there is no control over the vocabulary used in the papers, in their abstracts. and in the search system.

own document type definition. The university was forced to go to great lengths to reconcile the semantics of the DTDs, both to extract indexing information and to build a coherent user interface. This proved to be so complex that the university resorted to copying the information from the publishers' computers onto a single system and converting it to a common DTD. If a respected university research group encountered such difficulties with a relatively coherent body of information, it is not surprising that others face the same difficulties.

Online Catalogs and Z39.50

Many libraries have online catalogs of their holdings that are openly accessible over the Internet. These catalogs can be considered to form a federation. The catalog records follow the Anglo-American Cataloging Rules, using the MARC format, and the libraries share records to reduce the costs. The library community developed the Z39.50 protocol (described in panel 11.3) to meets its needs for record sharing and distributed searching. In the United States, where the Library of Congress, OCLC, and the Research Libraries Group have been active in developing and promulgating these standards, there have been numerous independent implementations of Z39.50 at academic sites and by commercial vendors. The high costs of belonging to this federation have been absorbed over decades, and they are balanced by the cost savings from shared cataloging.

One of the principal applications of Z39.50 is for communication between servers. A catalog system at a large library can use the protocol to search a group of peers to see if they have either a copy of a work or a catalog record for it. End users can use a single Z39.50 client to search several catalogs, sequentially or in parallel. Libraries and their patrons gain considerable benefits from sharing catalogs in these ways, yet interoperability among public access catalogs is still patchy. Some Z39.50 implementations have features that others lack, but the underlying cause of the patchiness is that the individual catalogs are maintained by people whose first loyalty is to their local communities. Supporting other institutions is never the first priority. Even though institutions share compatible versions of Z39.50, differences in how the catalogs are organized and presented to the outside world remain.

Panel 11.3
Z39.50

Z39.50 is a protocol, developed by the library community, that permits one computer (the client) to search and retrieve information on another (the database server). Z39.50 is important both technically and because it is widely used in library systems. In concept it is not tied to any particular category of information or any particular type of database, but much of the development has concentrated on bibliographic data. Most implementations emphasize searches that use bibliographic attributes to search databases of MARC catalog records and present them to the client.

Z39.50 is based on an abstract view of database searching. It assumes that the server stores a set of databases with searchable indexes. Interactions are based on the concept of a *session*. The client opens a connection with the server, carries out a sequence of interactions, then closes the connection. During the course of the session, both the server and the client remember the state of their interaction. It is important to understand that the client is a computer. End-user applications of Z39.50 require a user interface for communication with the user. The protocol makes no statements about the form of the user interface or about how it connects to the Z39.50 client.

A typical session begins with the client connecting to the server and exchanging initial information, using the *init* facility. This initial exchange establishes agreement on basics, such as the preferred message size; it can include authentication, but the actual form of the authentication is outside the scope of the standard. The client might then use the *explain* service to inquire of the server what databases are available for searching, what fields are available, what syntax and what formats are supported, and other options.

The *search* service allows a client to present a query to a database, as in the following example:

In the database named "Books" find all records for which the access point *title* contains the value "evangeline" and the access point *author* contains the value "longfellow."

The standard provides several choices of syntax for specifying searches, but only Boolean queries are widely implemented. The server carries out the search and builds a *results set*. One distinctive feature of Z39.50 is that the server saves the results set. A subsequent message from the client can reference the results set. Thus, the client can modify a large set by increasingly precise requests, or can request a presentation of any record in the set, without searching the entire database.

Depending on the parameters of the search request, one or more records may be returned to the client. The standard provides a variety of ways for clients to manipulate results sets, including services to *sort* them and to *delete* them. When the searching is complete, the next step is likely to be that the client sends a *present* request. This requests the server to send specified records from the results set to the client in a specified format. The present service has a wide range of options for controlling content and formats, and for managing large records or large results sets.

In addition to the basic services, Z39.50 has facilities for the browsing of indexes, for access control, and for resource management, and it supports extended services that allow a wide range of extensions. This is a large and flexible standard.

NCSTRL and Dienst

A *union catalog* is a single catalog that contains records of the materials in several libraries. Union catalogs (which were used by libraries long before computers) enable distributed searching by consolidating the information to be searched into a single catalog. A web search service can be considered to be a union catalogs for the web, albeit one with crude catalog records. An alternative method of distributed searching is for each collection to have its own searchable index. A search program sends queries to these separate indexes and combines the results for presentation to the user.

The Networked Computer Science Technical Reference Library (NCSTRL), a federation of digital library collections that are important to computer science researchers, uses a protocol called Dienst. To minimize the costs of acceptance, Dienst builds on a variety of technical standards that are familiar to computer scientists, who are typically heavy users of Unix, the Internet, and the web. The first version of Dienst sent search requests to all servers. As the number of servers grew, however, this approach broke down. If any server was unavailable, the entire system suffered. Dienst now has a master index, which is a type of union catalog.

Research on Alternative Approaches to Distributed Searching

In a federation, success or failure is at least as much an organizational challenge as a technical one. Inevitably, some members provide better service than others, and their levels of support differ widely; however, the quality of service must not be tied to the worst-performing organization. Panel 11.4 describes how the Dienst system, used by NCSTRL, was redesigned to address this need.

Panel 11.4
NCSTRL and the Dienst Model of Distributed Searching

The Networked Computer Science Technical Reference Library (NCSTRL) is a distributed library of research materials in computer science, notably technical reports. Cooperating organizations mount their collections on locally maintained servers. Access to these servers uses either FTP or Dienst. Dienst, a distributed library protocol developed by Jim Davis of the Xerox Corporation and Carl Lagoze of Cornell University, was developed as part of the Computer Science Technical Reports project, mentioned in chapter 4. At first there were five cooperating universities; by 1998, more than 100 organizations around the world were involved, 43 of which were operating Dienst servers. NCSTRL and Dienst combine day-to-day services with a test bed for distributed information management. NCSTRL is one of the few instances of a research group running an operational digital library service.

The Dienst architecture divides digital library services into four basic categories: repositories, indexes, collections, and user interfaces. It provides an open protocol that defines these services. The protocol supports distributed searching of independently managed collections. Each server has an index of the materials it stores. In early versions of Dienst, to search the collections, a user-interface program sent a query to all the Dienst sites seeking objects matching the query; the user interface then waited until it received replies from all the servers. This was distributed searching at its most basic, and it ran into problems when the number of servers grew large. The fundamental problem was that the quality of service seen by a user was determined by the service level provided by the worst of the Dienst sites. For a while, the server at Carnegie Mellon University was undependable. If it failed to respond, the user interface waited until an automatic time-out was triggered. Even when all the servers were operating, there were often long delays caused by erratic Internet connections to a few servers.

A slow search is tedious for the user. For a search to miss some of the collections is more serious. Failure to search all the indexes means that the researcher might miss important information, simply because of a server problem.

Dienst was redesigned to address these problems. NCSTRL is now divided into regions. At first there were two regional centers in the United States and four in Europe. With this regional model, a master index is maintained at a central location (Cornell University), and searchable copies of this index are stored at the regional centers. Everything a user needs to search for and locate information is at each regional site. The user contacts the individual collection sites only to retrieve materials stored there. Deciding which regional site to use is left to the individual user. (Because of the vagaries of the Internet, a user may get the best performance by using a regional site other than the nearest one geographically.)

Every information service makes some implicit assumptions about the scenarios it supports, the queries it accepts, and the kinds of answers it provides. These are implemented as facilities, such as search, browse, filter, and extract. The user desires coherent, personalized information; however, in the distributed world, information sources that are individually coherent may differ among themselves. How can a diverse set of organizations provide users with effective access to their information? How can services that are designed around different implied scenarios provide effective resource discovery without draconian standardization? There are tough technical questions for a single, centrally managed service. They become really difficult when the information sources are controlled by independent organizations.

The organizational challenges are so great that they constrain the technical options. Except within tight federations, the only hope for progress is to establish technical frameworks, with parallel acceptance strategies, that organizations can accept incrementally. For each of methods, there must be a low-level alternative (usually the status quo) so that services are not held back from doing anything worthwhile because of a few systems. Thus, in NCSTRL, although Dienst is the preferred protocol, more than half of the sites mount their collections on simple servers using the FTP protocol.

Much of the research in distributed searching sets out to build union catalogs from metadata provided by the creator or publisher. This was one of the motivations behind the Dublin Core. Computer systems are needed to assemble this metadata and consolidate it into a searchable index.

Another area of research aims to develop methods for restricting searches to the most promising collections. Users rarely want to search every source of information on the Internet. They want to search specific categories, such as monograph catalogs or indexes to medical research. Therefore, some means is needed for collections to provide summaries of their contents. This is particularly important where access is limited by authentication or payment mechanisms. If open access is provided to a source, an external program can (at least in theory) generate a statistical profile of the types of material and the vocabulary used. When an external user has access only through a search interface, such analysis is not possible.

Panel 11.5
The Harvest Architecture

Harvest was a research project in distributed searching led by Michael Schwartz, then at the University of Colorado. Although it ended in 1996, the architectural ideas it developed remain highly relevant. The underlying concept is to divide the principal functions of a centralized search system into separate subsystems. The Harvest project defined formats and protocols for communication among these subsystems and implemented software to demonstrate their use.

Central to Harvest is the concept of the *gatherer,* a program that collects indexing information from digital library collections. Gatherers are most effective when they are installed on the same system as the collections. Each gatherer extracts indexing information from the collections and transmits it in a standard format, by a standard protocol, to programs called *brokers*. A broker builds a combined index of information about many collections.

The Harvest architecture is much more efficient in its use of network resources than indexing methods that rely on web crawlers, and the team developed caches and methods of replication for added efficiency, but the real benefit is better searching and information discovery. All gatherers transmit information in a specified protocol, the Summary Object Interchange Format (SOIF), but how they gather the information can be tailored to the individual collections. Whereas web crawlers operate only on open-access information, gatherers can be given access privileges so they can be used to index restricted collections. They can be configured for specific databases, and they need not be restricted to web pages or any specific format. They can incorporate dictionaries or lexicons for specialized topic areas. In combination, these are major advantages.

Many benefits of the Harvest architecture are lost if the gatherer is not installed locally, with the digital library collections. For this reason, the Harvest architecture is particularly effective for federated digital libraries. In a federation, each library can run its own gatherer and can transmit indexing information to brokers that build consolidated indexes for the entire library, thus combining the benefits of local indexing with a central index for users.

In 1996, at Stanford University, Luis Gravano studied how a client can combine results from separate search services. Gravano developed a protocol known as STARTS for this purpose. STARTS was a joint project between Stanford University and several leading Internet companies. The willingness with which the companies joined in the STARTS effort shows that they see the concepts as fundamentally important to broad searching across the Internet. A small amount of standardization would lead to greatly improved searching.

In his analysis, Gravano viewed the information on the Internet as a large number of collection of materials, each organized differently and each with its own search engine. The fundamental concept is to enable clients to discover broad characteristics of the search engines and the collections that they maintain. The challenge is that the search engines are different and the collections have different characteristics. The difficulty is not simply that the interfaces have varying syntaxes, so that a query has to be reformulated to be submitted to different systems. The underlying algorithms are fundamentally different. Some use Boolean methods; others have methods of ranking results. Search engines that return a ranked list give little indication how the ranks were calculated. Indeed, the ranking algorithm is often a trade secret. As a result, it is impossible to merge ranking lists from several sources into a single list with sensible ranking. Ranking is strongly affected by the words used in a collection; thus, even merging results from two sources that use the same ranking algorithm is fraught with difficulty. The STARTS protocol enables search engines to report characteristics of their collections and the ranks that they generate, so that a client program can attempt to combine results from many sources.

Beyond Searching

Information discovery is more than searching. Most individuals use some combination of browsing and systematic searching. Chapter 10 discussed the range of requirements that users have when looking for information and the difficulty of evaluating the effectiveness of information retrieval in an interactive session with the user in the loop. Distributed digital libraries aggravate all these problems.

Browsing has always been an important way to discover information in libraries. Browsing can be as simple as looking at a library's shelves to see what books are stored together. A more systematic approach is to begin with one item and then move to the items to which that item refers. Most journal articles and some other materials include lists of references to other materials. Following these citations is an essentially part of research, but is a tedious task when the materials are physical objects that must be retrieved one at a time. With hyperlinks, following references becomes straightforward. A gross generalization is that following links and references is easier in digital libraries, but the quality of catalogs and indexes is higher in traditional libraries. Therefore, browsing is likely to be relatively more important in digital libraries.

If people follow a heuristic combination of browsing and searching, using a variety of sources and search engines, what confidence can they have in the results? The difficulties of comparing results obtained from searching different sets of information and deciding whether two items found in different sources are duplicates of the same information have already been noted in this chapter. Serious users of a digital library face a subtler but potentially more serious problem: It is often difficult to know how comprehensive a search is being carried out. A user who searches a central database, such as the National Library of Medicine's Medline system, can be confident of searching every record indexed in that system. Contrast this with a distributed search of a large number of data sets. What is the chance of missing important information because one data set is behind the others in supplying indexing information, or because one data set fails to reply to a search request?

Distributed searching epitomizes the current state of digital libraries. From one viewpoint, every technique has serious weaknesses. Technical standards have not emerged, the understanding of user needs is embryonic, and organizational difficulties are pervasive. Yet, at the same time, enormous volumes of material are accessible on the Internet, web search programs are freely available, and federations and commercial services are expanding rapidly. By intelligently combining searching and browsing, motivated users can usually find the information they seek.

12

Object Models, Identifiers, and Structural Metadata

Information comes in many forms and formats, each of which must be captured, stored, retrieved, and manipulated. Much of the early development of digital libraries concentrated on material that has a direct analog to some physical format. These materials can usually be represented as simply structured computer files. Digital libraries can go far beyond such simple digital objects; they include anything that can be represented in a digital format. The digital medium allows for new types of library objects, such as software, simulations, animations, movies, slide shows, and soundtracks, and for new ways to structure material. Computing has introduced its own types of objects, including spreadsheets, databases, symbolic mathematics, and hypertext. Increasingly, computers and networks support continuous streams of digital information—notably speech, music, and video. Even the simplest digital objects may come in many versions and be replicated many times.

Methods for managing this complexity fall into several categories: *identifiers* for digital objects; *data types,* which specify what the data represents; and *structural metadata,* which represent the relationship between digital objects and their component parts. In combination, these techniques create an *object model,* a description of some category of information that enables computer systems to store and provide access to complex information. Interoperability and long-term persistence are constant themes in studies of these topics. Information in today's digital libraries must be usable many years from now by people using computer systems that have not yet been imagined.

Works, Expressions, Manifestations, and Items

Users of a digital library usually want to refer to items at a higher level of abstraction than a file. Common English terms, such as *report, computer program*, or *musical work*, often refer to many digital objects that can be grouped together. The individual objects may have different formats, minor differences of content, different restrictions on their use, and so on, but usually the user considers them as equivalent. This requires a conceptual model that is able to describe content at various levels of abstraction.

Chapter 1 mentioned the importance of distinguishing between the underlying intellectual work and the individual items in a digital library, and the challenges of describing such differences in a manner that makes sense for all types of content. In 1998 the International Federation of Library Associations issued a report on the requirements for bibliographic records in which the following four levels for describing content were proposed:

Work   A work is the underlying abstraction, such as the *Iliad,* Beethoven's Fifth Symphony, or the Unix operating system.

Expression   A work is realized through an expression. The *Iliad* was first expressed orally; then it was written down as a fixed sequence of words. A musical work can be expressed as a printed score or by any one of many performances. Computer software, such as Unix, has separate expressions as source code and as machine code.

Manifestation   An expression is given form in one or more manifestations. The text of the *Iliad* has been manifest in numerous manuscripts and printed books. A musical performance can be distributed on a CD or broadcast on television. Software is manifest as files, which may be stored or transmitted in any digital medium.

Item   When many copies are made of a manifestation, each is a separate item, such as a specific copy of a book or a computer file.

Clearly there are many subtleties buried in these four levels. The distinctions among versions, editions, translations, and other variants are a matter for judgment, not for hard rules. Some works—such as jazz music (where each performance is a new creation) and paintings (where the item is the work)—are hard to fit into the model. Overall, however, the model holds great promise as a framework for describing this complicated subject.

Expressions

Multimedia

In chapters 9–11, particular attention was paid to works that are expressed as texts. Textual materials have special importance in digital libraries, but object models must support all media and all types of object. Some non-textual objects are files of fixed information, such as the digital equivalents of familiar objects (e.g., maps, audio recordings, video) and other objects that provide the user with a direct rendering of the stored form of a digital object. Even such apparently straightforward materials have many subtleties when the information is some medium other than text. This sections looks at three examples. Panel 12.1 describes the Alexandria Digital Library of *geospatial information* such as maps. Panel 12.2 describes how the Informedia digital library has combined several methods of information retrieval to build indexes automatically and search collections of *video*. Individually, each method is imprecise, but in combination quite good results are achieved. Panel 12.3 describes RealAudio, a way to deliver digitized *sound recordings* to users. Sound recordings require a special method of dissemination, so that a continuous stream of data is presented to the user at the appropriate pace. They are on the boundary of what can reasonably be transmitted over the Internet as it exists today.

Panel 12.1
The Geospatial Collections of the Alexandria Digital Library

The Alexandria Digital Library, located at the University of California at Santa Barbara and led by Terence Smith, was one of the six projects funded by the Digital Libraries Initiative from 1994 to 1998. The collections in Alexandria cover any data that is referenced by a geographical footprint. This includes all classes of terrestrial maps, aerial and satellite photographs, astronomical maps, databases, and related textual information. The project combines a broad program of research with practical implementation at the university's map library.

These collections have proved to be a fertile area for digital libraries research. Geospatial information is of interest in many fields: cartography, urban planning, navigation, environmental studies, agriculture, astronomy, and more. The data comes from many sources: survey data, digital photographs, printed maps, and analog images. A digital library of these collections faces many of the same issues as a digital library of textual documents, but it forces the researchers to examine every topic again to see which standard techniques can be used and which must be modified.

In the case of geospatial data, information retrieval concentrates on *coverage* or *scope*, whereas with other categories of material the focus is on subject matter or on bibliographic information (e.g., author or title). Coverage means the geographical area covered—e.g., the city of Santa Barbara or the Pacific Ocean. Scope describes the varieties of information—e.g., topographical features, political boundaries, population density. Alexandria provides several methods for capturing such information and using it for retrieval.

Latitude and longitude are basic metadata for maps and for geographical features. Systematic procedures have been developed for capturing such data from existing maps. A large gazetteer has been created. It consists of a database and a set of procedures that translate between different representations of geospatial references (e.g., place names, geographic features, coordinates, postal codes, census tracts). The Alexandria search engine is tailored to the peculiarities of searching for place names. Researchers are making steady progress at the difficult task of feature extraction, using automatic programs to identify objects in aerial photographs or printed maps.

The Alexandria researchers have applied methods of high-performance computing to digital libraries. *Wavelets* are one method they have exploited for storage and in user interfaces. Digitized maps and other geospatial information create large files of data. Wavelets provide a multi-level decomposition of an image, the first level being a small, coarse image that can be used as a thumbnail. Other levels provide greater detail and require larger volumes of data.

Alexandria has developed several user interfaces, each based on earlier experience. Two common themes have been the constraints imposed by the small size of computer displays and the slow rate at which the Internet delivers large files to users. Good design helps to mitigate the first, though it is impossible to fit a large image and a comprehensive search interface onto a single screen. To enhance performance, every attempt is made not to transmit the same information twice. The user interfaces retain state throughout a session, so a user can leave the system and return to the same place without having to repeat any steps.

Panel 12.2
Informedia: Multi-Modal Information Retrieval

Much of the research of the Informedia digital library project (introduced in chapter 8) is aimed at indexing and searching video segments without the assistance of human indexers or catalogers.

Informedia is multi-modal. It uses computer programs to analyze video tracks, sound tracks, closed captioning (if present), changes of scene, and other information. Analysis of each individual mode gives imperfect information, but combining the evidence from all modes can be surprisingly effective.

Informedia builds on methods developed in the field of artificial intelligence, including speech recognition, natural-language processing, and image recognition, bringing the work of independent research groups together to create something greater than the sum of its parts.

The first step in adding new materials to the Informedia collection is to take divide video material into topical segments. The computer program uses a variety of techniques of image and sound processing to look for clues as to when one topic ends and another begins. For example, in broadcast television programs the gaps intended for advertisements often coincide with changes of topic. The second step is to identify any text associated with each segment. This is done by recognizing speech on the sound track, by identifying any captions within the video stream, and by extracting any closed captioning. The final step is to process the raw text, using various tools of natural-language processing to create an approximate index record that is then loaded into the search system.

The methods of information discovery discussed in chapters 10 and 11 can be applied to audio tapes and to sound tracks of video material if the spoken words can be converted to computer text. Such conversion presents a tough computing problem, but steady progress has been made over the years with the help of ever-increasing computer power.

Informedia must tackle some of the hardest problems in speech recognition. Speech on a sound track may be indistinct, perhaps because of background noise or music. It may contain any word in the English language, proper nouns, slang, and foreign words. Even a human listener misses some words. Informedia successfully recognizes from about 50 percent to about 80 percent of the words, depending on the characteristics of the specific video segment.

To search the Informedia collection, a user either types a query or speaks it aloud so that it can be processed by the speech-recognition system. Since there may be errors in the recognition of a spoken query, and since the index is known to be built from inexact data, the apparent matches are ranked. The algorithm is based on the same research as the Lycos web search program, and the index uses the same underlying retrieval system.

Panel 12.3
RealAudio

An hour of digitized sound of compact disc quality requires 635 megabytes of storage if not compressed. This poses problems for digital libraries. The storage requirements for any substantial collection are huge, and transmission requires high-speed networks. Uncompressed sound of this quality challenges even links that run at 155 megabits per second. Since most local-area networks share Ethernets that run at less than a tenth of this speed, and dial-up links are much slower, some form of compression is needed.

RealAudio is a method of compression and an associated protocol for transmitting digitized sound. In the RealAudio format, an hour of sound requires about 5 megabytes of storage. Transmission makes use of a streaming protocol between the repository where the information is stored and a program running on the user's computer. When the user is ready, the repository transmits a steady sequence of sound packets. As they arrive at the user's computer, they are converted to sound and played. This is carried out at strict time intervals. There is no error checking. If a packet has not arrived when the time to play it is reached, it is ignored and the user hears a short gap in the sound. This process seems crude; however, if the network connection is reasonably clear, RealAudio transmits speech quite acceptably over dial-up lines at 28.8 kilobits per second. In an early experiment, RealAudio was used to store and transmit a collection of segments from National Public Radio programs.

RealAudio uses standard web methods except in two particulars, both of which are needed for the transmission of audio signals over the Internet in real time. First, the user's browser must accept streams of audio data in the RealAudio format. This requires the user to add a special player to his or her browser. (RealAudio players are available for downloading via the Internet.) Second, to achieve a steady flow of data, the library uses the UDP protocol instead of TCP. (Since some network security systems do not accept UDP data packets, RealAudio cannot be delivered everywhere.)

Dynamic and Complex Objects

Many of the digital objects that are now being considered for digital library collections cannot be represented as static files of data. Consider the following:

Dynamic objects   Dynamic or active library objects include computer programs, Java applets, simulations, data from scientific sensors, and video games. With these types of objects, what is presented to the user depends on the execution of computer programs or other external activities, so that the user gets different results every time the object is accessed.

Complex objects   A single library object can be made up of many inter-related elements. These elements can have various relationships to one another. They can be complementary elements of content, such as the audio and picture channels of a video recording; they can be alternative manifestations, such as a high-resolution or low-resolution satellite image; they can be surrogates, such as data and metadata. In practice these distinctions are often blurred—for example, is a thumbnail photograph an alternative manifestation, or is it metadata about a larger image?

Alternate disseminations   Digital objects may offer the user a choice of access methods. For example, a library object might provide the weather conditions at San Francisco Airport. When the user accesses this object, the information returned might be data (such as temperature, precipitation, wind speed and direction, and humidity), or it might be a photograph showing the cloud cover. And this information might be read directly from sensors (on request) or from regularly updated tables.

Databases   A database comprises many alternative records, with different individuals selected each time the database is accessed. Some databases can be best thought of as complete digital library collections, with the individual records as digital objects within the collections. Other databases, such as directories, are library objects in their own right.

The methods for managing these more general objects are still subjects of debate. Whereas the web provides a unifying framework that most people use for static files, there is no widely accepted framework for general objects. Even the terminology is rife with disputes. A set of conventions that relate the intellectual view of library materials to the internal structure is sometimes called a *document model*; however, since it applies to all aspects of digital libraries, *object model* seems a better term.

Identification

The first stage in building an object model is to have a method of identifying the materials. The identifier is used to refer to objects in catalogs and citations, to store and access them, to provide access management, and to archive them for the long term. This sounds simple, but identifiers must meet requirements that overlap and frequently contradict one another. Few topics in digital libraries cause as much heated discussion as names and identifiers. There is no universal approach to naming that satisfies every need.

One controversy is whether semantic information should be embedded in a name. Some people advocate completely semantic names. An example is the Serial Item and Contribution Identifier (SICI) standard. By a precisely defined set of rules, a SICI identifies either an issue of a serial or a specific article. It is usually possible to derive the SICI directly from a journal article or a citation; however, this is a daunting objective, and the SICI standard succeeds only because there is already a standard for identifying serial titles uniquely. The following, a typical SICI, identifies a journal article published by John Wiley and Sons.

0002-8231(199601)47:1<23:TDOMII>2.0.TX;2-2

Fully semantic names, such as SICIs, are inevitably restricted to narrow classes of information; they tend to be long and ugly because of the complexity of the rules that are used to generate them. Because of the difficulty of creating semantic identifiers for more general classes of objects (which is compounded by arguments over trademarks and other names), some people advocate the opposite: random identifiers that contain no semantic information about who assigned the name and what it references. Random strings used as identifiers can be shorter, but without any embedded information they are hard for people to remember and they may be difficult for computers to process.

In practice, many names are mnemonic—they contain information that makes them easy to remember. Consider the domain name www.apple.com. At first glance this appears to be a semantic name (the web site of a commercial organization called Apple), but this is just an informed guess. The prefix www is conventionally used for web sites, but this is merely a convention. There are several commercial organizations called Apple, and the name gives no hint whether this web site is managed by Apple Computer or some other company.

Another difficulty is to decide whether a name refers to a work, an expression, a manifestation, or an item. Consider International Standard Book Numbers (ISBNs), which were developed by publishers and the book trade for their own use. ISBNs distinguish separate products that can be bought or sold; for example, a hardcover edition will usually have a different ISBN than a paperback, even if the contents are identical. Libraries, however, may find this distinction unhelpful. For bibliographic purposes, the natural distinction is between versions in which the content differs, not the format; for the purposes of managing a collection, each individual copy is distinct and needs its own identifier.

Domain Names and Uniform Resource Locators

The most widely used identifiers on the Internet are domain names and Uniform Resource Locators (URLs). URLs extend the concept of domain names in several directions, but all are expansions of the basic concept of providing a name for a location on the Internet.

URLs have proved extremely successful. They permit any number of versatile applications to be built on the Internet. However, they pose a long-term problem for digital libraries: lack of persistence. Users of digital

Panel 12.4
Domain Names

The basic purpose of domain names is to identify computers on the Internet by name rather than by IP address. One advantage of this approach is that the name need not be changed if a computer system is changed. For example, over the years the domain name "library.dartmouth.edu" was assigned to a series of computers with different IP addresses, but users were not aware of the changes.

Over the years, domain names have become more flexible. A domain name need no longer refer to a specific computer. Several domain names can refer to the same computer, or one domain name can refer to a service that is spread over a set of computers.

The allocation of domain names forms a hierarchy. At the top are the root domain names. One set of root names are based on types of organization, such as .com (commercial), .edu (educational), .gov (government), .net (network services), and .org (other organizations). A second series of root domains are based on geography; typical examples are .ca (Canada), .jp (Japan), and .nl (Netherlands). Organizations are assigned domain names under one of these root domains. Typical examples are cmu.edu (Carnegie Mellon University), elsevier.nl (Elsevier Science), loc.gov (Library of Congress), and dlib.org (D-Lib Magazine).

In the United States, domain names have historically been assigned on a "first-come, first-served" basis. Controls on who could receive a domain name, and what the name might be, were minimal, and the fees were low. Thus, a person with no affiliation to the City of Pittsburgh could register the name pittsburgh.net. Aside from the proliferation of inappropriate names, the lack of controls has led to trademark disputes and other arguments.

Panel 12.5
Information Contained in a URL

The string of characters that comprises a URL is highly structured. A URL combines the specification of a protocol, a file name, and options that will be used to access a file. It may contain the following:

Protocols   The first part of a full URL is the name of a protocol or a service, ending with a colon. Typical examples are http:, mailto:, and ftp:.

Absolute and relative URLs   A URL may refer to a file by its domain name or by its location relative to another file. If the protocol is followed by a double slash, the URL contains a full domain name—e.g., http://www.dlib.org/figure.jpg. Otherwise, the address is relative to the current directory. For example, within an HTML page, the anchor <a href = "figure.jpg"> refers to a file "figure.jpg" in the same directory.

Files   A URL identifies a specific file on a specified computer system. In the URL http://www.dlib.org/contents.html, "www.dlib.org" is a domain name that identifies a computer on the Internet, and "contents.html" is a file on that computer.

Port   A server on the Internet may provide several services running concurrently. The TCP protocol provides a *port*, which identifies which service to use. The port is specified as a colon followed by a number at the end of the domain name. The URL http://www.dlib.org:80/index.html references port 80, which is the default port for the HTTP protocol and therefore could be omitted from this particular URL.

Parameters   A variety of parameters can be appended to a URL after either a # or a ?. These are passed to the server when the file is accessed.

libraries wish to be able to access material consistently over long periods of time. URLs identify resources by a location derived from a domain name. If the domain name no longer exists, or if the resource moves to a different location, the URL is no longer valid. A famous example comes dates back to the early days of the web. After the World Wide Web Consortium was established at the Massachusetts Institute of Technology, in 1994, the definitive documentation for the web was transferred from CERN's headquarters in Geneva to MIT, and every hyperlink that pointed to CERN became invalid. In such instances the convention is to leave behind a web page stating that the site has moved, but forwarding addresses tend to disappear with time or become long chains. If a domain name is canceled (perhaps because a company goes out of business), all URLs based on that domain name are broken forever. There are various forms of aliases that can be used with domain names and URLs to ameliorate this, but they are tricks rather than solutions.

Persistent Names and Uniform Resource Names

The digital library community and publishers of electronic materials have become interested in *persistent names*. These are sometimes called Uniform Resource Names (URNs). The idea is simple: Names should be globally unique and persist for all time—longer than any software system that exists today, longer even than the Internet.

A persistent name should be able to reference any Internet resource or set of resources. One application of URNs is to reference the current locations of copies of an object, defined by a list of URLs. Another is to provide electronic mail addresses that do not have to be changed when a person changes jobs or Internet service providers. Another possibility is to provide the public keys of named services. Panel 12.6 describes the "handle" system, which is a system to create and manage persistent names, and how publishers use it to manage Digital Object Identifiers.

Computer Systems for Resolving Names

Whatever system of identifiers is used, there must be a fast and efficient method by which a computer on the Internet can discover what a name refers to. This is known as *resolving* the name. Resolving a domain name provides the IP address or addresses of the computer system with that name. Resolving a URN provides the data associated with it—often a URL that specifies where is resource is currently stored.

Since almost every computer on the Internet has the software needed to resolve domain names and to manipulate URLs, several groups have attempted to use these existing mechanisms to build systems for identifying materials in digital libraries. One approach is OCLC's PURL system. A PURL (the P stands for 'persistent') is a URL such as the following.

http://purl.oclc.org/catalog/item1

In this identifier, purl.oclc.org is the domain name of a computer that is expected to be persistent. On this computer, the file catalog/item1 stores a URL to the location where the item is currently stored. If the item is moved, this URL must be changed, but the PURL (the external name) is unaltered.

Panel 12.6
Handles and Digital Object Identifiers

Handles is a naming system developed at CNRI as part of a general framework proposed by Robert Kahn of CNRI and Robert Wilensky of the University of California at Berkeley. Although this system was developed independently of the ideas of URNs, it is compatible with them, and it can be considered the first URN system to be used in digital libraries.

The handle system has a name scheme that allows independent authorities to create handle names with confidence that they are unique, a distributed computer system that stores handles along with data that they reference (e.g., the locations where material is stored), and administrative procedures to ensure high quality of information over long periods of time.

Here are two typical handles.

hdl:cnri.dlib/magazine

hdl:loc.music/musdi.139

Each of these handles has three parts. The first indicates that the string is of type hdl:. The next (e.g., cnri.dlib or loc.music) is called a *naming authority,* and is assigned hierarchically. The first part of a naming authority (e.g., cnri or loc) is assigned by the central authority; the rest (e.g., cnri.dlib) is assigned locally. The part following the slash may be any string of characters that is unique to the naming authority.

A handle is resolved by sending it to the computer system and receiving back the stored data. There is a central computer system known as the global handle registry. However, an organization is free to set up a local handle service on its own computers to maintain handles and provide resolution services. The only requirements are that the top-level naming authorities be assigned centrally and that all naming authorities be registered in the central service. For the sake of performance and reliability, each of these services may be spread over several computers, and the data may be automatically replicated. A variety of caching services are provided, as are plug-ins that enable web browsers to resolve handles.

In 1996, an initiative of the Association of American Publishers adopted handles as a means of identifying electronically published materials. These identifiers are called Digital Object Identifiers (DOIs). This initiative led to the creation of an international foundation which is developing DOIs further. Numeric naming authorities are assigned to publishers—e.g., 10.1006 was assigned to Academic Press. The following is the DOI of a book published by the Academic Press: doi:10.1006/0121585328. The use of numbers for naming authorities reflects a wish to minimize semantic information. Publishers often reorganize, merge, or transfer works to other publishers. Since the DOIs persist through such changes, they should not emphasize the name of the original publisher.

PURLs add an interesting twist to the management of names. Other naming systems set out to have a single coordinated set of names for a large community—perhaps the entire world. This can be considered a top-down approach. PURLs are bottom-up. Since each PURL server is separate, there is no need to coordinate the allocation of names among them. Names can be repeated or used with different semantics, depending entirely on decisions made locally. In contrast, when publishers create Digital Object Identifiers they are building a single set of names that are guaranteed to be globally unique.

Structural Metadata and Object Models

Data Types

Data types are structural metadata used to describe the different types of object in a digital library. Chapter 2 discussed the importance of the MIME standard for defining the data type of files that are exchanged by electronic mail or used in the web. MIME is a brilliant example of a standard that is flexible enough to cover a wide range of applications yet simple enough to be easily incorporated into computer systems.

The web object model consists of hyperlinked files of data, each with a MIME data type. The hyperlinks define relationships between the files; the data types tell the user interface how to render each file for presentation to the user.

Complex Objects

Many of the materials in digital libraries are more complex than files that can be represented by simple MIME types. For example, they may consist of several elements with different data types (such as images within a text, or separate audio and video tracks), or they may be related to other materials by relationships such as part/whole or sequence. A digitized text may consist of pages, chapters, frontmatter, an index, illustrations, and other elements. An article in an online periodical may be stored on a computer system as several files containing text and images, with complex links among them. Because digital materials are easy to change, different versions may be created continually.

Panel 12.7
MIME

The specification known as MIME (the name originally stood for Multipurpose Internet Mail Extensions) was developed by Nathaniel Borenstein and Ned Freed for electronic mail but proved useful in a wide range of Internet applications. It is one of the simple but flexible building blocks that led to the success of the web.

The full MIME specification is complicated by the need to fit with a wide variety of electronic mail systems, but for digital libraries the core is the concept that MIME calls Content-Type. MIME describes a data type as three parts, as in the following example: Content-Type: text/plain; charset = "US-ASCII".

A MIME data type consists of a type (e.g., "text"), a subtype ("plain"), and one or more optional parameters. The above example defines plain text using the ASCII character set. Commonly used types include text/plain, text/html, image/gif, image/jpeg, image/tiff, audio/basic, audio/wav, video/mpeg, and video/quickdraw.

The *application* type provides a data type for information that is to be used with some application program. The MIME types for files in PDF, Microsoft Word, and PowerPoint formats are, respectively, application/pdf, application/msword, and application/ppt. (Since a Microsoft Word file may contain information other than text and requires a specific computer program to interpret it, application/msword is not considered a text format.)

The above examples were approved through the formal process for registering MIME types. However, it is also possible to create unofficial types and subtypes with names beginning x-. An example of this is audio/x-pn-realaudio.

MIME's success is a lesson on how to turn a good concept into a widely adopted system. MIME goes to great lengths to be compatible with the systems that preceded it. Existing Internet mail systems needed no alterations to handle MIME messages. The processes for checking MIME versions, for registering new types and subtypes, and for changing the system were designed to fit naturally within standard Internet procedures. Most important, MIME does not attempt to solve all problems of data types and is not tightly integrated into any particular applications. It provides a flexible set of services that can be used in many different contexts. Its greatest triumph has been in the context of the World Wide Web, an application that did not exist when MIME was introduced.

A single item may be stored in several alternate digital formats. When existing material is converted to digital form, the same physical item may be converted several times. For example, a scanned photograph may have a high-resolution archival version, a medium-quality version, and a thumbnail. In some cases these formats are exactly equivalent (e.g., an uncompressed image and the same image stored with a lossless compression), and it is possible to convert from one to the other. In other cases, the different formats contain different information (e.g., differing representations of a page of text in SGML and PostScript formats).

Structural Types

To the user, an item appears as a single entity, and the internal representation is unimportant. A bibliography or an index will normally refer to such an item as a single object in a digital library. Yet the internal representation as stored within the digital library may be complex. Structural metadata is used to represent the various components and the relationships among them. The choice of structural metadata for a specific category of material creates an object model.

Different categories of objects require different object models—for example, text with SGML markup, web objects, computer programs, digitized sound recordings. Within each category, rules and conventions describe how to organize the information as sets of digital objects. For example, specific rules describe how to represent a digitized sound recording. For each category, the rules describe how to represent materials in the library, how the components are grouped as a set of digital objects, the internal structure of each component, the associated metadata, and the conventions for naming the digital objects. The categories are distinguished by *structural type*.

Object models for computer programs have been a standard part of computing for many years. A large computer program consists of many files of programs and data, with complex structure and interrelations. This relationship is described in a separate data structure that is used to compile and build the program. For a Unix program, this is called a *make file*.

Structural types must be distinguished from *genres*. For information retrieval, it is convenient to provide descriptive metadata that describes the genre. (For example, some of the genres of popular music are jazz, blues, rap, and rock.) Genre is a natural and useful way to describe materials for searching and other bibliographic purposes, but another categorization is required for managing distributed digital libraries. Though feature films, documentaries, and training videos are clearly different genres, their digitized equivalents may be encoded in precisely the same manner and processed identically; they are the same structural type. Conversely, two texts may be of the same genre, but if one is represented with SGML markup and the other in PDF format they have different structural types and object models.

Panel 12.8 describes an object model for a scanned image. This model was developed to represent digitized photographs, but the same structural type can be used for any bit-mapped image. For example, a map, a poster, a playbill, a technical diagram, and a baseball card represent different content, but they are stored and manipulated in a computer with the same

Panel 12.8
An Object Model for Scanned Images

In joint work with the Library of Congress, members of the Corporation for National Research Initiatives have developed object models for some types of material digitized by the National Digital Library Program. The first model was for digitized images, such as scanned photographs. When each image is converted, several digital versions are made. Typically, there is a high-resolution archival version, a medium resolution version for access via the web, and one or more thumbnails. Each of these versions has its own metadata in addition to the metadata shared by all the versions.

The first decision made in developing the object model was to store the bibliographic metadata that describes the content in separate catalog records. Structural metadata (which relates the various versions) and administrative metadata (used for access management) is stored with the scanned images and is part of the object model.

Since the individual digital versions may be used independently on some occasions, each version is stored as a separate digital object. Each of these is identified by a handle and has two elements: a digitized image and metadata. Another digital object, known as a *meta-object,* is used to bring the versions together. The main purpose of the meta-object is to provide a list of the versions. It also has a data-type field that describes the function of each image (e.g., for reference, for access, or as a thumbnail). The meta-object, which has its own handle, contains metadata that is shared by all the versions of the image.

structure. Current thinking suggests that even complicated digital library collections can be represented by a small number of structural types. It has been suggested that fewer than ten structural types would be adequate for all the categories of material being converted by the Library of Congress. Among these are digitized images, sets of page images, sets of page images with associated SGML text, digitized sound recordings, and digitized video recordings.

Object Models for Interoperability

Object models are evolving slowly. How the various parts should be grouped together can rarely be specified in a few dogmatic rules. The decision depends on the context, the specific objects, the type of content, and sometimes the actual content. After the introduction of printing, the structure of a book took decades to develop to the form that we know today, with its frontmatter, chapters, figures, and index. Not surprisingly, few conventions for object models and structural metadata have yet emerged in digital libraries. Structural metadata is still at the stage where every digital library is experimenting with its own specifications, making frequent modifications as experience suggests improvements.

This might appear to pose a problem for interoperability, since a client program will not know the structural metadata used to store a digital object in an independent repository. However, clients do not need to know the internal details of how repositories store objects; they need to know the functions that the repository can provide.

Consider the storage of printed materials that have been converted to digital formats. A single item in a digital library collection consists of a set of page images. If the material is also converted to SGML, there will be the SGML markup, the Document Type Definition, style sheets, and related information. Within the repository, structural metadata defines the relationship among the components, but a client program need not know these details. In chapter 8 we looked at a user-interface program that manipulates a sequence of page images. The functions included displaying a specified page and going to a page with a specific page number. A user interface that is aware of the functions supported for this structural type of information is able to present the material to the user without knowing how it is stored on the repository.

Dissemination

In a digital library, the form in which information is stored is rarely the form in which it is delivered to the user. In the web model of access, information is copied from the server to the user's computer, where it is then rendered for use by the user. The rendering typically takes the form of converting the data in the file into a screen image, using suitable fonts and colors, and embedding the image in a display with windows, menus, and icons.

Getting stored information and presenting it to the user of a digital library can be much more complicated than it is in the web model. At the very least, a general architecture must allow the stored information to be processed by computer programs on the server before being sent to the client, or on the client before being presented to the user. The data that is rendered need not have been stored explicitly on the server. Many servers run a computer program on a collection of stored data, extract certain information, and provide it to the user. This information may be fully formatted by the server, but often it is transmitted as a file that has been formatted in HTML or in some other intermediate format that can be recognized by the user's computer.

Important types of dissemination include direct interaction between the client and the stored digital objects and continuous streams of data. When a user interacts with the information, access by the user is not a single, discrete event. Video games are a well-known example of this; the same is true of any interactive material, such as a simulation of a physical situation. Access to such information consists of a series of interactions, which are guided by the user's control and by the structural metadata of the individual objects.

Often a client program may have a choice of disseminations. The selection may be determined by the equipment a user has—for example, users on a slow network sometimes choose to turn off images and receive only the text of web pages. It may be determined by the software on the user's computer—for example, if a text is available in both HTML and PostScript versions, a user whose computer does not have software capable of viewing PostScript will want the HTML dissemination. It may be determined on non-technical grounds, such as the user's wishes or convenience—for example, a user may prefer to see a short version of a video program rather than the full-length version.

One of the purposes of object models is to provide the user with a variety of dissemination options. Several research projects aim to enable a client computer to discover automatically the range of disseminations that are available and select the one that is most useful at any given time. Typically, one option will be a default dissemination—what the user receives unless a special request is made. Another option is a short summary; this is often a single line of text (perhaps author and title), but it can be something fancier, such as a thumbnail image or a short segment of video. Whatever method is chosen, the aim of the summary is to provide the user with a small amount of information that helps to identify and describe the object. This is still an area of research; there are few good examples of such systems in practical use.

13

Repositories and Archives

This chapter looks at methods for storing digital materials in repositories and archiving them for the long term. It also examines the protocols that provide access to materials stored in repositories. It may seem strange that such important topics should be addressed so late in the book, since long-term storage is central to digital libraries, but there is a reason. Throughout the book, the emphasis has been on what actually exists today. Research topics have been introduced where appropriate, but most of the discussion has been of systems that are used in libraries today. The topics in this chapter are less well established. Beyond the ubiquitous web server, there is little consensus about repositories for digital libraries and the field of digital archiving is new. The needs are beginning to be understood, but the methods are still embryonic—particularly in the field of archiving.

Repositories

A *repository* is any computer system whose primary function is to store digital material for use in a library. Repositories are the bookshelves of digital libraries. They can be huge or tiny, storing millions of digital objects or just a single object. In some contexts a mobile agent that contains a few digital objects can be considered a repository, but most repositories are straightforward computer systems that store information in a file system or database and present it to the world through a well-defined interface.

Web Servers
Currently, the most common form of repository is the web server. Several companies provide excellent web servers. The main differences between

Panel 13.1
Web Servers

A *web server* is a computer program whose tasks are to store files and to respond to requests in HTTP and associated protocols. A web server runs on a computer connected to the Internet. This computer can be a dedicated one, a shared one that also runs other applications, or a personal computer that provides a small web site.

At the heart of a web server is a process called httpd. The letter d stands for *daemon*. A daemon is a program that runs continuously but spends most of its time idling until a message arrives for it to process. The HTTP protocol runs on top of TCP, the Internet transport protocol. TCP provides several *ports* (addresses) for every computer. The web server is associated with one of these ports—usually port 80, although others can be specified. When a message arrives at this port, it is passed to the daemon. The daemon starts up a process to handle this particular message, and continues to listen for more messages to arrive. In this way, several messages can be processed at the same time without tying up the daemon with the details of their processing.

The actual processing that a web server carries out is tightly controlled by the HTTP protocol. Early web servers did little more than implement the *get* command. This command receives a message containing a URL from a client. The URL specifies a file stored on the server. The server retrieves the file and returns it to the client. The HTTP connection for the specific message then terminates.

As HTTP has added features and as web sites have grown larger, web servers have become more complex. In addition to the full set of HTTP commands, they have to support CGI scripts and other extensions. One of the requirements of web servers (and also of web browsers) is to continue to support older versions of the HTTP protocol. They have to be prepared to receive messages in any version of the protocol and to handle them appropriately. Furthermore, web servers have steadily added security features. Version 1.1 of the protocol also includes persistent connections, which permit several HTTP commands to be processed over a single TCP connection.

The biggest web sites are so busy that they need more than one computer. Several methods are used to share the load. One straightforward method is simply to replicate the data on several identical servers. This is feasible and convenient when the number of requests is high but the volume of data is moderate. A technique called "DNS round robin" is used to balance the load by means of an extension of the domain-name system that allows a domain name to refer to a group of computers with different IP addresses. For example, the domain name www.cnn.com refers to a set of computers each of which has a copy of the Cable News Network's web site. When a user accesses this site, the domain-name system chooses one of the computers to service the request. But replication of a web site is inconvenient if the volume of data is huge or if it is changing rapidly. Web search services provide an example. Some web search system use separate computers to carry out the search, to assemble the page that will be returned to the user, and to insert advertisements.

their products are in the associated programs that are linked to them, such as electronic mail, indexing programs, security systems, electronic payment mechanisms, and other network services.

For digital libraries, web servers provide moderate functionality with low costs. These attributes have led to broad acceptance and a basic level of interoperability. The web owes much of its success to its simplicity, and web servers are part of that success, but some of their simplifying assumptions are awkward for the implementers of digital libraries. Web servers support only one object model: a hierarchical file system in which information is organized into separate files. Their processing is inherently stateless; each message is received, processed, and forgotten.

Advanced Repositories

Although web servers are widely used, other types of storage systems are used as repositories in digital libraries. In business data processing, relational databases are the standard way to manage large volumes of data. Relational databases are based on an object model that consists of data tables and relations among them. These relations allow data from different tables to be joined or viewed in various ways. The tables and the data fields within a relational database are defined by a schema and a data dictionary. Relational databases are excellent at managing large amounts of data with a well-defined structure. Many of the large publishers mount collections on relational databases, with a web server providing the interface between the collections and the user.

Catalogs and indexes for digital libraries are usually mounted on commercial search systems. These systems have a set of indexes that refer to the digital objects. Typically, they have a flexible and sophisticated model for indexing information but a primitive model for the actual content. Many began as full-text systems, and their greatest strength lies in providing information retrieval for large bodies of text. Some systems have added relevance feedback, fielded searching, and other features that they hope will increase their functionality and hence their sales.

Relational databases and commercial search systems provide good tools for loading data, validating it, manipulating it, and protecting it. Access control is precise, and services that are important in business applications (such as audit trails) are provided. There is an industry-wide trend for database systems to add full-text searching, and for search systems to provide some parts of the relational database model. These extra features can be useful, but no company has yet created a system that combines the best of both approaches.

Although some digital libraries have used relational databases successfully, the relational model of data is not flexible enough for the rich object models that are emerging. The consensus among the leading digital libraries appears to be that more advanced repositories are needed. A possible set of requirements for such a repository is as follows.

Information hiding   The internal organization of the repository should be hidden from client computers. It should be possible to reorganize a collection, change its internal representation, or move it to a different computer without any external effect.

Object models   Repositories should support a flexible range of object models, with few restrictions on data, metadata, external links, and internal relationships. New categories of information should not require fundamental changes to other aspects of the digital library.

Open protocols and formats   Clients should communicate with the repository through well-defined protocols, data types, and formats. The repository architecture must allow incremental changes of protocols as they are enhanced over time. This applies, in particular, to access management. The repository must allow a broad set of policies to be implemented at all levels of granularity.

Reliability and performance   The repository should be able to store very large volumes of data, should be absolutely reliable, and should perform well.

Metadata in Repositories

Repositories store both data and metadata. The metadata can be considered as falling into the general classes of descriptive, structural, and administrative. Identifiers may need to distinguish elements of digital objects as well as the objects themselves. Storage of metadata in a repository requires flexibility, since there is a range of storage possibilities:

• Descriptive metadata often is stored in catalogs and indexes that are managed outside the repository. These catalogs and indexes may be held in separate repositories and may cover material in many independent digital libraries. Identifiers are used to associate the metadata with the corresponding data.

• Structural and administrative metadata is often stored with each digital object. Such metadata can be actually embedded within the object.

• Some metadata refers to a group of objects. Administrative metadata used for access management may apply to an entire repository or to a collection within a repository. Finding aids apply to many objects.

• Metadata may be stored as separate digital objects with links from the digital objects to which they apply. Some metadata is not stored explicitly but is generated when required.

Every digital library has its own ideas about the selection and specification of metadata, yet exchanging metadata is central to interoperability. The Warwick Framework, described in panel 13.2, is a conceptual framework that offers some semblance of order to this potentially chaotic situation.

Protocols for Interoperability

Interoperability requires protocols that clients can use to send messages to repositories and repositories can use to return information to clients. At the most basic level, functions are needed that deposit information in a repository and provide access. The implementation of effective systems requires that the client be able to discover the structure of the digital objects. Different types of objects require different access methods, and access management may require authentication or negotiation between client and repository. In addition, clients may wish to search indexes within the repository.

Currently, the most commonly used protocol in digital libraries is HTTP, the access protocol of the web. Another widely used protocol is Z39.50.

Object-Oriented Programming and Distributed Objects
One line of research aims to develop the simplest possible repository protocol that supports the necessary functions. If the repository protocol is simple, information about complex object types must be contained in the digital objects. (This has been called SODA, standing for "smart object, dumb archives.")

Several advanced projects are developing architectures that use the computing concept of *distributed objects*. In this context, the word 'object' has a precise technical meaning, which is different from its meaning in the terms

Panel 13.2
The Warwick Framework

The Warwick Framework had its genesis in some ideas that came out of a 1996 workshop at the University of Warwick in England. The basic aim of the Warwick Framework is to organize metadata. A vast array of metadata—including descriptive metadata such as MARC cataloging, access-management metadata, structural metadata, and identifiers—may apply to a single digital object. The members of the workshop suggested that the metadata might be organized into packages—e.g., one for Dublin Core, and one for geospatial data. This separation has obvious advantages for simplifying interoperability: if a client and a repository are both able to process packages of a specific type, they are able to interoperate to an extent even if the other metadata packages they support are not shared.

Carl Lagoze at Cornell University and Ron Daniel at the Los Alamos National Laboratory took this simple idea and developed an elegant way of looking at all the components of a digital object. Their first observation was that the distinction between data and metadata is often far from clear. Analogously, is a book's table of contents part of the book's content, or is it metadata about the book's content? In the Warwick Framework such distinctions are unimportant. Everything is divided into packages, and no distinction is made between data and metadata. Lagoze and Daniel's next observation was that not every package need be stored explicitly as part of a digital object. Descriptive metadata is often stored separately as a record in a catalog or an index. Terms and conditions that apply to many digital objects are often best stored in separate policy records, not embedded in each individual digital object. This separation can be achieved by allowing indirect packages. The package is stored wherever is most convenient, with a reference stored in the repository. The reference may be a simple pointer to a location, or it may invoke a computer program whose execution creates the package on demand.

Digital objects of the same structural type will usually be composed of a specific group of packages. This forms an object model for interoperability between clients and repositories for that type of digital object. The Warwick Framework has not been implemented explicitly in any large-scale system, but the ideas are appealing. Dividing information into well-defined packages simplifies the specification of digital objects and provides flexibility for interoperability.

Panel 13.3
HTTP

An HTTP *get* message is an instruction from a client to a server to return whatever information is identified by the URL included in the message. If the URL refers to a process that generates data, it is the data produced by the process that is returned.

The response to a *get* command begins with a three-digit *status* code. Some of these codes are familiar to users of the web as error codes–e.g., 404, which is returned when the resource addressed by the URL is not found. When there is no error, the status code is followed by technical information (used primarily to support proxies and caches) and then by metadata about the body of the response. The metadata gives the client the data type's length, language, and encoding, a hash, and date information. The client uses this metadata to process the *response body* (the final part of the message, which is usually the file referenced by the URL).

Two other HTTP message types are closely related to *get*. A *head* message requests the same data as a *get* message except that the message body itself is not sent. This is useful for testing hypertext links for validity, accessibility, or recent modification without transferring large files. A *post* message is used to extend the amount of information that a client sends to the server. Post messages are commonly used for a client to submit a block of data, such as an HTML form, that can then be processed by a CGI script or some other application at the server.

The primary use of HTTP is to retrieve information from a server, but it can also be used to change information on a server. A *put* message is used to store specified information at a given URL; a *delete* message is used to delete information. (Put and delete messages are rarely used. The normal way to add information to a web server is by means of separate programs that manipulate data on the server directly, not by means of HTTP messages sent from outside.)

Many of the changes to HTTP since its inception have been made to allow different versions of HTTP to coexist and to enhance performance over the Internet. HTTP recognizes that many messages are processed by proxies or by caches. Its later versions include a variety of data and services that support such intermediaries. There are also special message types, such as *options* (which allows a client to request information about the communications options that are available) and *trace* (used for diagnosis and testing).

HTTP has become more elaborate over the years, but it is still a simple protocol. The designers have done a good job of resisting pressure to add more and more features while making some practical enhancements to improve its performance. No two people will agree exactly what services a protocol should provide, but HTTP is clearly one of the Internet's success stories.

digital object and *library object* used elsewhere in this book. In modern computing, an object is an independent piece of computer code and associated data that can be used and reused in many contexts. The information and mechanisms within an object are encapsulated, so that all internal details are hidden. All that the outside world knows about a class of objects is a public interface consisting of *methods* (i.e., operations on the object) and *instance data*. The effect of a particular method may vary from class to class. For example, in a digital library, a "render" method may have different interpretations for different classes of objects.

After decades of development, object-oriented programming languages, such as C++ and Java, have become accepted as the most productive means of building computer systems. The driving force behind object-oriented programming is the complexity of computing. Object-oriented programming allows components to be developed and tested independently and does not require them to be revised for subsequent versions of a system. Microsoft is a heavy user of object-oriented programming. Various versions of Microsoft's object-oriented environment are known as OLE, COM, DCOM, and Active-X. They are all variants of the same key concepts.

Distributed objects generalize the idea of objects to a networked environment. The basic concept is that an object executing on one computer should be able to interact with an object executing on another through its published interface, defined in terms of methods and instance data. The leading software companies (with the notable exception of Microsoft) have developed a standard for distributed objects known as CORBA. CORBA provides the developers of distributed computing systems with many of the same programming amenities that object-oriented programming provides within a single computer.

The key notion in CORBA is that of an Object Request Broker (ORB). When an ORB is added to an application program, it establishes a client-server relationships between objects. Using an ORB, a client can transparently invoke a method on a server object, which might be on the same machine or across a network. The ORB intercepts the call, finds an object that can implement the request, passes the parameters to that object, invokes its method, and returns the results. The client does not have to be aware of where the object is located, its programming language, its operating system, or any other system aspects that are not part of the object's interface. Thus, the ORB provides interoperability between applications on different machines in heterogeneous distributed environments.

Data Hiding

Objects in the computing sense and digital objects in the library sense are different concepts, but they have features in common. The term *data hiding* comes from object-oriented programming but applies equally to digital objects in libraries. When a client accesses information in a repository, it needs to know the interface that the repository presents to the outside world, but it does not need to know how the information is stored in the repository. With a web server, the interface is a protocol (HTTP), an address scheme (URL), and a set of formats and data types. With other repositories, it can expressed in the terminology of object-oriented programming. What the user perceives as a single digital object may be stored in the repository as a complex set of files, as records in tables, or as active objects that are executed on demand.

Hiding the internal structure and providing all access through a clearly defined interface simplifies interoperability. Clients benefit because they do not need to know the internal organization of repositories. Two repositories may choose to organize similar information in different manners. One may store the soundtrack and the pictures of a digitized film as two separate digital objects, the other as a single object. A client program should be able to send a request to begin playback, unaware of these internal differences. Repositories benefit because internal reorganization is entirely a local concern. What the user sees as a single digital object may in fact be a page in HTML format with linked images and Java applets. With data hiding, it is possible to move the images to a different location or to change to a new version of Java, invisibly to the outside.

JSTOR and the National Digital Library Program at the Library of Congress both provide thumbnail images as scaled-down versions of larger images. The Library of Congress has decided to derive thumbnails in advance and to store them as separate data. JSTOR does not store thumbnails; instead, they are computed on demand from the stored forms of the larger images. Each approach is reasonable. These internal decisions should be hidden from the user interface and may be changed later. External systems need to know that the repository can supply a thumbnail; they do not need to know how it is created.

Legacy Systems

Conventional attempts at interoperability have followed a path based on agreed standards. The strategy is to persuade all organizations to decide on a set of technical and organizational standards. For complex system, such as digital libraries, this is an enormous undertaking. Standards are needed for networking, for data types, for methods of identification, for security, for search and retrieval, for the reporting of errors, and for exchanging payment. Each of these standards will have several parts, describing syntax, semantics, error procedures, extensions, and so forth. If a complete set of standards were to be agreed upon, and if every organization were to implement them in full, a wonderful level of interoperability might be achieved.

In practice, the pace of standardization is slower than the rate of change of technology. No organization ever completely integrates all the standards into its systems before it begins to change those systems to take advantage of new opportunities or to avoid new difficulties. Hence, a fundamental question in regard to interoperability is how systems of different generations can work together. Older systems are sometime given the disparaging name *legacy systems*, but many older systems do a fine job. Future plans always need to accommodate the existing systems and commitments.

Archiving

Archives are the raw material of history. In the United States, the National Archives and Records Administration has the task of keeping records "until the end of the republic." At the very least, archives must be prepared to keep library information longer than any computer system that exists today, and longer than any electronic or magnetic medium has ever been tested. Digital archiving is difficult. It is easier to state the issues that to resolve them, and there are few good examples. The foundation of modern work on digital archiving is the report of the Task Force on Archiving of Digital Information, described in panel 13.5.

Conventional archiving distinguishes between *conservation* (which looks after individual artifacts) and *preservation* (which retains the content even if the original artifact decays or is destroyed). The corresponding techniques in digital archiving are *refreshing* (which aims to preserve precise sequences of bits) and *migration* (which preserves the content at a semantic level, but

Panel 13.4
The Stanford InfoBus

One of the projects funded by the Digital Libraries Initiative was at Stanford University, under the leadership of Hector Garcia-Molina, Terry Winograd, and Andreas Paepcke. Their work, known as the InfoBus, tackled the challenging problem of interoperability between existing systems. Rather than define new standards and attempt to modify older systems, the InfoBus accepts systems as they are. The basic approach is to construct Library Service Proxies which are CORBA objects representing online services. These proxies communicate with existing services via whatever means of communication they support and convert messages to standard interfaces defined in terms of CORBA methods. For example, a client with a Z39.50 search interface might wish to search an online search service, such as Dialog. This requires two proxies: one to translate between the Z39.50 search protocol and the InfoBus model and one to translates between the Dialog interface and the InfoBus model. Using this pair of proxies, the client can search Dialog despite the different interfaces.

Perhaps the most interesting InfoBus tools are those that support Z39.50. Stanford has developed a proxy that allows Z39.50 clients to interact with search services that do not support Z39.50. Users can submit searches to this proxy through any user interface that was designed to communicate with a Z39.50 server. The proxy forwards the search requests through the InfoBus to any of the InfoBus-accessible sources, even sources that do not support Z39.50. The proxy converts the results into a format that Z39.50 clients can understand. In a parallel activity, researchers at the University of Michigan implemented another proxy that makes all Z39.50 servers accessible through the InfoBus. The Stanford project also constructed proxies for HTTP, for web search systems (Lycos, WebCrawler, AltaVista), and for other web services (including ConText, Oracle's document-summarization tool).

not the specific sequences of bits). This distinction was first articulated by the Task Force on Archiving of Digital Information, which recommended migration as the basic technique of digital archiving.

Both refreshing and migration require periodic effort. Business records are maintained over long periods of time because a team of people are paid to maintain them. It is their job, and they pay attention to the interrelated issues of security, backup, and long-term availability of data. Publishers have also come to realize that their digital information is an asset that can generate revenue for decades; however, for many digital collections no one is responsible for preserving information beyond its current usefulness. Some data that today appears to be of no consequence may be prized

Panel 13.5
The Task Force on Archiving of Digital Information

The Task Force on Archiving of Digital Information was established in late 1994 by the Commission on Preservation and Access and the Research Libraries Group to study the problems of digital preservation. It was chaired by John Garrett, then at CNRI, and Donald Waters, of Yale University. The 1995 report of this task force was the first comprehensive look at these issues from legal, economic, organizational, and technical viewpoints. It illustrated the dangers of technological obsolescence with some frightening examples. For example, the report noted, computer programs no longer exist to analyze the data collected by the New York Land Use and Natural Resources Inventory Project in the 1960s. The task force explored the possibility of establishing a national system of archives as a basis for long-term preservation. While it considers such a system desirable, perhaps even essential, it recognizes that it is not a panacea. The fundamental responsibility for maintaining information lies with the people and organizations who manage it. They need to consider themselves part of a larger system.

Archiving, the report stressed, is more than simply copying bits from one aging storage medium to another; methods for interpreting and manipulating the bits must also be preserved. For this reason, migration of information from one format to another and from one type of computer system to another is likely to be the dominant form of digital archiving.

The report's consideration of the legal issues associated with archiving is particularly interesting. Much of the information that should be archived is owned by organizations that value it as intellectual property for financial or other reasons. They are naturally hesitant to provide copies to archives. Archives, on the other hand, may have to be assertive about acquiring, for the public good, information that is in danger of being lost (perhaps because a company is going out of business).

This report remains the most complete study of the field. Although the financial calculations now appear dated, the analyses of the options and the choices available have not been seriously questioned.

centuries from now. Archiving such data is low on everyone's list of priorities, and it is the first thing to be cut when budgets are tight.

Storage

In the past, whether a physical artifact survived depended primarily on the physical longevity of its materials. Whether the artifacts were simple records from churches and governments or treasures such as the Rosetta Stone, the Dead Sea Scrolls, the Domesday Book, and the Gutenberg Bibles, the survivors have been those that were created with material that did not perish—notably high-quality paper.

None of today's digital media can be guaranteed to last long. Some, such as magnetic tape, have a frighteningly short life span. Others, such as compact discs, are more stable, but no one will predict their ultimate life. Unless someone pays attention, all digital information may be lost within a few decades. Panel 13.6 describes some of the methods that are used to store digital materials today. Notice that the emphasis is on minimizing the cost of equipment and on fast retrieval times, not on longevity.

Replication and Refreshing

Replication is a basic technique of data processing. Important data that exists only as a single copy on one computer is highly vulnerable. The hardware can fail; the data can be obliterated by faulty software; an

Panel 13.6
Storing Digital Information

Digital libraries use huge amounts of storage. A page of ASCII text may contain only a few thousand characters, but a scanned color image only one inch square requires more than a megabyte (a million bytes). An hour of digitized sound, as stored on a compact disk, consists of more than 600 megabytes, and a minute of video may consist of more than a gigabyte of data before compression. To reduce the storage requirements, large items (including almost all images, sound, and video) are *compressed*. The basic idea of compression is simple, though the math is complex. Digitized information contains redundancy. A page image has areas of white space; it is not necessary to encode every single pixel separately. Because successive frames of video differ only slightly, it is simpler to record the differences between them than to encode them separately.

Lossless compression removes redundant information in a manner that is completely reversible—the original data can be reconstructed exactly as it was. *Lossy* compression cannot be reversed—approximations lose some of the information. In some applications, compression must be lossless. In a physics experiment, a single dot on an image may be crucial evidence, so any modification of the image might undermine the validity of the experiment. In most applications, however, some losses are acceptable. JPEG compression (used for images) and MPEG (used for video) are lossy methods that are calibrated to provide images that are very satisfactory to the human eye.

Compression methods reduce the size of data considerably, but the files are still large. After compression, a monochrome page of scanned text is more than 50,000 bytes. MPEG compression reduces digitized video from 20 or 30 megabytes per second to 10 megabytes per minute. Since digital libraries may store millions of these items, storage capacity is important.

The ideal storage medium for digital libraries would allow vast amounts of data to be stored at low cost, would be fast to store and read information, and would be reliable and long lasting.

Rotating magnetic disks are the standard storage medium in modern computer systems. They range in size from a few hundred million bytes to units that hold thousands of gigabytes. (A gigabyte is 1000 million bytes.) Disks are fast enough for most digital library applications, since data can be read from disks faster than it can be transmitted over networks. When data is read from a disk, there is a slight delay (about 15 milliseconds) while the disk heads are aligned to begin reading; then data is read in large blocks (typically about 25 megabytes per second). These performance characteristics suit digital library applications, which typically read large blocks of data at a time.

The decline in the cost of disks is one of the marvels of technology. Magnetic disks are coming down in price even faster than semi-conductors. In 1998 the price of disks was a few hundred dollars per gigabyte. The technology is advancing so rapidly that digital libraries can confidently plan that in ten years the cost will be no more than 5 percent and very likely less than 1 percent of today's.

The weakness of disks is their unreliability. Data on disks is easily lost, either because of a hardware failure or because a program overwrites it. To guard against such losses, it is a standard practice to copy data regularly onto other media, usually magnetic tape. It is also common to have some redundancy in the disk stores so that simple errors can be corrected automatically. Neither disks nor magnetic tape can be relied on for long-term storage. Data is encoded on a thin magnetic film deposited on some surface, and sooner or later this film decays. Disks are excellent for current operations, but not for archiving.

Large digital library collections are sometimes stored in hierarchical stores. A typical store has three levels: magnetic disks, optical disks, and magnetic tapes. The magnetic disks are permanently online, so information can be read in a fraction of a second. The optical disks provide a cheaper way of storing huge amounts of data, but the disk platters are stored offline. Before an optical disk can be used, a robot must move it from the silo to a disk reader—a slow process. Magnetic tapes are also stored offline and loaded by a robot.

To the computers that use it, a hierarchical store appears to be a single coherent file system. Less frequently used data migrates from the faster but more expensive magnetic disks to the slower but cheaper media. As the cost and the capacity of magnetic disks continue to fall dramatically, the need for an intermediate level of storage becomes questionable. The magnetic disks and tapes serve distinctive functions and are both necessary, but the intermediate storage level may not by needed in the future.

incompetent or dishonest employee can remove the data; the building housing a computer may be destroyed by fire, flooding, or some other disaster. For these reasons, computer centers routinely make backup copies of all data and store them in safe locations. Good organizations go one step further and periodically consolidate important records for long-term storage. One approach is to retain copies of financial and legal records on microform (i.e., microfilm or microfiche), since archive-quality microform is exceptionally durable.

Because all types of media on which digital information is stored have short lives, digital libraries must plan to refresh their collections periodically in the same manner. Every few years the data must be moved onto new storage media. From a financial viewpoint this is not a vast challenge. In the next few decades, computing equipment will continue to tumble in price while increasing in capacity. The equipment that will be needed to migrate today's data ten years from now will cost a few percent of the cost today, and robots can minimize the labor involved. As is so often the case with digital libraries, the question is organizational: Will libraries and publishers by systematic in carrying out these processes?

Preserving Content by Migration

Even if we make the big assumption that bits are systematically refreshed from medium to medium, so that the technical necessity of preserving the raw data is resolved, the problems are just beginning. Digital information is useless unless the formats, protocols, and metadata can be recognized and processed. Ancient manuscripts can still be read, since languages and writing have changed slowly over the years. Considerable expertise is needed to interpret old documents, but this expertise has been passed down through generations, and scholars can decipher old materials through persistence and inspiration.

Computing formats change continually. File formats 10 years old may be hard to read. There is no computer in the world that can run programs for some computers that were widespread only a short time ago. Some formats are fairly simple. For example, if, at a future date, an archeologist stumbles onto a file of ASCII text, even if all knowledge of ASCII has been lost, the code is so simple that the text will probably be interpretable. But ASCII is an exception. Other formats are highly complex. It is hard to believe that anyone could ever decipher MPEG compression without a record of the underlying mathematics, or that anyone could understand a large computer program on the basis of its machine code.

Therefore, in addition to storing raw data, digital archiving must preserve ways to understand its type, its structure, and its format. If a computer program is needed to interpret the data, then the program and some device that can execute it must be preserved, or else the data must be migrated to a different form. In the near term it is possible to keep old computer systems for these purposes, but computers have a short life span. Sooner or later, a computer will break down, spare parts will no longer be available, and any program that depends on the computer will be useless. Therefore, migration of the content becomes necessary.

Migration has been a standard practice in data processing for decades. Pension funds, for example, maintain records of financial transactions over many years. In the United States, the Social Security Administration keeps a record of payroll taxes paid on behalf of all workers throughout their careers. These records are kept on computers, but the computer systems are changed periodically. Hardware is replaced and software systems are revised. When these changes take place, the data is migrated from computer to computer and from database to database. The basic principle of migration is that the formats and the structure of the data may be changed, but the semantics of the underlying content is preserved.

Another method that is sometimes suggested is *emulation*, The idea of emulation is to specify in complete detail the computing environment that is required to execute a program. Then, at any time in the future, an emulator can be built that will behave just like the original computing environment. In a few specialized circumstances, this is a sensible suggestion. For example, it is possible to provide such a specification for a program that renders a simple image format, such as JPEG. In all other circumstances, however, emulation is a chimera. Even simple computing environments are much too complex to be specified exactly. The exact combination of syntax, semantics, and special rules is beyond comprehension, yet subtle, esoteric aspects of a system are often crucial to correct execution.

Digital Archeology
Societies go through periods of stress, including recessions, wars, and political upheavals, when migrating archival material is of low priority. Physical

artifacts can lie forgotten for centuries in attics and storerooms and still be recovered. Digital information is less forgiving. Panel 13.7 describes how one such period of stress, the collapse of East Germany, came close to losing the archives of a state. The process of retrieving information from damaged, fragmentary, and archaic data sources is called *digital archeology*.

Creating Digital Libraries with Archiving in Mind

Since digital archiving has so many risks, what can we do today to enhance the likelihood that digital archeologists will be able to unscramble the bits we create? Some simple steps are likely to make a big difference. The first is to store the information in formats that are widely adopted today. This increases the chance that, when a format becomes obsolete, programs for conversion to new formats will be available. For example, HTML and PDF are so widely used in industry that viewers will surely be available many years from now.

One interesting suggestion is to create an archive that contains the definitions of formats, metadata standards, protocols, and the other building blocks of digital libraries. This archive should be maintained on a persistent medium (e.g., paper or microfilm), and everything should be described in simple text. If the formats and the encoding schemes are preserved, most information can be deciphered. Future digital archeologists may have a tough job creating an interpreter that can resolve long-obsolete formats or instruction sets, but it can be done. Modern computing formats are complex. Though a digital archeologist might be able to reverse engineer the entire architecture of an early IBM computer from a memory dump, the archeologist will be helpless with more complex materials unless the underlying specifications are preserved.

Perhaps the most important way that digital libraries can support archiving is through *selection*. Not everything should be preserved. Most information is intended to have a short life, and much information is ephemeral or valueless. Publishers have always made decisions about what to publish and what to reject, and even the biggest libraries acquire only a fraction of the world's output. Digital libraries are managed collections of information. A crucial part of that management is deciding what to collect, what to store, what to preserve for the future, and what to discard.

Panel 13.7
Digital Archeology in Germany

A 1998 article in the *New York Times* illustrates the challenges faced by archivists in a digital world unless data is maintained continuously from its initial creation.

In 1989, when the Berlin Wall was torn down and Germany was reunited, the digital records of East Germany were in disarray. The German Federal Archives acquired a mass of punched cards, magnetic disks, and computer tapes that represented the records of the Communist state. Much of the media was in poor condition, the data was in undocumented formats, and the computer centers that had maintained it were hastily shut down or privatized. Since then, a small team of German archivists have been attempting to reconstruct the records of East Germany. Appropriately, they call themselves "digital archeologists."

The first problem faced by the digital archeologists was to retrieve the data from the storage media. Data on even the best magnetic tape has a short life. This tape was in poor condition, so the archeologists could only read it once. In many cases the data was stored in a Russian system not supported by other computers. Though the archivists have obtained several of the Russian computers, some 30 percent of the data is unreadable.

When the data had been copied onto other media, the problems were far from solved. To save space, much of the data had been compressed in obscure and undocumented ways. An important database of Communist officials illustrates some of the difficulties. Since the database programs and the computers on which the data had been written were IBM clones, recovering the database itself was not too difficult; however, interpreting the data without documentation was extremely difficult. The archivists had one advantage: they were able to interview some of the people who built these databases, and they used the expertise of those individuals in interpreting much of the information and preserving it.

Michael Wettengel, the head of the German archivists, summarizes the situation clearly: "Computer technology is made for information processing, not for long-term storage."

14

Digital Libraries and Electronic Publishing Today

Digital libraries and electronic publishing are here. They are not an academic concept to debate, or a utopian dream. In this last chapter, the temptation is to predict what lies ahead, but the history of computing shows how fruitless such predictions can be. It is more profitable to celebrate the present.

This is not to ignore the future. The work that is in progress today will be in production soon. Not all new projects enter the mainstream, but understanding what is happening today helps us comprehend the potential of what lies ahead. This book was written over a twelve-month period in 1997 and 1998. Even during that short period, digital libraries developed at a rapid pace. This chapter looks at some of the current trends, not to forecast the future, but to understand the present.

One reason that predictions are so difficult is that at present the technology is more mature than the uses to which it is being put. In the past, forecasts of basic technology proved to be reasonably accurate. Every year, semiconductors and magnetic devices are smaller, cheaper, and faster, and their capacity increases. There are good engineering reasons to expect these trends to continue for the next five or ten years. Funds are already committed to high-speed networks that will be available in a few years. But predictions about new applications that will be developed have always been much less accurate. Such seminal applications as spreadsheets, desktop publishing, and web browsers emerged from obscurity with little warning. Even if no comparable breakthroughs take place, forecasts about how the applications will be used and the social effect of new technology are not dependable. The only reliable rule is this: When a pundit starts out with the words "It is inevitable that," the statement is inevitably wrong.

One possible interpretation of the current situation is that digital libraries are at the end of an initial phase and about to begin a new one. The first phase can be thought of as a movement of traditional publications and library collections to digital networks. Online newspapers, electronic versions of scientific journals, and the conversion of historic materials all fall into this category. Fundamentally, they use new technology to enhance established types of information. If the thinking is correct, the next phase will see new types of collections and services that have no analog in traditional media. The forms that they will take are almost impossible to anticipate.

A Myopic View of Digital Libraries

When one looks back on any period, trends and key events become apparent that were not obvious at the time. Those of us who work in digital libraries can only have a myopic view of the field, but here are some observations about how the field of digital libraries appears to an insider.

The contrast between a small boat and a supertanker is a useful metaphor. A small boat can accelerate and change direction quickly, but it has little momentum. The early digital library projects, such as the Mercury project at Carnegie Mellon University, were like small boats. They made fast progress, but when the initial enthusiasm ended or funding expired they lost their momentum. Established libraries, publishers, and commercial corporations are like supertankers. They move more deliberately, and changing direction is a slow process, but once they head in a new direction they move steadily in that direction. In the fields of digital libraries and electronic publishing, success requires attention to the thousands of details that transform good ideas into practical services. As the Internet and the World Wide Web mature, many organizations are making long-term investments in library collections, electronic publications, and online services. The supertankers are changing direction.

In the years 1997 and 1998, many developments matured that had been in progress for several years. Online versions of newspapers reached a high quality, and some of them began to rival print editions in readership. Major scientific publications from both commercial and society publishers became available online. It was also an important time for conversion projects in libraries, such as JSTOR and the Library of Congress; the volume of materials available from these projects accelerated sharply. The Dublin Core approach to metadata and the use of Digital Object Identifiers for electronic publications gained momentum and appear to be making the transition from the fringe to the mainstream.

On the technical front, products for automatic mirroring and caching reached the market, tools for web security became available, and the Java programming language at last became widely used. These developments were all begun in earlier years, and none can be considered research, yet in aggregate they represent tremendous progress.

In the United States, electronic commerce on the Internet grew rapidly. Buying books, airline tickets, stocks, and automobiles through Internet transactions has been widely accepted. The Internal Revenue Service now urges people to make income tax payments online. Congress passed a reasonable revision of the copyright law. Funds are available for entrepreneurial investments, and markets are open for the right new products. Internet stocks are the favorite of speculators on the stock market. Personal computers priced under $1000 are selling vigorously, bringing online information to an ever broader range of people.

No year is perfect, and pessimists can point out a few worrisome events. During 1997, junk electronic mail reached an annoying level. Leading manufacturers released incompatible versions of Java. The United States' policy on encryption continued to emulate an ostrich. These are short-term problems. By the time this book is published, one hopes, junk electronic mail will be controlled and Java will be standardized. There even appears to be some hope for the U.S. encryption policy.

For the next few years, incremental developments similar to those that occurred in 1997 in 1998 can be expected. They can be summarized succinctly. Large numbers of energetic individuals are exploiting the opportunities that the Internet provides to offer new products and services.

People

From a myopic viewpoint, it is easy to identify the individual activities. It is much harder to see the underlying changes of which they are part. The trend that is most fundamental in the long term may be the most difficult to measure in the short term. How are people's habits changing? Many people are writing for the web. Graphic designers are designing online materials. People are reading these materials. Who are these people? What would they be doing otherwise?

Habits clearly have changed. Visit a university campus or any organization that uses information intensively and it is obvious that people spend hours every week in front of computers, using online information. At home, there is evidence that some of the time people spend on the web is time that they once would have spent watching television. At work, are people reading more—or are they substituting online information for traditional activities, such as visits to the library? Ten years from now, when we look back at this period of change, these trends may be obvious. Today, however, we can only hypothesize or extrapolate wildly from small amounts of data. Here are some guesses, based on personal observation and private hunches.

The excitement of online information has brought large numbers of new people into the field of digital libraries. People who would have considered librarianship dull and publishing too bookish are enthralled by creating and designing online materials. The enthusiasm and the energy that these newcomers bring is influencing the older professions more fundamentally than anyone might have expected. Although every group has its Luddites, many people are reveling in their new opportunities.

When the web began, Internet expertise was in such short supply that anyone with a modicum of skill could command a high salary. Now, although real experts are still in great demand, the aggregate level of skill is quite high. One sign of this change is the growth of programs that help mid-career people learn about the new fields. In the United States, every community college is offering courses on the Internet and the web. Companies that provide computer training programs are booming. Programs specializing in digital libraries are oversubscribed.

In 1997, a Cornell student who was asked to find information in the university's library reportedly said "Please, can I use the web? I don't do libraries." More recently, a member of the faculty at the University of California at Berkeley mused that the term *digital library* is becoming a tautology. For the students she sees, the Internet is the library. In the future, will they think of Berkeley's fine conventional libraries as physical substitutes for the real thing? Are these the fringe opinions of a privileged minority, or are they insights into the next generation of library users? No one knows. The data is fragmentary and often contradictory. The following statistics have been culled from a number of sources and should be treated with healthy skepticism.

A survey taken in Pittsburgh in 1996 found that 56 percent of people between the ages of 18 and 24 used the Internet, versus only 7 percent of those over 55. Another poll, taken across the United States in 1997, found that 61 percent of teenagers (66 percent of boys, 56 percent of girls) used the web. In 1996, it was found that 72 percent of children between the ages of 8 and 12 had spent time on a computer during a given month.

The network that so many young people are beginning to use as their library had about 5.3 million computers in 1998. A careful study in late 1996 estimated that a million web site names were in common use, on 450,000 unique host machines. Of those names, 300,000 appeared to be stable. There were about 80 million HTML pages on public servers. Two years later, the number of web pages was estimated at about 320 million. Whatever the exact numbers, everyone agrees that they are large and that they are growing fast.

A pessimist would read these numbers as indicating that, in the United States, young people have embraced online information, mid-career people are striving to accept it, and the older people who make plans and control resources are obsolete. Observation, however, shows that this analysis is unduly gloomy. The fact that so many large organizations are investing heavily in digital information shows that at least some of the older leaders embrace the new world.

Organizations

Although many organizations are investing in digital libraries and electronic publications, no one can be sure what sort of organizations are likely to be most successful. In some circumstances, size may be an advantage; however, small, nimble organizations are also thriving.

A 1995 article in *The Economist* described control of the Internet in terms of giants and ants. The giants are big companies, such as the telephones companies and the media giants. The ants are individuals; separately they have little power, but in aggregate they have consistently succeeded in shaping the Internet, often in direct opposition to the perceived interests of the giants.

In particular, the community of ants has succeeded in keeping the Internet and its processes open. During the past few years, both digital libraries and electronic publishing have seen consolidation in large organizational units. In libraries this is seen as the movement to consortia; in publishing it has been a number of huge corporate mergers. Yet, even as these giants have been formed, the energy of the ants has continued. At present, it appears that giants and ants can coexist and are both thriving. Meanwhile, some of the ants, such as Yahoo and Amazon.com, are becoming the new giants.

Collections and Access

Two factors that will greatly influence the future of digital libraries are the rate at which well-managed collections become available on the Internet and the business models that emerge.

Materials are being mounted online at an enormous rate, and the growth of the web shows no sign of slowing. The number of good, online sites is clearly increasing. The sites run by newspapers and news agencies are fine examples of what is best; they also highlight the vulnerability of digital information. Online news services, such as those provided by the *Sydney Morning Herald*, the *New York Times*, and CNN, provides up-to-date, well-presented news at no charge to the users. Their combined readership probably exceeds that of any American newspaper. As sources of current information, they are excellent. However, they are ephemeral. The information is changed continually, and at the end of day most of it disappears. Conventional libraries collect newspapers and store them for centuries. No library or archive is storing these web sites.

It is hard to tell which disciplines have the largest proportion of their standard library materials available through digital libraries. Large portions of the current scientific and technical literature are now available, as is a great deal of government information. Legal information has long been online, albeit at a steep price. Business and medical information are patchy. Public libraries provide access to current information, such as newspapers, travel timetables, job advertisements, and tax forms; much of that material is available online, usually freely.

Many collections have current information available in digital form but not historic materials, although projects to convert traditional materials to digital format and mount them in digital libraries are flourishing. Libraries are converting their historic collections, and publishers are converting back runs of journals. Established projects are planning to increase their rate of conversion, and new projects are springing up. Several projects have already converted more than a million pages. The first plan to convert a billion pages was made public in 1998.

Perhaps the biggest gap is in commercial entertainment. Some of the major creators of entertainment—films, television, radio, novels, and magazines—have experimented with ways to use the Internet, but with little impact. This is due in part to the technical limitations of the Internet. Most people receive much better images from cable television than can be delivered over the network or rendered on moderately priced personal computers. In part, the rate of change is dictated by business practices. Entertainment is big business, and the entertainment business has not yet discovered how to use the Internet profitably.

Open access appears to be a permanent characteristic of digital libraries, but few services have yet discovered good business models for it. A few web sites make significant money from advertising, but most are supported by external funds. Digital libraries and electronic publishing require skilled professionals to create, organize, and manage information; they are expensive. Ultimately, an economic balance will emerge, with some collections offering open access and others paid for directly by their users, but it is not yet obvious what this balance will be.

Technology

The web technology, which has fueled so much recent growth, is maturing. During the mid 1990s, the web developed so rapidly that people coined the term *web year* for a short period of time packed with so much change that it seemed like a full calendar year. As the web has matured, the pace of change in the technology has slowed down to the normal rate in computing. Every year brings incremental change, and over a few years the incremental changes become substantial, but the hectic pace has slowed. This does not mean that the growth of the web has ended—far from it. The number of web sites continues to grow rapidly. Busy sites report that the volume of use is doubling every year. The quality of graphics and the standards of service improve steadily. For digital libraries and electronic publishing, several emerging technologies show promise: persistent names, such as Digital Object Identifiers; XML markup; the Resource Description Framework; Unicode. The success of these technologies will depend on the vagaries of the marketplace. Widespread acceptance of any or all would be highly beneficial to digital libraries.

The performance of the underlying Internet continues to improve spectacularly. The past few years have brought a series of governmental and commercial initiatives that aim to provide leaps in performance, reliability, and coverage over the next few years. We cannot predict how digital libraries will use this performance, but it provides remarkable opportunities.

Research and Development

Digital libraries now constitute an established field of research, with the usual paraphernalia of workshops and conferences. There have even been attempts to establish printed journals about digital libraries. More important, at least 1000 people consider it their job to carry out research in the field. Examples of projects funded by the National Science Foundation and by DARPA appear throughout this book. Many of the more recent ones were funded explicitly as digital libraries research.

A Concluding Note

While writing this book, I looked at hundreds of sources. Most were primary materials—descriptions written by researchers or by builders of digital libraries about their own work. One source was an exhibit at the U.S. Copyright Office; one was an out-of-print book; for a few topics, I sent electronic mail to friends. For everything else, my source was the Internet. Many of the relevant materials do not exist in conventional formats. In the field of digital libraries, the Internet already is the library.

Panel 14.1
The Santa Fe Workshop

In March of 1997, the National Science Foundation sponsored a workshop in Santa Fe, New Mexico, to discuss future research in digital libraries. This was part of a planning process that later led to the announcement of a major new digital libraries research program: phase 2 of the Digital Libraries Initiative. The workshop was an opportunity for researchers to describe their vision for the development of digital libraries and the research opportunities.

Many of the people at the meeting had been part of the first Digital Libraries Initiative or of other federally funded research projects. Of course they were interested in continuing their research, but they did not simply recommend a continuation of the same programs. The early projects constructed test collections and used them for research, mainly on technical topics. Some of the participants in the workshop argued that a valuable use of government funds would be to build large digital libraries. Many people agreed that archiving was worthy of serious research. Most of the discussion, however, was about making existing collections more usable. The participants in the workshop were senior researchers who needed not only to find information but also to escape from too much information. The discussions sometimes suggested that the central problem of digital libraries research was information overload. How could automatic methods be used to filter, extract, and consolidate information? The discussions embraced methods by which individuals could manage their private libraries and groups could carry out collaborative work over the Internet. How could digital libraries—managed collections of information—be managed for the convenience of the users?

Social, economic, and legal issues were also discussed. As ever in these areas, the question was how to articulate a coherent research strategy. While nobody denies the importance of these areas, there remains skepticism whether they can be tackled by large research projects.

Technical people at the meeting pointed out that digital libraries have become major users of supercomputers. In 1986, when the national supercomputing centers were established, the Internet's backbone ran at 56 kilobits per second and was shared by all users. Today that speed is provided by inexpensive dial-up modems used by individuals. Today's laptop computers have the performance of the supercomputers of 12 years ago. Twelve years from now, even smaller computers will have the performance of today's supercomputers.

After a few years, rapid incremental growth adds up to fundamental changes. The participants in the Santa Fe workshop were asked to explore assumptions about digital libraries that are so deeply rooted that they are taken for granted. The aim of this challenge was to set a creative agenda for the next generation of digital library research.

A dream of future libraries combines everything that we most prize about traditional methods with the best that online information can offer. In some nightmares, the worst aspects of each are combined. In the first years of the twentieth century, the philanthropy of Andrew Carnegie brought public libraries to the United States. Now a new form of library is emerging. It is to be hoped that digital libraries will attract the same passion and respect, and will serve the same deep needs, that have long been associated with the best of libraries and publishing.

Glossary

The field of digital libraries has absorbed terms from many other fields, including computing, libraries, publishing, and law. This glossary gives brief explanations of various terms as they are used today in the context of digital libraries. Some of these terms may have different meanings in other contexts.

AACR2 (Anglo-American Cataloging Rules)   A set of rules that describe the content that is contained in library catalog records.

abstracting and indexing services   Secondary information services that provide searching of scholarly and scientific information, in particular of individual journal articles.

access management   Control of access to material in digital libraries. Sometimes called *terms and conditions* or *rights management*.

ACM Digital Library   A digital library of the journals and conference proceedings published by the Association for Computing Machinery.

Alexandria Digital Library   A digital library of geospatial information, based at the University of California, Santa Barbara.

American Memory and National Digital Library Program   The Library of Congress's digital library of materials converted from its primary source materials related to American history.

applet   A small computer program that can be transmitted from a server to a client computer and executed on the client.

archives   Collections with related systems and services, organized to emphasize the long-term preservation of information.

Art and Architecture Thesaurus   A thesaurus for fine art, architecture, decorative art, and material culture, a project of the J. Paul Getty Trust.

artifact   A physical object in a library, archive, or museum.

ASCII (American Standard Code for Information Interchange)   A coding scheme that represents individual characters as seven or eight bits; *printable ASCII* is a subset of ASCII.

authentication   Validation of a user, a computer, or some digital object to ensure that it is what is claims to be.

authorization   Giving permission to a user or client computer to access specific information and carry out approved actions.

automatic indexing   Creation of catalog or indexing records using computer programs, not human catalogers.

Boolean searching   Methods of information retrieval where a query consists of a sequence of *search terms*, combined with operators, such as "and," "or," and "not."

browser   A general-purpose user interface, used with the web and other online information services. Also known as a *web browser.*

browse   To explore a body of information on the basis of the organization of the collections or by scanning lists, rather than by direct searching.

cache   A temporary store that is used to keep a readily available copy of recently used data or any data that is expected to be used frequently.

California Digital Library   A digital library that serves the nine campuses of the University of California.

catalog   A collection of bibliographic records created according to an established set of rules.

classification   An organization of library materials by a hierarchy of subject categories.

client   A computer that acts on behalf of a user, including a user's personal computer, or another computer that appears to a server to have that function.

CGI (Common Gateway Interface)   A programming interface that enables a web browser to be an interface to information services other than web sites.

Chemical Abstracts   A secondary information service for chemistry.

CNI (Coalition for Networked Information)   A partnership of the Association for Research Libraries and Educause to collaborate on academic networked information.

complex object   Library object that is made up from many interrelated elements or digital objects.

compression   Reduction in the size of digital materials by removing redundancy or by approximation; *lossless* compression can be reversed; *lossy* compression can not be reversed since information is lost by approximation.

computational linguistics   The branch of natural-language processing that deals with grammar and linguistics.

controlled vocabulary   A set of subject terms, and rules for their use in assigning terms to materials for indexing and retrieval.

conversion Transformation of information from one medium to another, including from paper to digital form.

CORBA A standard for distributed computing where an object on one computer invokes an *Object Request Broker (ORB)* to interact with an object on another computer.

CORE A project from 1991 to 1995 by Bellcore, Cornell University, OCLC, and the American Chemical Society to convert chemistry journals to digital form.

Cryptolope Secure container used to buy and sell content securely over the Internet, developed by IBM.

CSS (Cascading Style Sheets) System of style sheets for use with HTML, the basis of XLS.

CSTR (Computer Science Technical Reports project) A DARPA-funded research project with CNRI and five universities, from 1992 to 1996.

DARPA (Defense Advanced Research Projects Agency) A major sponsor of computer science research in the United States, including digital libraries. Formerly *ARPA*.

data type Structural metadata associated with digital data that indicates the digital format or the application used to process the data.

DES (Data Encryption Standard) A method for private-key encryption.

Dewey Decimal Classification A classification scheme for library materials which uses a numeric code to indicate subject areas.

desktop metaphor User interface concept on personal computers that represents information as files and folders on a desktop.

Dienst An architecture for digital library services and an open protocol that provides those services, developed at Cornell University, used in NCSTRL.

digital archeology The process of retrieving information from damaged, fragmentary, and archaic data sources.

Digital Libraries Initiative A digital libraries research program. In Phase 1, from 1994 to 1998, NSF, DARPA, and NASA funded six university projects. Phase 2 began in 1998.

digital object An item as stored in a digital library, consisting of data, metadata, and an identifier.

digital signature A cryptographic code consisting of a hash, to indicate that data has not changed, that is encrypted with the public key of the creator of the signature.

dissemination The transfer from the stored form of a digital object in a repository to a client.

distributed computing Computing systems in which services to users are provided by teams of computers collaborating over a network.

D-Lib Magazine A monthly online publication about digital libraries research and innovation.

DLITE   An experimental user interface used with the Stanford University InfoBus.

document   Digital object that is the analog of a physical document, especially textual materials; a *document model* is an object model for documents.

domain name   The name of a computer on the Internet; the *domain name service* (DNS) converts domain names to IP addresses.

DOI (Digital Object Identifier)   An identifier used by publishers to identify materials published electronically, a form of handle.

DSSSL (Document Style Semantics and Specification Language)   A general purpose system of *style sheets* for SGML.

DTD (Document Type Definition)   A markup specification for a class of documents, defined within the SGML framework.

Dublin Core   A simple set of metadata elements used in digital libraries, primarily to describe digital objects and for collections management, and for exchange of metadata.

dynamic object   Digital object where the dissemination presented to the user depends upon the execution of a computer program, or other external activity.

EAD (Encoded Archival Description)   A DTD used to encode electronic versions of finding aids for archival materials.

electronic journal   A online publication that is organized like a traditional printed journal, either an online version of a printed journal or a journal that has only an online existence.

eLib   A British program of innovation, around the theme of electronic publication.

emulation   Replication of a computing system to process programs and data from an early system that is no longer available.

encryption   Techniques for encoding information for privacy or security, so that it appears to be random data; the reverse process, *decryption,* requires knowledge of a digital key.

entities, elements   In a markup language, entities are the basic unit of information, including *character entities;* elements are strings of entities that form a structural unit.

expression   The realization of a work, by expressing the abstract concept as actual words, sounds, images, etc.

fair use   A concept in copyright law that allows limited use of copyright material without requiring permission from the rights holders, e.g., for scholarship or review.

federated digital library   A group of digital libraries that support common standards and services, thus providing interoperability and a coherent service to users.

field, subfield   An individual item of information in a structured record, such as a catalog or database record.

fielded searching   Methods for searching textual materials, including catalogs, where search terms are matched against the content of specified fields.

finding aid   A textual document that describes holdings of an archive, library, or museum.

firewall   A computer system that screens data passing between network segments, used to provide security for a private network at the point of connection to the Internet.

first sale   A concept in copyright law that permits the purchaser of a book or other object to transfer it to somebody else, without requiring permission from the rights holders.

FTP (File Transfer Protocol)   A protocol used to transmit files between computers on the Internet.

full text searching   Methods for searching textual materials where the entire text is matched against a query.

gatherer   A program that automatically assembles indexing information from digital library collections.

gazetteer   A database used to translate between different representations of geospatial references, such as place names and geographic coordinates.

genre   The class or category of an object when considered as an intellectual work.

geospatial information   Information that is reference by a geographic location.

GIF   A format for storing compressed images.

Google   A web search program that ranks web pages in a list of hits by giving weight to the links that reference a specific page.

gopher   A pre-web protocol used for building digital libraries, now largely obsolete.

handle   A system of globally-unique names for Internet resources and a computer system for managing them, developed by CNRI; a form of URN.

Harvest   A research project that developed an architecture for distributed searching, including protocols and formats.

hash   A short value calculated from digital data that serves to distinguish it from other data.

HighWire Press   A publishing venture, from Stanford University Libraries, that provides electronic versions of journals, on behalf of learned and professional societies.

hit   1. An incoming request to a web server or other computer system. 2. In information retrieval, a document that is discovered in response to a query.

home page   The introductory page to a collection of information on the web.

HTML (Hypertext Markup Language)   A simple markup and formatting language for text, with links to other objects, used with the web.

HTTP (Hypertext Transfer Protocol)   The basic protocol of the web, used for communication between browsers and web sites.

hyperlink   A network link from one item in a digital library or web site to another.

ICPSR (International Consortium for Political and Social Science Research)   An archive of social science data sets, based at the University of Michigan.

identifier   A string of characters that identifies a specific resource in a digital library or on a network.

IETF (Internet Engineering Task Force)   The body that coordinates the technological development of the Internet, including standards.

InfoBus   An approach to interoperability that uses proxies as interfaces between existing systems, developed at Stanford University.

information discovery   General term covering all strategies and methods of finding information in a digital library.

information retrieval   Searching a body of information for objects that match a search query.

Informedia   A research program and digital library of segments of video, based at Carnegie Mellon University.

Inspec   An indexing service for physics, engineering, computer science, and related fields.

Internet   An international network, consisting of independently managed networks using the *TCP/IP* protocols and a shared naming system. A successor to the *ARPAnet*.

Internet RFC series   The technical documentation of the Internet, provided by the Internet Engineering Task Force. *Internet Drafts* are preliminary versions of RFCs.

interoperability   The task of building coherent services for users from components that are technically different and independently managed.

inverted file   A list of the words in a set of documents and their locations within those documents; an *inverted list* is the list of locations for a given word.

item   A specific piece of material in a digital library; a single instance or copy of a manifestation.

Java   A programming language used for writing mobile code, especially for user interfaces, developed by Sun Microsystems.

JavaScript   A scripting language used to embed executable instructions in a web page.

JPEG   A format for storing compressed images.

JSTOR   A subscription service, initiated by the Andrew W. Mellon Foundation, to convert back runs of important journals and make them available to academic libraries.

key   A digital code used to encrypt or decrypt messages. *Private-key* encryption uses a single, secret key. *Dual-key (public-key)* encryption uses two keys of which one is secret and one is public.

legacy system   An existing system, usually a computer system, that must be accommodated in building new systems.

lexicon A linguistic tool with information about the morphological variations and grammatical usage of words.

Lexis A legal information service, a pioneer of full-text information online.

Los Alamos E-Print Archives An open-access site for rapid distribution of research papers in physics and related disciplines.

manifestation Form given to an expression of a work, e.g., by representing it in digital form.

MARC (Machine-Readable Cataloging) A format used by libraries to store and exchange catalog records.

markup language Codes embedded in a document that describe its structure and/or its format.

Medline An indexing service for research in medicine and related fields, provided by the National Library of Medicine.

MELVYL A shared digital library system for academic institutions in California; part of the California Digital Library.

Memex A concept of an online library suggested by Vannevar Bush in 1945.

Mercury An experimental digital library project to mount scientific journals online at Carnegie Mellon University from 1987 to 1993.

MeSH (Medical Subject Headings) A set of subject term and associated thesaurus used to describe medical research, maintained by the National Library of Medicine.

metadata Data about other data, commonly divided into *descriptive metadata* such as bibliographic information, *structural metadata* about formats and structures, and *administrative metadata*, which is used to manage information.

migration Preservation of digital content, where the underlying information is retained but older formats and internal structures are replaced by newer.

MIME (Internet Media Type) A scheme for specifying the data type of digital material.

mirror A computer system that contains a duplicate copy of information stored in another system.

mobile code Computer programs or parts of programs that are transmitted across a network and executed by a remote computer.

morphology Grammatical and other variants of words that are derived from the same root or stem.

Mosaic The first widely-used web browser, developed at the University of Illinois.

MPEG A family of formats for compressing and storing digitized video and sound.

multimedia A combination of several media types in a single digital object or collection, e.g., images, audio, video.

natural-language processing Use of computers to interpret and manipulate words as part of a language.

NCSTRL (Networked Computer Science Technical Reports Library)   An international distributed library of computer science materials and services, based at Cornell University.

Netlib   A digital library of mathematical software and related collections.

NSF (National Science Foundation)   A U.S. government agency that supports science and engineering, including digital libraries research.

object   A technical computing term for an independent piece of computer code with its data. Hence, *object-oriented programming*, and *distributed objects*, where objects are connected over a network.

object model   A description of the structural relationships among components of a library object including its metadata.

OCLC (Online Computer Library System)   An organization that provides, among other services, a bibliographic utility for libraries to share catalog records.

OPAC (online public access catalog)   An online library catalog used by library patrons.

open access   Resources that are openly available to users with no requirements for authentication or payment.

optical character recognition   Automatic conversion of text from a digitized image to computer text.

Pad++   A experimental user interface for access to large collections of information, based on semantic zooming.

page description language   A system for encoding documents that precisely describes their appearance when rendered for printing or display.

PDF (Portable Document Format)   A page description language developed by Adobe Corporation to store and render images of pages.

peer review   The procedure by which academic journal articles are reviewed by other researchers before being accepted for publication.

Perseus   A digital library of hyperlinked sources in classics and related disciplines, based at Tufts University.

policy   A rule established by the manager of a digital library that specifies which users should be authorized to have what access to which materials.

port   A method used by TCP to specify which program running on a computer should process a message arriving over the Internet.

PostScript   A programming language to create graphical output for printing, used as a page description language.

precision   In information retrieval, the percentage of hits found by a search that satisfy the request that generated the query.

presentation profile   Guidelines associated with a digital object that suggest how it might be presented to a user.

protocol   A set of rules that describe the sequence of messages sent across a network, specifying both syntax and semantics.

proxy A computer that acts as a bridge between two computer systems that use different standards, formats, or protocols.

publish To make information available and distribute it to the public.

PURL (Persistent URL) A method of providing persistent identifiers using standard web protocols, developed by OCLC.

query A textual string, possibly structured, that is used in information retrieval, the task being to find objects that match the words in the query.

ranked searching Methods of information retrieval that return a list of documents, ranked in order of how well each matches the query,

RDF (Resource Description Framework) A method for specifying the syntax of metadata, used to exchange metadata.

RealAudio A format and protocol for compressing and storing digitized sound, and transmitting it over a network to be played in real time.

recall In informational retrieval, the percentage of the items in a body of material which would satisfy a request that are actually found by a search.

refresh To make an exact copy of data from older media to newer for long-term preservation.

render To transform digital information in the form received from a repository into a display on a computer screen, or for other presentation to the user.

replication Make copies of digital material for backup, performance, reliability, or preservation.

repository A computer system used to store digital library collections and disseminate them to users.

RSA encryption A method of dual-key (public-key) encryption.

scanning Method of conversion in which a physical object, e.g., a printed page, is represented by a digital grid of pixels

search term A single term within a query, usually a single word or short phrase.

secondary information Information sources that describe other (primary) information, e.g., catalogs, indexes, and abstracts; used to find information and manage collections.

security Techniques and practices that preserve the integrity of computer systems, and digital library services and collections.

server Any computer on a network, other than a client, that stores collections or provides services.

SGML (Standard Generalized Markup Language) A system for creating markup languages that represent the structure of a document.

SICI (Serial Item and Contribution Identifier) An identifier for an issue of a serial or an article contained within a serial.

speech recognition Automatic conversion of spoken words to computer text.

STARTS   An experimental protocol for use in distributed searching, which enables a client to combine results from several search engines.

stemming   In informational retrieval, reduction of morphological variants of a word to a common stem.

stop word   A word that is so common that it is ignored in information retrieval. A set of such words is called a *stop list*.

structural type   Metadata that indicates the structural category of a digital object.

style sheet   A set of rules that specify how markup in a document translates into the appearance of the document when rendered.

subscription   In a digital library, a payment made by a person or an organization for access to specific collections and services, usually for a fixed period, e.g., one year.

subsequent use   Use made of digital materials after they leave the control of a digital library.

tag   A special string of characters embedded in marked-up text to indicate the structure or format.

TCP/IP   The base protocols of the Internet. IP uses numeric IP addresses to join network segments; TCP provides reliable delivery of messages between networked computers.

TEI (Text Encoding Initiative)   A project to represent texts in digital form, emphasizing the needs of humanities scholars. Also the DTD used by the program.

TeX   A method of encoding text that precisely describes its appearance when printed, especially good for mathematical notation. *LaTeX* is a version of TeX.

thesaurus   A linguistic tool that relates words by meaning.

Ticer Summer School   A program at Tilburg University to educate experienced librarians about digital libraries.

Tipster   A DARPA program of research to improve the quality of text processing methods, including information retrieval.

transliteration   A systematic way to convert characters in one script or alphabet into another.

TREC (Text Retrieval Conferences)   Annual conferences in which methods of text processing are evaluated against standard collections and tasks.

truncation   Use of the first few letters of a word as a search term in information retrieval.

Tulip   An experiment in which Elsevier Science scanned material science journals and a group of universities mounted them on local computers.

UDP   An Internet protocol which transmits data packets without error checking.

Unicode   A 16-bit code to represent the characters used in most of the world's scripts. *UTF-8* is an alternative encoding in which one or more 8-bit bytes represents each Unicode character.

union catalog   A single catalog that contains records about materials in several collections or libraries.

URL (Uniform Resource Locator)   A reference to a resource on the Internet, specifying a protocol, a computer, a file on that computer, and parameters. An *absolute URL* specifies a location as a domain name or IP address; a *relative URL* specifies a location relative to the current file.

URN (Uniform Resource Name)   Location-independent name for Internet resources.

WAIS   An early version of Z39.50, used in digital libraries before the web, now largely obsolete.

Warwick Framework   A general model that describes the various parts of a complex object, including the various categories of metadata.

watermark   A code embedded into digital material that can be used to establish ownership, may be visible or invisible to the user.

web crawler   A web indexing program that builds an index by following hyperlinks continuously from web page to web page.

webmaster   A person who manages web sites.

web search services   Commercial services that provide searching of the web, including: Yahoo, AltaVista, Excite, Lycos, Infoseek, etc.

web site   A collection of information on the web; usually stored on a *web server*.

Westlaw   A legal information service provided by West Publishing.

World Wide Web (web)   An interlinked set of information sources on the Internet, and the technology they use, including HTML, HTTP, URLs, and MIME.

World Wide Web Consortium (W3C)   A international consortium based at MIT that coordinates technical developments of the web.

work   The underlying intellectual abstraction behind some material in a digital library.

Xerox Digital Property Rights Language   Syntax and rules for expressing rights, conditions, and fees for digital works.

XLS (eXtensible Style Language)   System of style sheets for use with XML, derived from CSS.

XML (eXtensible Markup Language)   A simplified version of SGML intended for use with online information.

Z39.50   A protocol that allows a computer to search collections of information on a remote system, create sets of results for further manipulation, and retrieve information; mainly used for bibliographic information.

Index